Great American Speeches

★

Great American Speeches

★

EDITED, WITH INTRODUCTIONS, BY
Gregory R. Suriano

GRAMERCY BOOKS
NEW YORK • AVENEL

ACKNOWLEDGMENTS

The following sources are gratefully acknowledged for their permission to print the texts of a number of speeches: The ALF-CIO, for the speeches of Samuel Gompers and George Meany; the Philosophical Library, for Albert Einstein's speech, originally published in *Out of My Later Years*; Ralph Nader; the Institute for Intercultural Studies, Inc., New York, for Margaret Mead's speech; and the National Rainbow Coalition for Jesse Jackson's speech.

The March on Washington Address by Martin Luther King, Jr., is reprinted by arrangement with the heirs of the estate of Martin Luther King, Jr., c/o Joan Daves Agency as agent for the proprietor. Copyright © 1963 by Martin Luther King, Jr.; copyright renewed 1991 by Coretta Scott King.

Published by Gramercy Books,
distributed by
Random House Value Publishing, Inc.,
40 Engelhard Avenue, Avenel, New Jersey 07001.

Random House
New York • Toronto • London • Sydney • Auckland

Printed and bound in the United States of America

Designed by Helene Berinsky

Library of Congress Cataloging-in-Publication Data
Great american speeches / edited by Gregory R. Suriano.
p.   cm.—(Library of Freedom)
ISBN 0-517-09117-8
1. United States—Politics and government—Sources.
2. Speeches, addresses, etc., American.   I. Suriano, Gregory R., 1951–
II. Series.
E183.G68   1993   92-37536
973—dc20   CIP

8   7   6   5   4

CONTENTS

INTRODUCTION

THE SPOKEN WORDS of great Americans echo through the years of the republic to reveal, better than any history text, the nation's triumphs and crises, its soul and its deeds, its anguish and its dreams. *Great American Speeches* is a collection that reflects the important issues confronting the country at significant moments from the Revolution to the day before yesterday. The speeches have been organized chronologically so that the history of the United States unfolds decade by decade, year by year, through the personal responses of the individuals who shaped events and ideas.

Each speech has been chosen according to a number of criteria: Does the address reveal one of the significant issues facing the American people at a particular time? Is the speaker considered an important figure in the political, social, literary, cultural, or military life of the nation? Is the speaker a renowned orator? Did he or she make frequent public addresses? Was the speech memorable—have its phrases remained in the hearts of Americans since its delivery, or has its very existence become part of the collective consciousness?

Often, not all of these elements converge in one speech. Robert E. Peary, for example, has not been remembered for his oratorical skills or any specific addresses; yet, the inclusion of a 1907 talk on his arctic expeditions is merited because of the almost mythical character of his discovery of the North Pole, which has come to symbolize the American spirit of exploration. A similar significance underlies the choice of astronaut John Glenn's address to Congress, which was broadcast to the nation following his history-making orbit of the earth in 1962.

And certainly many Americans do not recall a famous speech made by John La Farge; but La Farge, a prominent cultural figure at the turn of the century, deserves a place in this collection because his lectures reflect the first flowering of pride in American art.

On the other hand, the speeches of such notables as George Washington, James Madison, Ralph Waldo Emerson, Henry Clay, Daniel Webster, Frederick Douglass, Lucy Stone, Abraham Lincoln, Mark Twain, Theodore Roosevelt, Woodrow Wilson, Franklin Delano Roosevelt, John F. Kennedy, and Martin Luther King, Jr., obviously combine elements of personal importance, oratorical skill, topical consequence, and memorable presentation.

The speeches in this collection are not merely patriotic or political but are representative of the entire life of the nation, of specific moments in history. Each address has been prefaced by a concise introduction that places the words firmly in their historical context and provides background on the life and accomplishments of the speaker.

To ensure as representative a collection as possible, many of the speeches have been shortened; great care has been taken, however, to retain all the essential points and exceptional turns-of-phrase in a given speech. Any deleted passages within a text have been indicated by ellipses. Editing has been limited to modernization of punctuation and capitalization. About a third of the speeches are printed in full.

GREGORY R. SURIANO

New York
1993

PATRICK HENRY

——— ★ ———

Liberty or Death

VIRGINIA CONVENTION, ST. JOHN'S CHURCH,
RICHMOND, VIRGINIA; MARCH 23, 1775

---

*Patrick Henry's famous speech, delivered in the year before the
signing of the Declaration of Independence, was a fiery call to
arms against British oppression. In defense of a "great and arduous struggle for liberty," Henry argued for a "well-regulated
militia" for the colony of Virginia, and the convention subsequently passed his resolution. Henry (1736–1799) was a member
of the First Continental Congress and was the first governor of
the state of Virginia. William Wirt re-created the address in his
Life of Patrick Henry (1817).*

Mr. President: No man thinks more highly than I do of the
patriotism, as well as abilities, of the very worthy gentlemen who have just addressed the House. But different men often
see the same subjects in different lights; and, therefore, I hope
that it will not be thought disrespectful to those gentlemen, if,
entertaining as I do, opinions of a character very opposite to
theirs, I shall speak forth my sentiments freely and without
reserve. This is no time for ceremony. The question before the
House is one of awful moment to this country. For my own part
I consider it as nothing less than a question of freedom or
slavery, and in proportion to the magnitude of the subject ought
to be the freedom of the debate. It is only in this way that we
can hope to arrive at truth and fulfill the great responsibility

which we hold to God and our country. Should I keep back my opinions at such a time, through fear of giving offense, I should consider myself as guilty of treason toward my country and of an act of disloyalty toward the majesty of heaven, which I revere above all earthly kings.

Mr. President, it is natural to man to indulge in the illusions of hope. We are apt to shut our eyes against a painful truth and listen to the song of that siren, till she transforms us into beasts. Is this the part of wise men, engaged in a great and arduous struggle for liberty? Are we disposed to be of the number of those who, having eyes, see not, and having ears, hear not, the things which so nearly concern their temporal salvation? For my part, whatever anguish of spirit it may cost, I am willing to know the whole truth, to know the worst and to provide for it.

I have but one lamp by which my feet are guided, and that is the lamp of experience. I know of no way of judging of the future but by the past. And judging by the past, I wish to know what there has been in the conduct of the British ministry for the last ten years to justify those hopes with which gentlemen have been pleased to solace themselves and the House? Is it that insidious smile with which our petition has been lately received? Trust it not, sir; it will prove a snare to your feet. Suffer not yourselves to be betrayed with a kiss. Ask yourselves how this gracious reception of our petition comports with these warlike preparations which cover our waters and darken our land. Are fleets and armies necessary to a work of love and reconciliation? Have we shown ourselves so unwilling to be reconciled that force must be called in to win back our love? Let us not deceive ourselves, sir. These are the implements of war and subjugation, the last arguments to which kings resort. I ask gentlemen, sir, what means this martial array, if its purpose be not to force us to submission? Can gentlemen assign any other possible motives for it? Has Great Britain any enemy, in this quarter of the world, to call for all this accumulation of navies and armies? No, sir, she has none. They are meant for us; they can be meant for no other. They are sent over to bind and rivet upon us those chains which the British ministry have been so long forging. And what have we to oppose to them? Shall we try argument? Sir, we have been trying that for the last ten years. Have we anything new to offer on the subject? Nothing. We have held the subject up in every light of which it is capable, but it has been all in vain. Shall we resort to entreaty and humble supplication? What terms shall we find which have not been already exhausted? Let us not, I beseech you, sir, deceive ourselves longer. Sir, we have done everything that could be done to avert the storm which is now coming on. We have petitioned; we have remonstrated; we have supplicated; we have prostrated ourselves before the tyrannical hands of the ministry and parliament. Our petitions have been slighted; our remonstrances have produced additional violence and insult; our supplications have been disregarded; and we have been spurned, with contempt, from the foot of the throne. In vain, after these things, may we indulge the fond hope of peace and reconciliation. There is no longer any room for hope. If we wish to be free—if we mean to preserve inviolate those inestimable privileges for which we have been so long contending—if we mean not basely to abandon the noble struggle in which we have been so long engaged, and which we have pledged ourselves never to abandon until the glorious object of our contest shall be obtained, we must fight! I repeat it, sir, we must fight! An appeal to arms and to the God of Hosts is all that is left us!

They tell us, sir, that we are weak, unable to cope with so formidable an adversary. But when shall we be stronger? Will it be the next week, or the next year? Will it be when we are totally disarmed, and when a British guard shall be stationed in every house? Shall we gather strength by irresolution and inaction? Shall we acquire the means of effectual resistance by lying supinely on our backs and hugging the delusive phantom of hope, until our enemies shall have bound us hand and foot? Sir, we are not weak, if we make a proper use of the means which the God of nature hath placed in our power. Three millions of people, armed in the holy cause of liberty, and in such a country as that which we possess, are invincible by any force which our enemy can send against us. Besides, sir, we shall not fight our battles alone. There is a just God who presides over the destinies of nations, and who will raise friends to fight our battles for us. The battle, sir, is not to the strong alone; it is to the vigilant, the active, the brave. Besides, sir, we have no election. If we were base enough to desire it, it is now too late to retire from the contest. There is no retreat but in submission and slavery! Our chains are forged! Their clanking may be heard on the plains of Boston! The war is inevitable—and let it come! I repeat it, sir, let it come!

It is in vain, sir, to extenuate the matter. Gentlemen may cry, peace, peace!—but there is no peace. The war is actually begun! The next gale that sweeps from the north will bring to our ears the clash of resounding arms! Our brethren are already in the field! Why stand we here idle? What is it that gentlemen wish? What would they have? Is life so dear, or peace so sweet, as to be purchased at the price of chains and slavery? Forbid it, Almighty God! I know not what course others may take, but as for me: *Give me liberty, or give me death!*

James Madison

★

In Favor of the
Federal Constitution

Virginia Ratification Convention,
Richmond, Virginia; June 6, 1788

James Madison's argument in favor of the adoption of the Constitution was essentially a rebuttal to a speech against ratification made on the previous day by Patrick Henry. Madison's support was instrumental in reversing opinion against a federal constitution. In addition to writing The Federalist *(1787) with John Jay and Alexander Hamilton, Madison (1751–1836) served as secretary of state under Thomas Jefferson, whom he succeeded as president in 1809.*

We ought, sir, to examine the Constitution on its own merits solely. We are to inquire whether it will promote the public happiness; its aptitude to produce this desirable object ought to be the exclusive subject of our present researches. In this pursuit, we ought not to address our arguments to the feelings and passions but to those understandings and judgments which were selected by the people of this country, to decide this great question by a calm and rational investigation.

I hope that gentlemen, in displaying their abilities on this occasion, instead of giving opinions and making assertions, will condescend to prove and demonstrate by a fair and regular discussion. It gives me pain to hear gentlemen continually distorting the natural construction of language; for it is sufficient if any human production can stand a fair discussion. Before I proceed to make some additions to the reasons which have been adduced by my honorable friend over the way, I must take the liberty to make some observations on what was said by another gentleman [Patrick Henry].

He told us that this Constitution ought to be rejected because it endangered the public liberty, in his opinion, in many instances. Give me leave to make answer to that observation. Let the dangers which this system is supposed to be replete with be clearly pointed out. If any dangerous and unnecessary powers be given to the general legislature, let them be plainly demonstrated; and let us not rest satisfied with general assertions of danger, without examination. If powers be necessary, apparent danger is not a sufficient reason against conceding them. He has suggested that licentiousness has seldom produced the loss of liberty, but that the tyranny of rulers has almost always affected it. Since the general civilization of mankind I believe there are more instances of the abridgment of the freedom of the people by gradual and silent encroachments of those in power than by violent and sudden usurpations; but, on a candid examination of history, we shall find that turbulence, violence, and abuse of power, by the majority trampling on the rights of the minority, have produced factions and commotions which, in republics, have more frequently than any other cause, produced despotism. If we go over the whole history of ancient and modern republics we shall find their destruction to have generally resulted from those causes. If we consider the peculiar situation of the United States, and what are the sources of that diversity of sentiment which pervades its inhabitants, we shall find great danger to fear that the same causes may terminate here in the same fatal effects which they produced in those republics. This danger ought to be wisely guarded against. . . .

I must confess I have not been able to find his usual consistency in the gentleman's argument on this occasion. He informs us that the people of the country are at perfect repose; that is, every man enjoys the fruits of his labor peaceably and securely, and that everything is in perfect tranquility and safety. I wish sincerely that this were true. If this be their happy situation, why has every state acknowledged the contrary? Why were deputies from all the states sent to the general convention? Why have complaints of national and individual distresses been echoed and reechoed throughout the continent? Why has our general government been so shamefully disgraced and our Constitution violated? Wherefore have laws been made to authorize a change, and wherefore are we now assembled here? A federal government is formed for the protection of its individual members. Ours has attacked itself with impunity. Its authority has been disobeyed and despised.

I think I perceive a glaring inconsistency in another of his arguments. He complains of this Constitution because it requires the consent of at least three-fourths of the states to introduce amendments which shall be necessary for the happiness of the people. . . . In the first case, he asserts that a majority ought to have the power of altering the government when found to be inadequate to the security of public happiness. In the last case, he affirms that even three-fourths of the community have not a right to alter a government which experience has proved to be subversive of national felicity! nay, that the most necessary and urgent alterations cannot be made without the absolute unanimity of all the states! Does not the thirteenth article of the Confederation expressly require that no alteration shall be made without the unanimous consent of all the states? Could anything in theory be more perniciously improvident and injudicious than this submission of the will of the majority to the most trifling minority? Have not experience and practice actually manifested this theoretical inconvenience to be extremely impolitic? . . .

The power of raising and supporting armies is exclaimed against as dangerous and unnecessary. I wish there were no necessity of vesting this power in the general government. But suppose a foreign nation were to declare war against the United States; must not the general legislature have the power of defending the United States? Ought it to be known to foreign nations that the general government of the United States of America has no power to raise and support an army, even in the utmost danger, when attacked by external enemies? Would not their knowledge of such a circumstance stimulate them to fall upon us? If, sir, Congress be not invested with this power, any powerful nation, prompted by ambition or avarice, will be invited by our weakness to attack us; and such an attack by disciplined veterans would certainly be attended with success, when only opposed by irregular, undisciplined militia. . . .

Give me leave to say something of the nature of the government and to show that it is safe and just to vest it with the power of taxation. There are a number of opinions, but the principal question is whether it be a federal or a consolidated government. In order to judge properly of the question before us, we must consider it minutely in its principal parts. I conceive myself that it is of a mixed nature; it is in a manner unprecedented; we cannot find one express example in the experience of the world. It stands by itself. In some respects it is a government of a federal nature; in others, it is of a consolidated nature. Even if we attend to the manner in which the Constitution is investigated, ratified, and made the act of the people of America, I can say, notwithstanding what the honorable gentleman has alleged, that this government is not completely consolidated, nor is it entirely federal. Who are parties to it? The people—but not the people as composing one great body, but the people as composing thirteen sovereignties. Were it, as the gentleman asserts, a consolidated government, the assent of a majority of the people would be sufficient for its establishment; and, as a majority have adopted it already, the remaining states would be bound by the act of the majority, even if they unanimously rejected it. Were it such a government as is suggested it would be now binding on the people of this state without their having had the privilege of deliberating on it. But, sir, no state is bound by it, as it is, without its own consent. Should all the states adopt it, it will be then a government established by the thirteen states of America, not through the intervention of the legislatures, but by the people at large. In this particular respect the distinction between the existing and the proposed governments is very material. The existing system has been derived from the dependent derivative authority of the legislatures of the states; whereas, this is derived from the superior power of the people.

If we look at the manner in which alterations are to be made in it, the same idea is, in some degree, attended to. By the new system a majority of the states cannot introduce amendments, nor are all the states required for that purpose; three-fourths of them must concur in alterations. In this there is a departure from the federal idea. The members of the national House of Representatives are to be chosen by the people at large, in proportion to the numbers in the respective districts. When we come to the Senate, its members are elected by the states in their equal and political capacity. But had the government been completely consolidated, the Senate would have been chosen by the people in their individual capacity, in the same manner as the members of the other house. Thus it is of a complicated nature; and this complication, I trust, will be found to exclude the evils of absolute consolidation, as well as of a mere confederacy. . . .

Those who wish to become federal representatives must depend on their credit with that class of men who will be the most popular in their counties, who generally represent the people in the state governments; they can, therefore, never succeed in any measure contrary to the wishes of those on whom they depend. It is almost certain, therefore, that the deliberations of the members of the federal House of Representatives will be directed to the interests of the people of America. As to the other branch, the senators will be appointed by the legislatures; and, though elected for six years, I do not conceive they will so soon forget the source from whence they derive their political existence. This election of one branch of the federal by the state legislatures secures an absolute dependence of the former on the latter. The biennial exclusion of one-third will lessen the facility of a combination and may put a stop to intrigues. I appeal to our past experience whether they will attend to the interests of their constituent states. Have not those gentlemen who have been honored with seats in Congress, often signalized themselves by their attachment to their seats?

I wish this government may answer the expectation of its friends and foil the apprehension of its enemies. I hope the patriotism of the people will continue and be a sufficient guard to their liberties. I believe its tendency will be that the state governments will counteract the general interest and ultimately prevail. The number of the representatives is yet sufficient for our safety and will gradually increase; and, if we consider their different sources of information, the number will not appear too small.

George Washington

★

First Inaugural Address

Federal Hall, New York, New York; April 30, 1789

Although the first Congress was to begin operations on March 4, 1789, it was not until April 5 that a sufficient number of senators was available to count electoral votes. On April 6 George Washington (1732–1799) was declared president and John Adams vice president. Washington's popularity was such that he was honored by crowds and officials in villages all along the route of his journey from Mount Vernon to New York for the inauguration. The president's dignified bearing and words gave the impression of a grandfather gently presiding over the upbringing of a young child. A striking feature of his speech is the repeated references to the homage owed "the Almighty Being . . . the Great Author of every public and private good" for the success and blessings of the people of the United States.

Fellow Citizens of the Senate and of the House of Representatives: Among the vicissitudes incident to life, no event could have filled me with greater anxieties than that of which the notification was transmitted by your order and received on the fourteenth day of the present month.

On the one hand, I was summoned by my country, whose voice I can never hear but with veneration and love, from a retreat which I had chosen with the fondest predilection, and, in my flattering hopes, with an immutable decision, as the asylum of my declining years—a retreat which was rendered every day more necessary as well as more dear to me by the addition of habit to inclination, and of frequent interruptions in my health to the gradual waste committed on it by time.

On the other hand, the magnitude and difficulty of the trust to which the voice of my country called me, being sufficient to awaken in the wisest and most experienced of her citizens a distrustful scrutiny into his qualifications, could not but overwhelm with despondence one who (inheriting inferior endowments from nature and unpracticed in the duties of civil administration) ought to be peculiarly conscious of his own deficiencies.

In this conflict of emotions all I dare aver is that it has been my faithful study to collect my duty from a just appreciation of every circumstance by which it might be affected. All I dare hope is that if, in executing this task, I have been too much swayed by a grateful remembrance of former instances, or by an affectionate sensibility to this transcendent proof of the confidence of my fellow citizens, and have thence too little consulted my incapacity as well as disinclination for the weighty and untried cares before me, my error will be palliated by the motives which misled me, and its consequences be judged by my country, with some share of the partiality in which they originated.

Such being the impressions under which I have, in obedience to the public summons, repaired to the present station, it would be peculiarly improper to omit in this first official act, my fervent supplications to that Almighty Being who rules over the universe, who presides in the councils of nations, and whose providential aids can supply every human defect, that His benediction may consecrate to the liberties and happiness of the people of the United States, a government instituted by themselves for these essential purposes, and may enable every instrument employed in its administration to execute with success the functions allotted to his charge.

In tendering this homage to the Great Author of every public and private good, I assure myself that it expresses your sentiments not less than my own, nor those of my fellow citizens at large, less than either. No people can be bound to acknowledge and adore the Invisible Hand which conducts the affairs of men more than the people of the United States. Every step by which they have advanced to the character of an independent nation seems to have been distinguished by some token of providential agency. And in the important revolution just accomplished in the system of their united government, the tranquil deliberations and voluntary consent of so many distinct communities, from which the event has resulted, cannot be compared with the means by which most governments have been established, without some return of pious gratitude, along with an humble anticipation of the future blessings which the past seem to presage.

These reflections, arising out of the present crisis, have forced themselves too strongly on my mind to be suppressed. You will join with me, I trust, in thinking that there are none under the influence of which the proceedings of a new and free government can more auspiciously commence.

By the article establishing the executive department it is made the duty of the president "to recommend to your consideration such measures as he shall judge necessary and expedient." The circumstances under which I now meet you will acquit me from entering into that subject farther than to refer to the great constitutional charter under which you are assembled and which, in defining your powers, designates the objects to which your attention is to be given.

It will be more consistent with those circumstances, and far more congenial with the feelings which actuate me, to substitute, in place of a recommendation of particular measures, the tribute that is due to the talents, the rectitude, and the patriotism which adorn the characters selected to devise and adopt them. In these honorable qualifications I behold the surest pledges that as on one side, no local prejudices or attachments, no separate views nor party animosities, will misdirect the comprehensive and equal eye which ought to watch over this great assemblage of communities and interests: so, on another, that the foundations of our national policy will be laid in the pure and immutable principles of private morality; and the preeminence of free government be exemplified by all the attributes which can win the affections of its citizens and command the respect of the world.

I dwell on this prospect with every satisfaction which an ardent love for my country can inspire, since there is no truth more thoroughly established than that there exists in the economy and course of nature an indissoluble union between virtue and happiness—between duty and advantage—between the genuine maxims of an honest and magnanimous policy and the solid rewards of public prosperity and felicity; since we ought to be no less persuaded that the propitious smiles of heaven can never be expected on a nation that disregards the external rules of order and right which heaven itself has ordained; and since the preservation of the sacred fire of liberty and the destiny of the republican model of government are justly considered as deeply, perhaps as finally staked, on the experiment entrusted to the hands of the American people.

Besides the ordinary objects submitted to your care, it will remain with your judgment to decide how far an exercise of the occasional power delegated by the fifth article of the Constitution is rendered expedient, at the present juncture, by the nature of objections which have been urged against the system, or by the degree of inquietude which has given birth to them.

Instead of undertaking particular recommendations on this subject, in which I could be guided by no lights derived from official opportunities, I shall again give way to my entire confidence in your discernment and pursuit of the public good; for I assure myself that whilst you carefully avoid every alteration which might endanger the benefits of an united and effective government, or which ought to await the future lessons of experience, a reverence for the characteristic rights of freemen and a regard for the public harmony will sufficiently influence your deliberations on the question how far the former can be impregnably fortified or the latter be safely and advantageously promoted.

To the foregoing observations I have one to add, which will

be most properly addressed to the House of Representatives. It concerns myself and will therefore be as brief as possible.

When I was first honored with a call into the service of my country, then on the eve of an arduous struggle for its liberties, the light in which I contemplated my duty required that I should renounce every pecuniary compensation. From this resolution I have in no instance departed. And being still under the impressions which produced it, I must decline as inapplicable to myself, any share in the personal emoluments which may be indispensably included in a permanent provision for the executive department, and must accordingly pray that the pecuniary estimates for the station in which I am placed may, during my continuance in it, be limited to such actual expenditures as the public good may be thought to require.

Having thus imparted to you my sentiments as they have been awakened by the occasion which brings us together, I shall take my present leave; but not without resorting once more to the benign Parent of the Human Race, in humble supplication that since He has been pleased to favor the American people with opportunities for deliberating in perfect tranquillity and dispositions for deciding with unparalleled unanimity on a form of government for the security of their union, and the advancement of their happiness, so His divine blessing may be equally conspicuous in the enlarged views, the temperate consultations, and the wise measures on which the success of this government must depend.

George Washington

—— ★ ——

Farewell Address

To His Cabinet, Philadelphia, Pennsylvania;
September 17, 1796

*By 1796 George Washington had served two terms as president
and did not wish to serve a third. His immense popularity had
dwindled—over his opposition to aid for the French Revolution,
his suppression of the Whiskey Rebellion, and his perceived pro-
British leanings in the settlement of differences with England
through the 1794 Jay Treaty. He was opposed to the formation
of political parties, which were emerging, and was tired of being
lampooned in satirical prints. Washington considered his fare-
well statement so important that he had the full text published in
the Philadelphia* Daily American Advertiser *on September 19,
1796, so that it would reach a large segment of the public.
The address warned against foreign involvements, political factions, and sectionalism and promoted religion, morality, and
education.*

Friends and Fellow Citizens: The period for a new election of
a citizen to administer the executive government of the
United States being not far distant, and the time actually arrived
when your thoughts must be employed in designating the person
who is to be clothed with that important trust, it appears to me
proper, especially as it may conduce to a more distinct expression of the public voice, that I should now apprise you of the
resolution I have formed to decline being considered among the
number of those out of whom a choice is to be made. . . .

In looking forward to the moment which is intended to
terminate the career of my political life, my feelings do not
permit me to suspend the deep acknowledgment of that debt of
gratitude which I owe to my beloved country for the many

honors it has conferred upon me; still more for the steadfast confidence with which it has supported me, and for the opportunities I have thence enjoyed of manifesting my inviolable attachment by services faithful and persevering, though in usefulness unequal to my zeal. . . .

Here, perhaps, I ought to stop. But a solicitude for your welfare, which cannot end but with my life, and the apprehension of danger natural to that solicitude urge me on an occasion like the present to offer to your solemn contemplation and to recommend to your frequent review some sentiments which are the result of much reflection, of no inconsiderable observation, and which appear to me all important to the permanency of your felicity as a people. . . .

The unity of government which constitutes you one people is also now dear to you. It is justly so, for it is a main pillar in the edifice of your real independence, the support of your tranquility at home, your peace abroad, of your safety, of your prosperity, of that very liberty which you so highly prize.

But as it is easy to foresee that from different causes and from different quarters much pains will be taken, many artifices employed, to weaken in your minds the conviction of this truth, as this is the point in your political fortress against which the batteries of internal and external enemies will be most constantly and actively (though often covertly and insidiously) directed, it is of infinite moment that you should properly estimate the immense value of your national union to your collective and individual happiness. . . .

The name of American, which belongs to you in your national capacity, must always exalt the just pride of patriotism more than any appellation derived from local discriminations. With slight shades of difference, you have the same religion, manners, habits, and political principles. You have in a common cause fought and triumphed together. The independence and liberty you possess are the work of joint councils and joint efforts, of common dangers, sufferings, and successes.

But these considerations, however powerfully they address

themselves to your sensibility, are greatly outweighed by those which apply more immediately to your interest. Here every portion of our country finds the most commanding motives for carefully guarding and preserving the union of the whole. . . .

In contemplating the causes which may disturb our Union, it occurs as matter of serious concern that any ground should have been furnished for characterizing parties by geographical discriminations—Northern and Southern, Atlantic and Western—whence designing men may endeavor to excite a belief that there is a real difference of local interests and views. One of the expedients of party to acquire influence within particular districts is to misrepresent the opinions and aims of other districts. You cannot shield yourselves too much against the jealousies and heartburnings which spring from these misrepresentations. They tend to render alien to each other those who ought to be bound together by fraternal affection. . . .

To the efficacy and permanency of your Union a government for the whole is indispensable. No alliances, however strict, between the parts can be an adequate substitute. They must inevitably experience the infractions and interruptions which all alliances in all times have experienced. Sensible of this momentous truth, you have improved upon your first essay by the adoption of a constitution of government better calculated than your former for an intimate union, and for the efficacious management of your common concerns. . . .

Toward the preservation of your government and the permanency of your present happy state, it is requisite not only that you steadily discountenance irregular oppositions to its acknowledged authority, but also that you resist with care the spirit of innovation upon its principles, however specious the pretexts. One method of assault may be to effect in the forms of the Constitution alterations which will impair the energy of the system, and thus to undermine what cannot be directly overthrown. . . .

I have already intimated to you the danger of parties in the state, with particular reference to the founding of them on geographical discriminations. Let me now take a more comprehensive view and warn you in the most solemn manner against the baneful effects of the spirit of party generally. . . .

The alternate domination of one faction over another, sharpened by the spirit of revenge natural to party dissension, which in different ages and countries has perpetrated the most horrid enormities, is itself a frightful despotism. But this leads at length to a more formal and permanent despotism. The disorders and miseries which result gradually incline the minds of men to seek security and repose in the absolute power of an individual, and sooner or later the chief of some prevailing faction, more able or more fortunate than his competitors, turns this disposition to the purposes of his own elevation on the ruins of public liberty. . . .

Of all the dispositions and habits which lead to political prosperity, religion and morality are indispensable supports. In vain would that man claim the tribute of patriotism who should labor to subvert these great pillars of human happiness, these firmest props of the duties of men and citizens. The mere politician, equally with the pious man, ought to respect and to cherish them. A volume could not trace all their connections with private and public felicity. Let it simply be asked: Where is the security for property, for reputation, for life, if the sense of religious obligation desert the oaths which are the instruments of investigation in courts of justice? And let us with caution indulge the supposition that morality can be maintained without religion. Whatever may be conceded to the influence of refined education on minds of peculiar structure, reason and experience both forbid us to expect that national morality can prevail in exclusion of religious principle.

'Tis substantially true that virtue or morality is a necessary spring of popular government. The rule indeed extends with more or less force to every species of free government. Who that is a sincere friend to it can look with indifference upon attempts to shake the foundation of the fabric? Promote, then, as an object of primary importance, institutions for the general diffusion of knowledge. In proportion as the structure of a government gives force to public opinion, it is essential that public opinion should be enlightened. . . .

Observe good faith and justice toward all nations. Cultivate peace and harmony with all. Religion and morality enjoin this conduct; and can it be that good policy does not equally enjoin it? It will be worthy of a free, enlightened, and at no distant period, a great nation, to give to mankind the magnanimous and too novel example of a people always guided by an exalted justice and benevolence. Who can doubt that in the course of time and things the fruits of such a plan would richly repay any temporary advantages which might be lost by a steady adherence to it? Can it be that Providence has not connected the permanent felicity of a nation with its virtues? The experiment, at least, is recommended by every sentiment which ennobles human nature. Alas! is it rendered impossible by its vices?

In the execution of such a plan nothing is more essential than that permanent, inveterate antipathies against particular nations and passionate attachments for others should be excluded, and that in place of them just and amicable feelings toward all should be cultivated. . . .

Harmony, liberal intercourse with all nations are recommended by policy, humanity, and interest. But even our commercial policy should hold an equal and impartial hand, neither seeking nor granting exclusive favors or preferences. . . . There can be no greater error than to expect or calculate upon real favors from nation to nation. 'Tis an illusion which experience must cure, which a just pride ought to discard.

In offering to you, my countrymen, these counsels of an old and affectionate friend, I dare not hope they will make the strong and lasting impression I could wish, that they will control the usual current of the passions or prevent our nation from running the course which has hitherto marked the destiny of nations. But if I may even flatter myself that they may be productive of some partial benefit, some occasional good—that they may now and then recur to moderate the fury of party spirit, to warn against the mischiefs of foreign intrigue, to guard against the impostures of pretended patriotism—this hope will be a full recompense for the solicitude for your welfare by which they have been dictated. . . .

Though in reviewing the incidents of my administration I am unconscious of intentional error, I am nevertheless too sensible of my defects not to think it probable that I may have committed many errors. Whatever they may be, I fervently beseech the Almighty to avert or mitigate the evils to which they may tend. I shall also carry with me the hope that my country will never cease to view them with indulgence, and that after forty-five years of my life dedicated to its service, with an upright zeal, the faults of incompetent abilities will be consigned to oblivion, as myself must soon be to the mansions of rest.

Relying on its kindness in this as in other things, and actuated by that fervent love toward it which is so natural to a man who views in it the native soil of himself and his progenitors for several generations, I anticipate with pleasing expectation that retreat in which I promise myself to realize, without alloy, the sweet enjoyment of partaking, in the midst of my fellow citizens, the benign influence of good laws under a free government—the ever favorite object of my heart and the happy reward, as I trust, of our mutual cares, labors, and dangers.

THOMAS JEFFERSON

———— ★ ————

Second Inaugural Address

CAPITOL, WASHINGTON, D.C.; MARCH 4, 1805

Elected the third president of the United States in 1800, Thomas Jefferson (1743–1826) and his Democratic-Republican party offered a clear alternative to the previous administrations' policies that had fostered the central government's powers over those of the states. President Jefferson had authorized the purchase of the Louisiana Territory from the French for $15 million in 1803. In his second inaugural address, he defended the acquisition of this land and noted with pride that "the suppression of unnecessary offices, of useless establishments and expenses, enabled us to discontinue our internal taxes. . . . What farmer, what mechanic, what laborer ever sees a tax gatherer of the United States?" Jefferson brilliantly struck a balance in tone between the philosophical concerns of a man of great intellect and the specific, clearly enunciated public issues of his previous and future terms.

P roceeding, fellow citizens, to that qualification which the Constitution requires before my entrance on the charge again conferred upon me, it is my duty to express the deep sense I entertain of this new proof of confidence from my fellow citizens at large, and the zeal with which it inspires me, so to conduct myself as may best satisfy their just expectations.

On taking this station on a former occasion, I declared the principles on which I believed it my duty to administer the affairs of our commonwealth. My conscience tells me that I have, on every occasion, acted up to that declaration, according to its obvious import, and to the understanding of every candid mind.

In the transaction of your foreign affairs, we have endeavored to cultivate the friendship of all nations, and especially of those with which we have the most important relations. We have done them justice on all occasions, favored where favor was lawful, and cherished mutual interests and intercourse on fair and equal terms. We are firmly convinced, and we act on that conviction, that with nations, as with individuals, our interests soundly calculated, will ever be found inseparable from our moral duties; and history bears witness to the fact that a just nation is taken on its word when recourse is had to armaments and wars to bridle others.

At home, fellow citizens, you best know whether we have done well or ill. The suppression of unnecessary offices, of useless establishments and expenses, enabled us to discontinue our internal taxes. These covering our land with officers, and opening our doors to their intrusions, had already begun that process of domiciliary vexation which, once entered, is scarcely to be restrained from reaching successively every article of produce and property. If among these taxes some minor ones fell which had not been inconvenient, it was because their amount would not have paid the officers who collected them, and because, if they had any merit, the state authorities might adopt them instead of others less approved.

The remaining revenue on the consumption of foreign articles is paid cheerfully by those who can afford to add foreign luxuries to domestic comforts, being collected on our seaboards and frontiers only and incorporated with the transactions of our mercantile citizens; it may be the pleasure and pride of an American to ask, What farmer, what mechanic, what laborer, ever sees a tax gatherer of the United States? These contributions enable us to support the current expenses of the government, to fulfill contracts with foreign nations, to extinguish the native right of soil within our limits, to extend those limits, and to apply such a surplus to our public debts, as places at a short day their final redemption, and that redemption once effected, the revenue thereby liberated may, by a just repartition among the states and a corresponding amending of the Constitution, be applied, in time of peace, to rivers, canals, roads, arts, manufactures, education, and other great objects within each state. In time of war, if injustice, by ourselves or others, must sometimes produce war, increased as the same revenue will be increased by population and consumption, and aided by other resources reserved for that crisis, it may meet within the year all the expenses of the year, without encroaching on the rights of future generations by burdening them with the debts of the past. War will then be but a suspension of useful works, and a return to a state of peace a return to the progress of improvement.

I have said, fellow citizens, that the income reserved had enabled us to extend our limits; but that extension may possibly pay for itself before we are called on, and in the meantime, may keep down the accruing interest; in all events, it will repay the advances we have made. I know that the acquisition of Louisiana has been disapproved by some, from a candid apprehension that the enlargement of our territory would endanger its union. But who can limit the extent to which the federative principle may operate effectively? The larger our association, the less will it be shaken by local passions; and in any view, is it not better that the opposite bank of the Mississippi should be settled by our own brethren and children, than by strangers of another family? With which shall we be most likely to live in harmony and friendly intercourse?

In matters of religion, I have considered that its free exercise is placed by the Constitution independent of the powers of the general government. I have therefore undertaken, on no occasion, to prescribe the religious exercises suited to it, but have left them, as the Constitution found them, under the direction and discipline of state or church authorities acknowledged by the several religious societies.

The aboriginal inhabitants of these countries I have regarded with the commiseration their history inspires. Endowed with the faculties and the rights of men, breathing an ardent love of liberty and independence, and occupying a country which left them no desire but to be undisturbed, the stream of overflowing population from other regions directed itself on these shores; without power to divert, or habits to contend against, they have been overwhelmed by the current, or driven before it; now reduced within limits too narrow for the hunter's state, humanity enjoins us to teach them agriculture and the domestic arts; to encourage them to that industry which alone can enable them to maintain their place in existence, and to prepare them in time for that state of society, which to bodily comforts adds the improvement of the mind and morals. We have therefore liberally furnished them with the implements of husbandry and household use; we have placed among them instructors in the arts of first necessity; and they are covered with the aegis of the law against aggressors from among ourselves.

But the endeavors to enlighten them on the fate which awaits their present course of life, to induce them to exercise their reason, follow its dictates, and change their pursuits with the change of circumstances, have powerful obstacles to encounter; they are combated by the habits of their bodies, prejudice of their minds, ignorance, pride, and the influence of interested and crafty individuals among them, who feel themselves something in the present order of things and fear to become nothing in any other. These persons inculcate a sanctimonious reverence for the customs of their ancestors; that whatsoever they did must be done through all time; that reason is a false guide, and to advance under its counsel, in their physical, moral, or political condition, is perilous innovation; that their duty is to remain as their Creator made them, ignorance being safety, and knowledge full of danger; in short, my friends, among them is seen the action and counteraction of good sense and bigotry; they, too, have their antiphilosophers, who find an interest in keeping things in their present state, who dread reformation and exert all their faculties to maintain the ascendancy of habit over the duty of improving our reason and obeying its mandates.

In giving these outlines, I do not mean, fellow citizens, to arrogate to myself the merit of the measures; that is due, in the first place, to the reflecting character of our citizens at large, who, by the weight of public opinion, influence and strengthen the public measures; it is due to the sound discretion with which they select from among themselves those to whom they confide the legislative duties; it is due to the zeal and wisdom of the characters thus selected, who lay the foundations of public happiness in wholesome laws, the execution of which alone remains for others; and it is due to the able and faithful auxiliaries, whose patriotism has associated with me in the executive functions.

During this course of administration, and in order to disturb it, the artillery of the press has been levelled against us, charged with whatsoever its licentiousness could devise or dare. These abuses of an institution so important to freedom and science are deeply to be regretted, inasmuch as they tend to lessen its usefulness and to sap its safety; they might, indeed, have been corrected by the wholesome punishments reserved and provided by the laws of the several states against falsehood and defamation; but public duties more urgent press on the time of public servants, and the offenders have therefore been left to find their punishment in the public indignation.

Nor was it uninteresting to the world that an experiment could be fairly and fully made, whether freedom of discussion, unaided by power, is not sufficient for the propagation and protection of truth—whether a government, conducting itself in the true spirit of its constitution, with zeal and purity, and doing no act which it would be unwilling the whole world should witness, can be written down by falsehood and defamation. The experiment has been tried; you have witnessed the scene; our fellow citizens have looked on, cool and collected; they saw the latent source from which these outrages proceeded; they gathered around their public functionaries, and when the Constitution called them to the decision by suffrage, they pronounced their verdict, honorable to those who had served them, and consolatory to the friend of man, who believes he may be entrusted with his own affairs.

No inference is here intended that the laws, provided by the state against false and defamatory publications, should not be enforced; he who has time renders a service to public morals and public tranquillity, in reforming these abuses by the salutary coercions of the law; but the experiment is noted to prove that, since truth and reason have maintained their ground against false opinions in league with false facts, the press, confined to truth, needs to other legal restraint; the public judgment will correct false reasonings and opinions, on a full hearing of all parties; and no other definite line can be drawn between the inestimable liberty of the press and its demoralizing licentiousness. If there be still improprieties which this rule would not restrain, its supplement must be sought in the censorship of public opinion.

Contemplating the union of sentiment now manifested so generally, as auguring harmony and happiness to our future course, I offer to our country sincere congratulations. With those, too, not yet rallied to the same point, the disposition to do so is gaining strength; facts are piercing through the veil drawn over them, and our doubting brethren will at length see that the mass of their fellow citizens, with whom they cannot yet resolve to act, as to principles and measures, think as they think and desire what they desire; that our wish, as well as theirs, is that the public efforts may be directed honestly to the public good, that peace be cultivated, civil and religious liberty unassailed, law and order preserved, equality of rights maintained, and that state of property, equal or unequal, which results to every man from his own industry, or that of his fathers. When satisfied of these views, it is not in human nature that they should not approve and support them; in the meantime, let us cherish them with patient affection; let us do them justice, and more than justice, in all competitions of interest; and we need not doubt that truth, reason, and their own interests will at length prevail, will gather them into the fold of their country, and will complete their entire union of opinion, which gives to a nation the blessing of harmony and the benefit of all its strength.

I shall now enter on the duties to which my fellow citizens have again called me and shall proceed in the spirit of those principles which they have approved. I fear not that any motives of interest may lead me astray; I am sensible of no passion which could seduce me knowingly from the path of justice; but the weakness of human nature and the limits of my own understanding will produce errors of judgment sometimes injurious to your interests. I shall need, therefore, all the indulgence I have heretofore experienced—the want of it will certainly not lessen with increasing years. I shall need, too, the favor of that Being in whose hands we are, who led our forefathers, as Israel of old, from their native land, and planted them in a country flowing with all the necessaries and comforts of life; who has covered our infancy with His providence, and our riper years with His wisdom and power; and to whose goodness I ask you to join with me in supplications, that He will so enlighten the minds of your servants, guide their councils, and prosper their measures, that whatsoever they do shall result in your good and shall secure to you the peace, friendship, and approbation of all nations.

RALPH WALDO EMERSON

——— ★ ———

The American Scholar

FIRST PARISH CHURCH, CAMBRIDGE, MASSACHUSETTS;
AUGUST 31, 1837

Ralph Waldo Emerson (1803–1882) was an essayist, philosopher, poet, prominent public lecturer, and leader of the transcendentalist movement. In his 1837 Phi Beta Kappa address to the Harvard community, Emerson espoused the primacy of the individual as thinker, upon which state there are four main influences: nature; the knowledge, culture, and institutions of the past; society, which the thinking person must actively engage; and the application of self-trust and duty to the world. "The world—this shadow of the soul, or other me—lies wide around," Emerson stated in the poetic tone that characterized the lecture. "Its attractions are the keys which unlock my thoughts and make me acquainted with myself. I run eagerly into this resounding tumult."

M r. President and Gentlemen: I greet you on the recommencement of our literary year. Our anniversary is one of hope, and, perhaps, not enough of labor. We do not meet for games of strength or skill, for the recitation of histories, tragedies, and odes, like the ancient Greeks; for parliaments of love and poesy, like the troubadors; nor for the advancement of science, like our contemporaries in the British and European capitals. Thus far, our holiday has been simply a friendly sign of the survival of the love of letters amongst a people too busy to give to letters any more. As such it is precious as the sign of an indestructible instinct. Perhaps the time is already come when it ought to be, and will be, something else; when the sluggard intellect of this continent will look from under its iron lids and fill the postponed expectation of the world with something better than the exertions of mechanical skill. Our day of dependence, our long apprenticeship to the learning of other lands, draws to a close. The millions that around us are rushing into life cannot always be fed on the sere remains of foreign harvests. Events, actions arise that must be sung, that will sing themselves. Who can doubt that poetry will revive and lead in a new age, as the star in the constellation Harp, which now flames in our zenith, astronomers announce, shall one day be the pole star for a thousand years?

In this hope I accept the topic which not only usage but the nature of our association seem to prescribe to this day—the American Scholar. Year by year we come up hither to read one more chapter of his biography. Let us inquire what light new days and events have thrown on his character and his hopes. . . . The state of society is one in which the members have suffered amputation from the trunk and strut about so many walking monsters—a good finger, a neck, a stomach, an elbow, but never a man.

Man is thus metamorphosed into a thing, into many things. The planter, who is man sent out into the field to gather food, is seldom cheered by any idea of the true dignity of his ministry. He sees his bushel and his cart, and nothing beyond, and sinks into the farmer, instead of man on the farm. The tradesman scarcely ever gives an ideal worth to his work but is ridden by the routine of his craft, and the soul is subject to dollars. The priest becomes a form; the attorney a statute-book; the mechanic a machine; the sailor a rope of the ship.

In this distribution of functions the scholar is the delegated intellect. In the right state he is *Man Thinking*. In the degenerate state, when the victim of society, he tends to become a mere thinker, or still worse, the parrot of other men's thinking.

In this view of him, as Man Thinking, the theory of his office is contained. Him Nature solicits with all her placid, all her monitory pictures; him the past instructs; him the future invites. Is not indeed every man a student, and do not all things exist for the student's behoof? And, finally, is not the true scholar the only true master? But the old oracle said, "All things have two handles: beware of the wrong one." In life, too often, the scholar errs with mankind and forfeits his privilege. Let us see him in his school and consider him in reference to the main influences he receives.

1. The first in time and the first in importance of the influences upon the mind is that of nature. Every day, the sun; and, after sunset, Night and her stars. Ever the winds blow; ever the grass grows. Every day, men and women, conversing—beholding and beholden. The scholar is he of all men whom this spectacle most engages. He must settle its value in his mind. What is nature to him? There is never a beginning, there is never an end, to the inexplicable continuity of this web of God, but always circular power returning into itself. Therein it resembles his own spirit, whose beginning, whose ending, he never can find—so entire, so boundless. Far too as her splendors shine, system on system shooting like rays, upward, downward, without center, without circumference—in the mass and in the particle, Nature hastens to render account of herself to the mind. Classification begins. To the young mind everything is individual, stands by itself. By and by, it finds how to join two things and see in them one nature; then three, then three thousand; and so, tyrannized over by its own unifying instinct, it goes on tying things together, diminishing anomalies, discovering roots running under ground whereby contrary and remote things cohere and flower out from one stem. . . .

Thus to him, to his schoolboy under the bending dome of day, is suggested that he and it proceed from one root; one is leaf and one is flower; relation, sympathy, stirring in every vein. And what is that root? Is not that the soul of his soul? A thought too bold; a dream too wild. Yet when this spiritual light shall have revealed the law of more earthly natures—when he has learned to worship the soul and to see that the natural philosophy that now is, is only the first gropings of its gigantic hand, he shall look forward to an ever expanding knowledge as to a becoming creator. He shall see that nature is the opposite of the soul, answering to it part for part. One is seal and one is print. Its beauty is the beauty of his own mind. Its laws are the laws of his own mind. Nature then becomes to him the measure of his attainments. So much of nature as he is ignorant of, so much of his own mind does he not yet possess. And, in fine, the ancient precept "Know thyself" and the modern precept "Study nature" become at last one maxim.

2. The next great influence into the spirit of the scholar is the mind of the past—in whatever form, whether of literature, of art, of institutions, that mind is inscribed. Books are the best type of the influence of the past, and perhaps we shall get at the truth—learn the amount of this influence more conveniently—by considering their value alone.

The theory of books is noble. The scholar of the first age received into him the world around; brooded thereon; gave it the new arrangement of his own mind, and uttered it again. It came into him life; it went out from him truth. It came to him short-lived actions; it went out from him immortal thoughts. It came to him business; it went from him poetry. It was dead fact; now, it is quick thought. It can stand, and it can go. It now endures, it now flies, it now inspires. Precisely in proportion to the depth of mind from which it issued, so high does it soar, so long does it sing. . . .

Books are the best of things, well used; abused, among the worst. What is the right use? What is the one end which all means go to effect? They are for nothing but to inspire. I had better never see a book than to be warped by its attraction clean out of my own orbit and made a satellite instead of a system. The one thing in the world, of value, is the active soul. This every man is entitled to; this every man contains within him, although in almost all men obstructed and as yet unborn. The soul active sees absolute truth and utters truth, or creates. In this action it is genius—not the privilege of here and there a favorite, but the sound estate of every man. In its essence it is progressive. The book, the college, the school of art, the institution of any kind, stop with some past utterance of genius. This is good, say they—let us hold by this. They pin me down. They look backward and not forward. But genius looks forward. . . .

Undoubtedly there is a right way of reading, so it be sternly subordinated. Man Thinking must not be subdued by his instruments. Books are for the scholar's idle times. When he can read God directly, the hour is too precious to be wasted in other men's transcripts of their readings. But when the intervals of darkness come, as come they must—when the sun is hid and the stars withdraw their shining—we repair to the lamps which were kindled by their ray, to guide our steps to the east again, where the dawn is. We hear, that we may speak. . . .

3. There goes in the world a notion that the scholar should be a recluse, a valetudinarian—as unfit for any handiwork or public labor as a penknife for an axe. . . . Action is with the scholar subordinate, but it is essential. Without it he is not yet man. Without it thought can never ripen into truth. Whilst the world hangs before the eye as a cloud of beauty, we cannot even see its beauty. Inaction is cowardice, but there can be no scholar without the heroic mind. The preamble of thought, the transition through which it passes from the unconscious to the conscious, is action. . . .

The world—this shadow of the soul, or *other me*—lies wide around. Its attractions are the keys which unlock my thoughts and make me acquainted with myself. I run eagerly into this resounding tumult. I grasp the hands of those next me and take my place in the ring to suffer and to work, taught by an instinct that so shall the dumb abyss be vocal with speech. I pierce its order; I dissipate its fear; I dispose of it within the circuit of my expanding life. So much only of life as I know by experience, so much of the wilderness have I vanquished and planted, or so far have I extended my being, my dominion. I do not see how any man can afford, for the sake of his nerves and his nap, to spare any action in which he can partake. It is pearls and rubies to his discourse. Drudgery, calamity, exasperation, want are instructors in eloquence and wisdom. The true scholar grudges every opportunity of action passed by as a loss of power. It is the raw material out of which the intellect moulds her splendid products. A strange process, too, this by which experience is converted into thought, as a mulberry leaf is converted into satin. The manufacture goes forward at all hours. . . .

I have now spoken of the education of the scholar by nature, by books, and by action. It remains to say somewhat of his duties. They are such as become Man Thinking. They may all be comprised in self-trust. The office of the scholar is to cheer, to raise, and to guide men by showing them facts amidst appearances. . . . For all this loss and scorn, what offset? He is to find consolation in exercising the highest functions of human nature. He is one who raises himself from private considerations and breathes and lives on public and illustrious thoughts. He is the world's eye. He is the world's heart. He is to resist the vulgar prosperity that retrogrades ever to barbarism, by preserving and communicating heroic sentiments, noble biographies, melodious verse, and the conclusions of history. . . .

These being his functions, it becomes him to feel all confidence in himself, and to defer never to the popular cry. He and he only knows the world. The world of any moment is the merest appearance. Some great decorum, some fetish of a government, some ephemeral trade, or war, or man, is cried up by half mankind and cried down by the other half, as if all depended on this particular up or down. The odds are that the whole question is not worth the poorest thought which the scholar has lost in listening to the controversy. . . .

But I have dwelt perhaps tediously upon this abstraction of the scholar. I ought not to delay longer to add what I have to say of nearer reference to the time and to this country. . . .

Our age is bewailed as the age of introversion. Must that needs be evil? We, it seems, are critical; we are embarrassed with second thoughts; we cannot enjoy anything for hankering to know whereof the pleasure consists. . . . It is so bad then? Sight is the last thing to be pitied. Would we be blind? Do we fear lest we should outsee nature and God, and drink truth dry? I look

upon the discontent of the literary class as a mere announcement of the fact that they find themselves not in the state of
mind of their fathers and regret the coming state as untried—as
a boy dreads the water before he has learned that he can swim.
If there is any period one would desire to be born in, is it not
the age of revolution; when the old and the new stand side by
side and admit of being compared; when the energies of all men
are searched by fear and by hope; when the historic glories of
the old can be compensated by the rich possibilities of the new
era? This time, like all times, is a very good one, if we but know
what to do with it.

I read with some joy of the auspicious signs of the coming
days, as they glimmer already through poetry and art, through
philosophy and science, through church and state.

One of these signs is the fact that the same movement which
effected the elevation of what was called the lowest class in the
state assumed in literature a very marked and as benign an
aspect. Instead of the sublime and beautiful, the near, the low,
the common was explored and poetized. That which had been
negligently trodden under foot by those who were harnessing
and provisioning themselves for long journeys into far countries
is suddenly found to be richer than all foreign parts. The literature of the poor, the feelings of the child, the philosophy of the
street, the meaning of household life are the topics of the time.
It is a great stride. It is a sign—is it not?—of new vigor when
the extremities are made active, when currents of warm life run
into the hands and the feet. . . .

Another sign of our times, also marked by an analogous
political movement, is the new importance given to the single
person. Everything that tends to insulate the individual—to
surround him with barriers of natural respect, so that each man
shall feel the world is his, and man shall treat with man as a
sovereign state with a sovereign state—tends to true union as
well as greatness. . . . The scholar is that man who must take up
into himself all the ability of the time, all the contributions of
the past, all the hopes of the future. He must be a university of

knowledges. If there be one lesson more than another which should pierce his ear, it is: The world is nothing, the man is all; in yourself is the law of all nature, and you know not yet how a globule of sap ascends; in yourself slumbers the whole of reason; it is for you to know all; it is for you to dare all. Mr. President and gentlemen, this confidence in the unsearched might of man belongs, by all motives, by all prophecy, by all preparation, to the American Scholar.

Angelina Grimké

———— ★ ————

Antislavery Convention Address

National Antislavery Convention, Philadelphia, Pennsylvania; May 16, 1838

Angelina and Sarah Grimké, sisters from South Carolina who moved to Philadelphia and became Quakers, were active in the abolitionist movement and were frequent lecturers on the evils of slavery and the right of women to speak and work publicly for social issues. In 1836 Angelina Grimké (1805–1879) caused a furor with her widely distributed pamphlet An Appeal to the Christian Women of the South, *which was burned in South Carolina. The building in which she addressed an antislavery convention in May 1838 was surrounded by an angry mob and pelted with stones during her speech and consumed by fire a few days later.*

D o you ask, "What has the North to do with slavery?" Hear it, hear it! Those voices without tell us that the spirit of slavery is *here* and has been roused to wrath by our conventions; for surely liberty would not foam and tear herself with rage, because her friends are multiplied daily, and meetings are held in quick succession to set forth her virtues and extend her peaceful kingdom. This opposition shows that slavery has done its deadliest work in the hearts of our citizens. Do you ask, then, "What has the North to do?" I answer, cast out first the spirit of slavery from your own hearts, and then lend your aid to convert the South. Each one present has a work to do, be his or her situation what it may, however limited their means or insignificant their supposed influence. The great men of this country will not do this work; the church will never do it. A desire to please the world, to keep the favor of all parties and of all conditions, makes them dumb on this and every other unpopular subject.

As a Southerner, I feel that it is my duty to stand up here tonight and bear testimony against slavery. I have seen it! I have seen it! I know it has horrors that can never be described. I was brought up under its wing. I witnessed for many years its demoralizing influences and its destructiveness to human happiness. I have never seen a happy slave. I have seen him dance in his chains, it is true, but he was not happy. There is a wide difference between happiness and mirth. Man cannot enjoy happiness while his manhood is destroyed. Slaves, however, may be, and sometimes are mirthful. When hope is extinguished, they say, "Let us eat and drink, for tomorrow we die."

What is a mob? What would the breaking of every window be? What would the leveling of this hall be? Any evidence that we are wrong, or that slavery is a good and wholesome institution? What if the mob should now burst in upon us, break up our meeting, and commit violence upon our persons? Would that be anything compared with what the slaves endure? No, no; and we do not remember them, "as bound with them," if we shrink in the time of peril, or feel unwilling to sacrifice ourselves, if need be, for their sake. I thank the Lord that there is yet life enough left to feel the truth, even though it rages at it; that conscience is not so completely seared as to be unmoved by the truth of the living God.

How wonderfully constituted is the human mind! How it

resists, as long as it can, all efforts to reclaim it from error! I feel that all this disturbance is but an evidence that our efforts are the best that could have been adopted, or else the friends of slavery would not care for what we say and do. The South knows what we do. I am thankful that they are reached by our efforts. Many times have I wept in the land of my birth over the system of slavery. I knew of none who sympathized in my feelings; I was unaware that any efforts were made to deliver the oppressed; no voice in the wilderness was heard calling on the people to repent and do works meet for repentance, and my heart sickened within me. Oh, how should I have rejoiced to know that such efforts as these were being made. I only wonder that I had such feelings. But in the midst of temptation I was preserved, and my sympathy grew warmer, and my hatred of slavery more inveterate, until at last I have exiled myself from my native land, because I could no longer endure to hear the wailing of the slave.

I fled to the land of Penn; for here, thought I, sympathy for the slave will surely be found. But I found it not. The people were kind and hospitable, but the slave had no place in their thoughts. I therefore shut up my grief in my own heart. I remembered that I was a Carolinian, from a state which framed this iniquity by law. Every Southern breeze wafted to me the discordant tones of weeping and wailing, shrieks and groans, mingled with prayers and blasphemous curses. My heart sank within me at the abominations in the midst of which I had been born and educated. What will it avail, cried I, in bitterness of spirit, to expose to the gaze of strangers the horrors and pollutions of slavery, when there is no ear to hear nor heart to feel and pray for the slave? But how different do I feel now! Animated with hope, nay, with an assurance of the triumph of liberty and good will to man, I will lift up my voice like a trumpet, and show this people what they can do to influence the Southern mind and overthrow slavery.

We often hear the question asked: "What shall we do?" Here is an opportunity. Every man and every woman present may do something, by showing that we fear not a mob, and in the midst of revilings and threatenings, pleading the cause of those who are ready to perish. Let me urge everyone to buy the books written on this subject; read them and lend them to your neighbors. Give your money no longer for things which pander to pride and lust, but aid in scattering "the living coals of truth upon the naked heart of the nation," in circulating appeals to the sympathies of Christians in behalf of the outraged slave.

But it is said by some, our "books and papers do not speak the truth"; why, then, do they not contradict what we say? They cannot. Moreover, the South has entreated, nay, commanded us, to be silent; and what greater evidence of the truth of our publications could be desired?

Women of Philadelphia! allow me as a Southern woman, with much attachment to the land of my birth, to entreat you to come up to this work. Especially, let me urge you to petition. Men may settle this and other questions at the ballot-box, but you have no such right. It is only through petitions that you can reach the legislature. It is, therefore, peculiarly your duty to petition. Do you say, "It does no good!" The South already turns pale at the number sent. They have read the reports of the proceedings of Congress and there have seen that among other petitions were very many from the women of the North on the subject of slavery. Men who hold the rod over slaves rule in the councils of the nation; and they deny our right to petition and remonstrate against abuses of our sex and our kind. We have these rights, however, from our God. Only let us exercise them, and, though often turned away unanswered, let us remember the influence of importunity upon the unjust judge and act accordingly. The fact that the South looks jealously upon our measures shows that they are effectual. There is, therefore, no cause for doubting or despair.

It was remarked in England that women did much to abolish slavery in her colonies. Nor are they now idle. Numerous petitions from them have recently been presented to the queen to abolish apprenticeship, with its cruelties, nearly equal to those of the system whose place it supplies. One petition, two miles and a quarter long, has been presented. And do you think these labors will be in vain? Let the history of the past answer. When the women of these states send up to Congress such a petition our legislators will arise, as did those of England, and say: "When all the maids and matrons of the land are knocking at our doors we must legislate." Let the zeal and love, the faith and works of our English sisters quicken ours; that while the slaves continue to suffer, and when they shout for deliverance, we may feel the satisfaction of "having done what we could."

James K. Polk
——— ★ ———
Inaugural Address

CAPITOL, WASHINGTON, D.C.; MARCH 4, 1845

James K. Polk (1795–1849), in his inaugural address, clearly stated his new administration's objectives: the reintegration of Texas into the U.S. and the "right of the United States to that portion of territory which lies beyond the Rocky Mountains." Within three years his objectives were achieved: Britain relinquished claims to Oregon in 1846, and the area was organized as a territory in 1848; California declared itself independent in 1846, and the Polk-instigated Mexican War resulted in the annexation by the United States of California and the New Mexico Territory in 1848. Texas, an independent republic since 1836, became a U.S. state in 1845.

The Republic of Texas has made known her desire to come into our Union, to form a part of our confederacy and enjoy with us the blessings of liberty secured and guaranteed by our Constitution. Texas was once a part of our country—was unwisely ceded away to a foreign power—is now independent, and possesses an undoubted right to dispose of a part or the whole of her territory and to merge her sovereignty as a separate and independent state in ours. I congratulate my country that by an act of the late Congress of the United States the assent of this government has been given to the reunion, and it only remains for the two countries to agree upon the terms to consummate an object so important to both.

I regard the question of annexation as belonging exclusively to the United States and Texas. They are independent powers competent to contract, and foreign nations have no right to interfere with them or to take exceptions to their reunion. Foreign powers do not seem to appreciate the true character of our government. Our Union is a confederation of independent states, whose policy is peace with each other and all the world. To enlarge its limits is to extend the dominions of peace over additional territories and increasing millions. The world has nothing to fear from military ambition in our government. . . .

Foreign powers should therefore look on the annexation of Texas to the United States not as the conquest of a nation seeking to extend her dominions by arms and violence, but as the peaceful acquisition of a territory once her own, by adding another member to our confederation, with the consent of that member, thereby diminishing the chances of war and opening to them new and ever-increasing markets for their products.

To Texas the reunion is important, because the strong protecting arm of our government would be extended over her, and the vast resources of her fertile soil and genial climate would be speedily developed. . . .

Is there one among our citizens who would not prefer perpetual peace with Texas to occasional wars, which so often occur between bordering independent nations? Is there one who would not prefer free intercourse with her to high duties on all our products and manufactures which enter her ports or cross her frontiers? Is there one who would not prefer an unrestricted communication with her citizens to the frontier obstructions which must occur if she remains out of the Union? Whatever is good or evil in the local institutions of Texas will remain her own whether annexed to the United States or not. None of the present states will be responsible for them any more than they are for the local institutions of each other. They have confederated together for certain specified objects. Upon the same principle that they would refuse to form a perpetual union with Texas because of her local institutions our forefathers would have been prevented from forming our present Union. . . . I shall on the broad principle which formed the basis and produced the adoption of our Constitution, and not in any narrow spirit of sectional policy, endeavor by all constitutional, honorable, and appropriate means to consummate the expressed will of the people and government of the United States by the reannexation of Texas to our Union at the earliest practicable period.

Nor will it become in a less degree my duty to assert and maintain by all constitutional means the right of the United States to that portion of our territory which lies beyond the Rocky Mountains. Our title to the country of the Oregon is "clear and unquestionable," and already are our people preparing to perfect that title by occupying it with their wives and children. But eighty years ago our population was confined on the west by the ridge of the Alleghanies. Within that period—within the lifetime, I might say, of some of my hearers—our people, increasing to many millions, have filled the eastern valley of the Mississippi, adventurously ascended the Missouri to its headsprings, and are already engaged in establishing the blessings of self-government in valleys of which the rivers flow to the Pacific. The world beholds the peaceful triumphs of the industry of our emigrants. To us belongs the duty of protecting them adequately wherever they may be upon our soil. The jurisdiction of our laws and the benefits of our republican institutions should be extended over them in the distant regions which they have selected for their homes.

Henry Clay

— ★ —

The Compromise of 1850

U.S. Senate, Washington, D.C.;
February 5 and 6, 1850

---

*Henry Clay (1777–1852), congressman, Speaker of the House of
Representatives, U.S. senator, secretary of state under President
John Quincy Adams, and three-time candidate for the presidency, was respected throughout the country for his stirring
speeches. In the face of a severe crisis between Northern and
Southern states, Clay, as a representative of Kentucky and a
fervent Unionist, proposed compromise legislation to define the
status of slavery in the new territories acquired as a result of the
Mexican War. He spoke on behalf of the plan on two successive
days.*

If the Union is to be dissolved for any existing causes, it will
be dissolved because slavery is interdicted or not allowed to
be introduced into the ceded territories; because slavery is
threatened to be abolished in the District of Columbia, and
because fugitive slaves are not returned, as in my opinion they
ought to be, and restored to their masters. These, I believe, will
be the causes, if there be any causes, which can lead to the
direful event to which I have referred.

Well, now, let us suppose that the Union has been dissolved.
What remedy does it furnish for the grievances complained
of in its united condition? Will you be able to push slavery into
the ceded territories? How are you to do it, supposing the
North—all the states north of the Potomac, and which are
opposed to it—in possession of the navy and army of the United
States? Can you expect, if there is a dissolution of the Union,
that you can carry slavery into California and New Mexico?
You cannot dream of such a purpose. If it were abolished in the

District of Columbia, and the Union were dissolved, would the dissolution of the Union restore slavery in the District of Columbia? Are you safer in the recovery of your fugitive slaves, in a state of dissolution or of severance of the Union, than you are in the Union itself? Why, what is the state of the fact in the Union? You lose some slaves. You recover some others. Let me advert to a fact which I ought to have introduced before, because it is highly creditable to the courts and juries of the free states. In every case, so far as my information extends, where an appeal has been made to the courts of justice for the recovery of fugitives, or for the recovery of penalties inflicted upon persons who have assisted in decoying slaves from their masters and aiding them in escaping from their masters—as far as I am informed, the courts have asserted the rights of the owner, and the juries have promptly returned adequate verdicts in favor of the owner. Well, this is some remedy. What would you have if the Union were dissevered? Why, sir, then the severed parts would be independent of each other—foreign countries! Slaves taken from the one into the other would be then like slaves now escaping from the United States into Canada. There would be no right of extradition; no right to demand your slaves; no right to appeal to the courts of justice to demand your slaves which escape, or the penalties for decoying them. Where one slave escapes now, by running away from his owner, hundreds and thousands would escape if the Union were severed in parts—I care not where nor how you run the line, if independent sovereignties were established. . . .

But, I must take the occasion to say that, in my opinion, there is no right on the part of one or more of the states to secede from the Union. War and the dissolution of the Union are identical and inseparable. There can be no dissolution of the Union, except by consent or by war. No one can expect, in the existing state of things, that that consent would be given, and war is the only alternative by which a dissolution could be accomplished. And, Mr. President, if consent were given—if possibly we were to separate by mutual agreement and by a given line, in less than sixty days after such an agreement had been executed, war would break out between the free and slave-holding portions of this Union—between the two independent portions into which it would be erected in virtue of the act of separation. . . .

But how are you going to separate them? In my humble opinion, Mr. President, we should begin at least with three confederacies—the Confederacy of the North, the Confederacy of the Atlantic Southern States (the slaveholding states), and the Confederacy of the Valley of the Mississippi. My life upon it, sir, that vast population that has already concentrated, and will concentrate, upon the headwaters and tributaries of the Mississippi, will never consent that the mouth of that river shall be held subject to the power of any foreign state whatever. Such, I believe, would be the consequences of a dissolution of the Union. But other confederacies would spring up, from time to time, as dissatisfaction and discontent were disseminated over the country. There would be the Confederacy of the Lakes— perhaps the Confederacy of New England and of the Middle States. . . .

Mr. President, I am directly opposed to any purpose of secession, of separation. I am for staying within the Union and defying any portion of this Union to expel or drive me out of the Union. I am for staying within the Union and fighting for my rights—if necessary, with the sword—within the bounds and under the safeguard of the Union. I am for vindicating these rights, but not by being driven out of the Union rashly and unceremoniously by any portion of this confederacy. Here I am within it, and here I mean to stand and die; as far as my individual purposes or wishes can go—within it to protect myself and to defy all power upon earth to expel me or drive me from the situation in which I am placed. Will there not be more safety in fighting within the Union than without it? . . .

I said that I thought that there was no right on the part of one or more of the states to secede from this Union. I think that the Constitution of the thirteen states was made, not merely for the generation which then existed, but for posterity, undefined, unlimited, permanent, and perpetual—for their posterity, and for every subsequent state which might come into the Union, binding themselves by that indissoluble bond. It is to remain for that posterity now and forever. Like another of the great relations of private life, it was a marriage that no human authority can dissolve or divorce the parties from; and, if I may be allowed to refer to this same example in private life, let us say what man and wife say to each other: "We have mutual faults; nothing in the form of human beings can be perfect. Let us then be kind to each other, forbearing, conceding; let us live in happiness and peace."

Mr. President, I have said what I solemnly believe—that the dissolution of the Union and war are identical and inseparable; that they are convertible terms.

Such a war, too, as that would be, following the dissolution of the Union! . . . And what would be its termination? Standing armies and navies, to an extent draining the revenues of each portion of the dissevered empire, would be created; exterminating wars would follow—not a war of two nor three years, but of interminable duration—an exterminating war would follow, until some Philip or Alexander, some Caesar or Napoleon would rise to cut the Gordian knot, and solve the problem of the capacity of man for self-government, and crush the liberties of both the dissevered portions of this Union. Can you doubt it? Look at history—consult the pages of all history, ancient or modern; look at human nature—look at the character of the contest in which you would be engaged in the supposition of a war following the dissolution of the Union such as I have suggested—and I ask you if it is possible for you to doubt that the final but perhaps distant termination of the whole will be some despot treading down the liberties of the people?—that the final result will be the extinction of this last and glorious light, which is leading all mankind, who are gazing upon it, to cherish hope and anxious expectation that the liberty which prevails here will sooner or later be advanced throughout the civilized world? Can you, Mr. President, lightly contemplate the consequences? Can you yield yourself to a torrent of passion, amidst dangers which I have depicted in colors far short of what would be the reality, if the event should ever happen? I conjure gentlemen—whether from the South or the North, by all they hold dear in this world—by all their love of liberty—by all their veneration for their ancestors—by all their regard for posterity—by all their gratitude to him who has bestowed upon them such unnumbered blessings—by all the duties which they owe to mankind, and all the duties they owe to themselves—by all these considerations I implore them to pause—solemnly to pause—at the edge of the precipice before the fearful and disastrous leap is taken in the yawning abyss below, which will inevitably lead to certain and irretrievable destruction.

And, finally, Mr. President, I implore, as the best blessing which heaven can bestow upon me on earth, that if the direful and sad event of the dissolution of the Union shall happen, I may not survive to behold the sad and heart-rending spectacle.

Daniel Webster

— ★ —

Slavery in the
Western Territories

U.S. Senate, Washington, D.C.;
March 7, 1850

---

*Daniel Webster's career as an orator, congressman, U.S. senator,
and secretary of state (under President Fillmore) paralleled that
of Henry Clay; their deaths even occurred in the same year. On
March 7, 1850, Webster (1782–1852) spoke in the Senate in support of Clay's compromise proposal for the treatment of slavery
in the new western territories, California, New Mexico, and
Utah, as well as in the District of Columbia. Partisans of both
Northern and Southern positions were not pleased with the plan,
but the legislation passed. Together, Clay and Webster had postponed the inevitable conflict for another decade.*

Mr. President, in the excited times in which we live, there
is found to exist a state of crimination and recrimination
between the North and South. There are lists of grievances
produced by each; and those grievances, real or supposed, alien-
ate the minds of one portion of the country from the other,
exasperate the feelings, and subdue the sense of fraternal affection, patriotic love, and mutual regard. I shall bestow a little
attention, sir, upon these various grievances existing on the one
side and on the other. I begin with complaints of the South. I
will not answer, further than I have, the general statements of
the honorable senator from South Carolina, that the North has
prospered at the expense of the South in consequence of the
manner of administering the government, in the collecting of its
revenues, and so forth. These are disputed topics, and I have no
inclination to enter into them. But I will allude to other com-

plaints of the South, and especially to one which has in my opinion just foundation; and that is, that there has been found at the North, among individuals and among legislators, a disinclination to perform fully their constitutional duties in regard to the return of persons bound to service who have escaped into the free states. In that respect, the South, in my judgment, is right, and the North is wrong.

Every member of every Northern legislature is bound by oath, like every other officer in the country, to support the Constitution of the United States; and the article of the Constitution which says to these states they shall deliver up fugitives from service is as binding in honor and conscience as any other article. No man fulfills his duty in any legislature who sets himself to find excuses, evasions, escapes from this constitutional obligation. I have always thought that the Constitution addressed itself to the legislatures of the states or to the states themselves. It says that these persons escaping to other states "shall be delivered up," and I confess I have always been of the opinion that it was an injunction upon the states themselves. When it is said that a person escaping into another state, and coming therefore within the jurisdiction of that state, shall be delivered up, it seems to me the import of the clause is that the state itself, in obedience to the Constitution, shall cause him to be delivered up. That is my judgment. I have always entertained that opinion, and I entertain it now. But when the subject, some years ago, was before the Supreme Court of the United States, the majority of the judges held that the power to cause fugitives from service to be delivered up was a power to be exercised under the authority of this government. I do not know, on the whole, that it may not have been a fortunate decision. My habit is to respect the result of judicial deliberations and the solemnity of judicial decisions.

As it now stands, the business of seeing that these fugitives are delivered up resides in the power of Congress and the national judicature, and my friend at the head of the Judiciary Committee has a bill on the subject now before the Senate, which, with some amendments to it, I propose to support, with all its provisions, to the fullest extent. And I desire to call the attention of all sober-minded men at the North, of all conscientious men, of all men who are not carried away by some fanatical idea or some false impression, to their constitutional obligations. I put it to all the sober and sound minds at the North as a question of morals and a question of conscience. What right have they, in their legislative capacity or any other capacity, to endeavor to get round this Constitution, or to embarrass the free exercise of the rights secured by the Constitution to the persons whose slaves escape from them? None at all; none at all. . . .

Then, sir, there are the abolition societies, of which I am unwilling to speak, but in regard to which I have very clear notions and opinions. I do not think them useful. I think their operations for the last twenty years have produced nothing good or valuable. At the same time, I believe thousands of their members to be honest and good men, perfectly well-meaning men. They have excited feelings; they think they must do something for the cause of liberty; and, in their sphere of action, they do not see what else they can do than to contribute to an abolition press, or an abolition society, or to pay an abolition lecturer. I do not mean to impute gross motives even to the leaders of these societies, but I am not blind to the consequences of their proceedings. I cannot but see what mischiefs their interference with the South has produced. And is it not plain to every man? Let any gentleman who entertains doubts on this point recur to the debates in the Virginia House of Delegates in 1832, and he will see with what freedom a proposition made by Mr. Jefferson Randolph for the gradual abolition of slavery was discussed in that body. Every one spoke of slavery as he thought, very ignominious and disparaging names and epithets were applied to it. The debates in the House of Delegates on that occasion, I believe, were all published. They were read by every colored man who could read, and to those who could not read, those debates were read by others. At that time Virginia was not unwilling or afraid to discuss this question, and to let that part of her population know as much of the discussion as they could learn. That was in 1832. As has been said by the honorable member from South Carolina, these abolition societies commenced their course of action in 1835. It is said, I do not know how true it may be, that they sent incendiary publications into the slave states; at any rate, they attempted to arouse, and did arouse, a very strong feeling; in other words, they created great agitation in the North against Southern slavery. Well, what was the result? The bonds of the slaves were bound more firmly than before, their rivets were more strongly fastened. Public opinion, which in Virginia had begun to be exhibited against slavery, and was opening out for the discussion of the question, drew back and shut itself up in its castle. . . .

Mr. President, I should much prefer to have heard from every member on this floor declarations of opinion that this Union could never be dissolved, than the declaration of opinions by any body, that, in any case, under the pressure of any circumstances, such a dissolution was possible. I hear with distress and anguish the word "secession," especially when it falls from the lips of those who are patriotic, and known to the country, and known all over the world, for their political services. Secession! Peaceable secession! Sir, your eyes and mine are never destined to see that miracle. The dismemberment of this vast country without convulsion! The breaking up of the fountains of the great deep without ruffling the surface! Who is so foolish, I beg everybody's pardon, as to expect to see any such thing? Sir, he who sees these states, now revolving in harmony around a common center, and expects to see them quit their places and fly off without convulsion, may look the next hour to see the heavenly bodies rush from their spheres and jostle against each other in the realms of space, without causing the wreck of the universe. There can be no such thing as a peaceable secession. Peaceable secession is an utter impossibility. Is the great Constitution under which we live, covering this whole country, is it to be thawed and melted away by secession, as the snows on the mountain melt under the influence of a vernal sun, disappear almost unobserved, and run off? No, sir! No, sir! . . .

Peaceable secession! Peaceable secession! The concurrent agreement of all the members of this great republic to separate! A voluntary separation, with alimony on one side and on the other. Why, what would be the result? Where is the line to be drawn? What states are to secede? What is to remain American? What am I to be? An American no longer? Am I to become a sectional man, a local man, a separatist, with no country in common with the gentlemen who sit around me here, or who fill the other house of Congress? Heaven forbid! Where is the flag of the republic to remain? Where is the eagle still to tower? or is he to cower, and shrink, and fall to the ground? . . .

What is to become of the army? What is to become of the navy? What is to become of the public lands? How is each of the thirty states to defend itself? I know, although the idea has not been stated distinctly, there is to be, or it is supposed possible that there will be, a Southern Confederacy. I do not mean, when I allude to this statement, that any one seriously contemplates such a state of things. I do not mean to say that it is true, but I have heard it suggested elsewhere, that the idea has been entertained, that, after the dissolution of this Union, a Southern Confederacy might be formed. I am sorry, sir, that it has ever been thought of, talked of, or dreamed of, in the wildest flights of human imagination. But the idea, so far as it exists, must be of a separation, assigning the slave states to one side and the free states to the other. Sir, I may express myself too strongly perhaps, but there are impossibilities in the natural as well as in the physical world, and I hold the idea of a separation of these states, those that are free to form one government, and those that are slave-holding to form another, as such an impossibility. We could not separate the states by any such line, if we were to draw it. We could not sit down here today and draw a line of separation that would satisfy any five men in the country. There are natural causes that would keep and tie us together, and there are social and domestic relations which we could not break if we would, and which we should not if we could. . . .

And now, Mr. President, instead of speaking of the possibility or utility of secession, instead of dwelling in those caverns of darkness, instead of groping with those ideas so full of all that is horrid and horrible, let us come out into the light of day; let us enjoy the fresh air of liberty and union; let us cherish those hopes which belong to us; let us devote ourselves to those great objects that are fit for our consideration and our action; let us raise our conceptions to the magnitude and the importance of the duties that devolve upon us; let our comprehension be as broad as the country for which we act, our aspirations as high as its certain destiny; let us not be pigmies in a case that calls for men. Never did there devolve on any generation of men higher trusts than now devolve upon us, for the preservation of this Constitution and the harmony and peace of all who are destined to live under it. Let us make our generation one of the strongest and brightest links in that golden chain which is destined, I fondly believe, to grapple the people of all the states to this Constitution for ages to come.

SOJOURNER TRUTH

★

On Women's Rights

OHIO WOMEN'S RIGHTS CONVENTION,
AKRON, OHIO; 1851

---

*Sojourner Truth (1797–1883) was born a slave in New York State
and was emancipated by the state in 1828. She traveled throughout the North preaching religion, abolitionism, and women's
rights. In 1850 she attended the First National Women's Rights
Convention in Worcester, Massachusetts, and the following year
she spoke at the Ohio Women's Rights Convention. Her words
were transcribed by Frances Gage, the convention's organizer, and printed in the 1878 edition of the* Narrative of
Sojourner Truth.

Well, children, where there is so much racket there must be
something out of kilter. I think that 'twixt the Negroes
of the South and the women at the North, all talking about
rights, the white men will be in a fix pretty soon.

But what's all this here talking about? That man over there
says that women need to be helped into carriages, and lifted over
ditches, and to have the best place everywhere. Nobody ever
helps me into carriages, or over mud-puddles, or gives me any
best place. And aren't I a woman? Look at me! Look at my arm.
I have plowed and planted and gathered into barns, and no man
could head me. And aren't I a woman? I could work as much
and eat as much as a man—when I could get it—and bear the
lash as well. And aren't I a woman? I have borne thirteen
children, and seen them most all sold off into slavery, and when
I cried out with a mother's grief, none but Jesus heard me! And
aren't I a woman?

Then they talk about this thing in the head; what's this they
call it? ["Intellect," whispered someone near.] That's it, honey.

What's that got to do with women's rights or Negroes' rights? If my cup won't hold but a pint and yours holds a quart, wouldn't you be mean not to let me have my little half-measure full?

Then that little man in black there, he says women can't have as much rights as men, 'cause Christ wasn't a woman. Where did your Christ come from? Where did your Christ come from? *Where did your Christ come from?* From God and a woman! Man had nothing to do with Him.

If the first woman God ever made was strong enough to turn the world upside down all alone, these together ought to be able to turn it back and get it right side up again. And now they is asking to do it, the men better let them.

Obliged to you for hearing on me, and now old Sojourner hasn't got nothing more to say.

Frederick Douglass

— ★ —

Independence Day Address

Rochester, New York; July 4, 1852

Frederick Douglass (1817–1895), born into slavery in Tuckahoe, Maryland, escaped to New Bedford, Massachusetts, in 1836. His gifts as an orator were first revealed five years later when he spoke at an antislavery convention in Nantucket, Massachusetts. He wrote his autobiography, Narrative of the Life of Frederick Douglass, an American Slave, *in 1845 and founded the abolitionist newspaper* North Star *in 1847 in Rochester, New York, where he was invited to speak on Independence Day 1852.*

F ellow citizens, pardon me, allow me to ask, Why am I called upon to speak here today? What have I, or those I represent, to do with your national independence? Are the great principles of political freedom and of natural justice, embodied in that Declaration of Independence, extended to us? And am I, therefore, called upon to bring our humble offering to the national altar and to confess the benefits and express devout gratitude for the blessings resulting from your independence to us?

Would to God, both for your sakes and ours, that an affirmative answer could be truthfully returned to these questions! Then would my task be light and my burden easy and delightful. For who is there so cold that a nation's sympathy could not warm him? Who so obdurate and dead to the claims of gratitude that would not thankfully acknowledge such priceless benefits? Who so stolid and selfish that would not give his voice to swell the hallelujahs of a nation's jubilee, when the chains of servitude had been torn from his limbs? I am not that man. In a case like that the dumb might eloquently speak and the "lame man leap as a hart."

But such is not the state of the case. I say it with a sad sense of the disparity between us. I am not included within the pale of this glorious anniversary! Your high independence only reveals the immeasurable distance between us. The blessings in which you, this day, rejoice are not enjoyed in common. The rich inheritance of justice, liberty, prosperity, and independence bequeathed by your fathers is shared by you, not by me. The sunlight that brought light and healing to you has brought stripes and death to me. This Fourth of July is yours, not mine. You may rejoice, I must mourn. To drag a man in fetters into the grand illuminated temple of liberty, and call upon him to join you in joyous anthems, were inhuman mockery and sacrilegious irony. Do you mean, citizens, to mock me by asking me to speak today? If so, there is a parallel to your conduct. And let me warn you that it is dangerous to copy the example of a nation whose crimes, towering up to heaven, were thrown down by the breath of the Almighty, burying that nation in irrevocable ruin! I can today take up the plaintive lament of a peeled and woe-smitten people! . . .

Fellow citizens, above your national, tumultuous joy, I hear the mournful wail of millions!—whose chains, heavy and grievous yesterday, are, today, rendered more intolerable by the jubilee shouts that reach them. If I do forget, if I do not faithfully remember those bleeding children of sorrow this day, "may my right hand forget her cunning, and may my tongue cleave to the roof of my mouth"! To forget them, to pass lightly over their wrongs, and to chime in with the popular theme would be treason most scandalous and shocking, and would make me a reproach before God and the world.

My subject, then, fellow citizens, is American slavery. I shall see this day and its popular characteristics from the slave's point of view. Standing there identified with the American bondman, making his wrongs mine. I do not hesitate to declare with all my soul that the character and conduct of this nation never looked blacker to me than on this Fourth of July! Whether we turn to the declarations of the past or to the professions of the present, the conduct of the nation seems equally hideous and revolting.

America is false to the past, false to the present, and solemnly binds herself to be false to the future. Standing with God and the crushed and bleeding slave on this occasion, I will, in the name of humanity which is outraged, in the name of liberty which is fettered, in the name of the Constitution and the Bible which are disregarded and trampled upon, dare to call in question and to denounce, with all the emphasis I can command, everything that serves to perpetuate slavery—the great sin and shame of America! . . .

But I fancy I hear someone of my audience say, "It is just in this circumstance that you and your brother abolitionists fail to make a favorable impression on the public mind. Would you argue more and denounce less, would you persuade more and rebuke less, your cause would be much more likely to succeed." But, I submit, where all is plain, there is nothing to be argued. What point in the antislavery creed would you have me argue? On what branch of the subject do the people of this country need light? Must I undertake to prove that the slave is a man? That point is conceded already. Nobody doubts it. The slaveholders themselves acknowledge it in the enactment of laws for their government. They acknowledge it when they punish disobedience on the part of the slave. There are seventy-two crimes in the state of Virginia which, if committed by a black man (no matter how ignorant he be), subject him to the punishment of death; while only two of the same crimes will subject a white man to the like punishment. What is this but the acknowledgment that the slave is a moral, intellectual, and responsible being? The manhood of the slave is conceded. It is admitted in the fact that the Southern statute books are covered with enactments forbidding, under severe fines and penalties, the teaching of the slave to read or to write. When you can point to any such laws in reference to the beasts of the field, then I may consent to argue the manhood of the slave. When the dogs in your streets, when the fowls of the air, when the cattle on your hills, when the fish of the sea and the reptiles that crawl shall be unable to distinguish the slave from a brute, then will I argue with you that the slave is a man!

For the present, it is enough to affirm the equal manhood of the Negro race. Is it not astonishing that, while we are plowing, planting, and reaping, using all kinds of mechanical tools, erecting houses, constructing bridges, building ships, working in metals of brass, iron, copper, silver, and gold; that, while we are reading, writing, and ciphering, acting as clerks, merchants, and secretaries, having among us lawyers, doctors, ministers, poets, authors, editors, orators, and teachers; that, while we are engaged in all manner of enterprises common to other men, digging gold in California, capturing the whale in the Pacific, feeding sheep and cattle on the hillside, living, moving, acting, thinking, planning, living in families as husbands, wives, and children, and above all, confessing and worshiping the Christian's God, and looking hopefully for life and immortality beyond the grave, we are called upon to prove that we are men! . . .

What, am I to argue that it is wrong to make men brutes, to rob them of their liberty, to work them without wages, to keep them ignorant of their relations to their fellow men, to beat them with sticks, to flay their flesh with the lash, to load their limbs with irons, to hunt them with dogs, to sell them at auction, to sunder their families, to knock out their teeth, to burn their flesh, to starve them into obedience and submission to their masters? Must I argue that a system thus marked with blood, and stained with pollution, is wrong? No! I will not. I have better employment for my time and strength than such arguments would imply.

What, then, remains to be argued? Is it that slavery is not divine; that God did not establish it; that our doctors of divinity are mistaken? There is blasphemy in the thought. That which is inhuman cannot be divine! Who can reason on such a proposition? They that can may; I cannot. The time for such argument is past. . . .

What, to the American slave, is your Fourth of July? I answer: a day that reveals to him, more than all other days in the year, the gross injustice and cruelty to which he is the constant victim. To him, your celebration is a sham; your boasted liberty, an unholy license; your national greatness, swelling vanity; your sounds of rejoicing are empty and heartless; your denunciation of tyrants, brass-fronted impudence; your shouts of liberty and equality, hollow mockery; your prayers and hymns, your sermons and thanksgivings, with all your religious parade and solemnity, are, to him, mere bombast, fraud, deception, impiety, and hypocrisy—a thin veil to cover up crimes which would disgrace a nation of savages. There is not a nation of savages. There is not a nation on the earth guilty of practices more shocking and bloody than are the people of the United States at this very hour.

Go where you may, search where you will, roam through all the monarchies and despotisms of the Old World, travel through South America, search out every abuse, and when you have found the last, lay your facts by the side of the everyday practices of this nation, and you will say with me that, for revolting barbarity and shameless hypocrisy, America reigns without a rival.

ELIZABETH CADY STANTON

———— ★ ————

Temperance and Women's Rights

WOMEN'S STATE TEMPERANCE SOCIETY CONVENTION,
ROCHESTER, NEW YORK; 1853

*From 1851 Susan B. Anthony and Elizabeth Cady Stanton (1815–
1902) were partners in the combined crusade for women's suffrage, abolitionism, and temperance. In the earlier years Stanton,
unlike Anthony, was busy raising a large family; she nevertheless
served as president of the Women's State Temperance Society in
New York and spoke publicly on these important issues.*

We have been obliged to preach woman's rights because
many, instead of listening to what we had to say on
temperance, have questioned the right of a woman to speak on
any subject. In courts of justice and legislative assemblies, if the
right of the speaker to be there is questioned, all business waits
until that point is settled. Now, it is not settled in the mass of
minds that woman has any rights on this footstool, and much
less a right to stand on an even pedestal with man, look him in
the face as an equal, and rebuke the sins of her day and generation. Let it be clearly understood, then, that we are a woman's
rights society; that we believe it is woman's duty to speak whenever she feels the impression to do so; that it is her right to be
present in all the councils of church and state. The fact that our
agents are women settles the question of our character on this
point.

Again, in discussing the question of temperance, all lecturers, from the beginning, have made mention of the drunkards'
wives and children, of widows' groans and orphans' tears. Shall
these classes of sufferers be introduced but as themes for rhetori-
cal flourish, as pathetic touches of the speaker's eloquence? Shall
we passively shed tears over their condition, or by giving them

their rights, bravely open to them the doors of escape from a wretched and degraded life? Is it not legitimate in this to discuss the social degradation, the legal disabilities of the drunkard's wife? If in showing her wrongs, we prove the right of all womankind to the elective franchise; to a fair representation in the government; to the right in criminal cases to be tried by peers of her own choosing—shall it be said that we transcend the bounds of our subject? If in pointing out her social degradation, we show you how the present laws outrage the sacredness of the marriage institution; if in proving to you that justice and mercy demand a legal separation from drunkards, we grasp the higher idea that a unity of soul alone constitutes and sanctifies true marriage, and that any law or public sentiment that forces two immortal, high-born souls to live together as husband and wife, unless held there by love, is false to God and humanity—who shall say that the discussion of this question does not lead us legitimately into the consideration of the important subject of divorce?

CHIEF SEATTLE

Oration

OREGON TERRITORY; DECEMBER 1854

Dr. Henry A. Smith wrote down the speech given by Chief Seattle before an assemblage, which included territorial governor Isaac I. Stevens, Native Americans, and white settlers, in December 1854 on the site of the city that would bear the tribal leader's name. Chief Seattle accepted the U.S. government's terms for buying tribal lands and establishing reservations but spoke sadly of "two distinct races with separate origins and separate destinies." He added, "It matters little where we pass the remnant of our days. They will not be many. The Indians' night promises to be dark."

There was a time when our people covered the land as the waves of a wind-ruffled sea cover its shell-paved floor, but that time long since passed away with the greatness of tribes that are now but a mournful memory. I will not dwell on, nor mourn over, our untimely decay, nor reproach my pale-faced brothers with hastening it as we too may have been somewhat to blame. . . .

Our good father at Washington—for I presume he is now our father as well as yours, since King George has moved his boundaries further north—our great and good father, I say, sends us word that if we do as he desires he will protect us. . . .

Your God is not our God! Your God loves your people and hates mine. He folds his strong protecting arms lovingly about the pale face and leads him by the hand as a father leads his infant son; but He has forsaken His red children—if they really are his. Our God, the Great Spirit, seems also to have forsaken us. Your God makes your people wax strong every day. Soon they will fill all the land. Our people are ebbing away like a rapidly receding tide that will never return. The white man's

God cannot love our people or He would protect them. . . . We are two distinct races with separate origins and separate destinies. There is little in common between us.

To us the ashes of our ancestors are sacred and their resting place is hallowed ground. You wander far from the graves of your ancestors and seemingly without regret. Your religion was written upon tables of stone by the iron finger of your God so that you could not forget. The red man could never comprehend nor remember it. Our religion is the traditions of our ancestors—the dreams of our old men, given them in solemn hours of night by the Great Spirit, and the visions of our sachems—and is written in the hearts of our people.

Your dead cease to love you and the land of their nativity as soon as they pass the portals of the tomb and wander away beyond the stars. They are soon forgotten and never return. Our dead never forget the beautiful world that gave them being. They still love its verdant valleys, its murmuring rivers, its magnificent mountains, sequestered vales and verdant lined lakes and bays, and ever yearn in tender, fond affection over the lonely hearted living, and often return from the Happy Hunting Ground to visit, guide, console, and comfort them.

Day and night cannot dwell together. The red man has ever fled the approach of the white man, as the morning mist flees before the morning sun.

However, your proposition seems fair and I think that my people will accept it and will retire to the reservation you offer them. Then we will dwell apart in peace, for the words of the Great White Chief seem to be the words of nature speaking to my people out of dense darkness.

It matters little where we pass the remnant of our days. They will not be many. The Indians' night promises to be dark. Not a single star of hope hovers above his horizon. Sad-voiced winds moan in the distance. Grim fate seems to be on the red man's trail, and wherever he goes he will hear the approaching footsteps of his fell destroyer and prepare stolidly to meet his doom, as does the wounded doe that hears the approaching footsteps of the hunter. . . .

But why should I mourn at the untimely fate of my people? Tribe follows tribe, and nation follows nation, like the waves of the sea. It is the order of nature, and regret is useless. Your time of decay may be distant, but it will surely come, for even the white man whose God walked and talked with him as friend with friend, cannot be exempt from the common destiny. We may be brothers after all. We will see.

We will ponder your proposition and when we decide we will let you know. But should we accept it, I here and now make this condition—that we will not be denied the privilege without molestation of visiting at any time the tombs of our ancestors, friends, and children. Every part of this soil is sacred in the estimation of my people. Every hillside, every valley, every plain and grove has been hallowed by some sad or happy event in days long vanished. . . .

And when the last red man shall have perished, and the memory of my tribe shall have become a myth among the white men, these shores will swarm with the invisible dead of my tribe, and when your children's children think themselves alone in the field, the store, the shop, upon the highway, or in the silence of the pathless woods, they will not be alone. In all the earth there is no place dedicated to solitude. At night when the streets of your cities and villages are silent and you think them deserted, they will throng with the returning hosts that once filled them and still love this beautiful land. The white man will never be alone.

Let him be just and deal kindly with my people, for the dead are not powerless. Dead, did I say? There is no death, only a change of worlds.

LUCY STONE

—— ★ ——

A Disappointed Woman

NATIONAL WOMAN'S RIGHTS CONVENTION, CINCINNATI, OHIO; 1855

Like Susan B. Anthony and Elizabeth Cady Stanton, Lucy Stone (1818–1893) was a pioneering champion of women's rights and was active as well in the temperance and abolitionist movements. Stone was well-known for her decision to retain her own name after marriage. She was a founder of the American Woman's Suffrage Association and was editor of Boston's Women's Jour- nal, *assisted by her husband, Henry Brown Blackwell, and her daughter, Alice Stone Blackwell.*

The last speaker alluded to this movement as being that of a few disappointed women. From the first years to which my memory stretches, I have been a disappointed woman. When, with my brothers, I reached forth after the sources of knowledge, I was reproved with "It isn't fit for you; it doesn't belong to women." Then there was but one college in the world where women were admitted, and that was in Brazil. I would have found my way there, but by the time I was prepared to go, one was opened in the young state of Ohio—the first in the United States where women and Negroes could enjoy oppor- tunities with white men. I was disappointed when I came to seek a profession worthy an immortal being—every employment was closed to me, except those of the teacher, the seamstress, and the housekeeper. In education, in marriage, in religion, in everything, disappointment is the lot of woman. It shall be the business of my life to deepen this disappointment in every woman's heart until she bows down to it no longer. I wish that women, instead of being walking showcases, instead of begging of their fathers and brothers the latest and gayest new bonnet, would ask of them their rights.

The question of woman's rights is a practical one. The notion has prevailed that it was only an ephemeral idea, that it was but women claiming the right to smoke cigars in the streets and to frequent barrooms. Others have supposed it a question of comparative intellect; others still, of sphere. Too much has already been said and written about woman's sphere. Trace all the doctrines to their source and they will be found to have no basis except in the usages and prejudices of the age. This is seen in the fact that what is tolerated in woman in one country is not tolerated in another. In this country women may hold prayer meetings, etcetera, but in Mohammedan countries it is written upon their mosques, "Women and dogs, and other impure animals, are not permitted to enter." Wendell Phillips says, "The best and greatest thing one is capable of doing, that is his sphere."

I have confidence in the Father to believe that when He gives us the capacity to do anything He does not make a blunder. Leave women, then, to find their sphere. And do not tell us before we are born even, that our province is to cook dinners, darn stockings, and sew on buttons. We are told woman has all the rights she wants; and even women, I am ashamed to say, tell us so. They mistake the politeness of men for rights—seats while men stand in this hall tonight, and their adulations; but these are mere courtesies. We want rights. The flour merchant, the house builder, and the postman charge us no less on account of our sex; but when we endeavor to earn money to pay all these, then, indeed, we find the difference. . . . Women working in tailor shops are paid one-third as much as men. Someone in Philadelphia has stated that women make fine shirts for twelve and a half cents apiece; that no woman can make more than nine a week, and the sum thus earned, after deducting rent, fuel, etcetera, leaves her just three and a half cents a day for bread. Is it a wonder that women are driven to prostitution? Female teachers in New York are paid fifty dollars a year, and for every such situation there are five hundred applicants. I know not what you believe of God, but I believe He gave yearnings and longings to be filled, and that He did not mean all our time should be devoted to feeding and clothing the body.

The present condition of woman causes a horrible perversion of the marriage relation. It is asked of a lady, "Has she married well?" "Oh, yes, her husband is rich." Woman must marry for a home, and you men are the sufferers by this; for a woman who loathes you may marry you because you have the means to get money which she cannot have. But when woman can enter the lists with you and make money for herself, she will marry you only for deep and earnest affection.

A woman undertook in Lowell to sell shoes to ladies. Men laughed at her, but in six years she has run them all out and has a monopoly of the trade. Sarah Tyndale, whose husband was an importer of china and died bankrupt, continued his business, paid off his debts, and has made a fortune and built the largest china warehouse in the world. Mrs. Tyndale, herself, drew the plan of her warehouse, and it is the best plan ever drawn. A laborer to whom the architect showed it, said: "Don't she know e'en as much as some men?" I have seen a woman at manual labor turning out chair legs in a cabinet shop, with a dress short enough not to drag in the shavings. I wish other women would imitate her in this. . . . The widening of woman's sphere is to improve her lot. Let us do it, and if the world scoff, let it scoff—if it sneer, let it sneer—but we will go on emulating the example of the sisters Grimké and Abby Kelley. When they first lectured against slavery they were not listened to as respectfully as you listen to us. So the first female physician meets many difficulties, but to the next the path will be made easy.

ABRAHAM LINCOLN

— ★ —

Seventh Lincoln-Douglas Debate, Illinois Campaign for the U.S. Senate

ALTON, ILLINOIS; OCTOBER 15, 1858

Abraham Lincoln (1809–1865) had served in the Illinois legisla-
ture from 1834 to 1842 and in the U.S. House of Representatives
from 1847 to 1849. A lawyer in private practice, he was nomi-
nated by the Republican party to oppose Stephen Douglas in the
campaign for the U.S. Senate in 1858. While Douglas's final
speech in the series of seven debates held throughout Illinois
contained cogent legal and political points about the problems of
slavery and states' rights, Lincoln's argument centered persua-
sively on the moral evil of slavery: "The sentiment that contem-
plates the institution of slavery in this country as a wrong is the
sentiment of the Republican party."

I have stated upon former occasions, and I may as well state
again, what I understand to be the real issue in this contro
versy between Judge Douglas and myself. On the point of my
wanting to make war between the free and the slave states, there
has been no issue between us. So, too, when he assumes that I
am in favor of introducing a perfect social and political equality
between the white and black races. These are false issues, upon
which Judge Douglas has tried to force the controversy. There
is no foundation in truth for the charge that I maintain either of
these propositions. The real issue in this controversy—the one
pressing upon every mind—is the sentiment on the part of one
class that looks upon the institution of slavery *as a wrong,* and
of another class that *does not* look upon it as a wrong. The

sentiment that contemplates the institution of slavery in this country as a wrong is the sentiment of the Republican party. It is the sentiment around which all their actions, all their arguments, circle, and from which all their propositions radiate. They look upon it as being a moral, social, and political wrong; and while they contemplate it as such, they nevertheless have due regard for its actual existence among us, and the difficulties of getting rid of it in any satisfactory way, and to all the constitutional obligations thrown about it. Yet having a due regard for these, they desire a policy in regard to it that looks to its not creating any more danger. They insist that it should, as far as may be, be treated as a wrong, and one of the methods of treating it as a wrong is to make provision that it shall grow no larger. They also desire a policy that looks to a peaceful end of slavery at some time, as being wrong. These are the views they entertain in regard to it as I understand them; and all their sentiments, all their arguments and propositions, are brought within this range. I have said, and I repeat it here, that if there be a man among us who does not think that the institution of slavery is wrong in any one of the aspects of which I have spoken, he is misplaced and ought not to be with us. . . .

On this subject of treating it as a wrong, and limiting its spread, let me say a word. Has anything ever threatened the existence of this Union save and except this very institution of slavery? What is it that we hold most dear among us? Our own liberty and prosperity. What has ever threatened our liberty and prosperity, save and except this institution of slavery? If this is true, how do you propose to improve the condition of things by enlarging slavery—by spreading it out and making it bigger? You may have a wen or a cancer upon your person and not be able to cut it out lest you bleed to death; but surely it is no way to cure it to ingraft it and spread it over your whole body. That is no proper way of treating what you regard as a wrong. You see this peaceful way of dealing with it as a wrong—restricting the spread of it and not allowing it to go into new countries where it has not already existed. That is the peaceful way, the old-fashioned way, the way in which the fathers themselves set us the example.

On the other hand, I have said there is a sentiment which treats it as *not* being wrong. That is the Democratic sentiment of this day. I do not mean to say that every man who stands within that range positively asserts that it is right. That class will include all who positively assert that it is right, and all who, like Judge Douglas, treat it as indifferent and do not say it is either right or wrong. . . . You may turn over everything in the Democratic policy from beginning to end, whether in the shape it takes on the statute book, in the shape it takes in the *Dred Scott* decision, in the shape it takes in conversation, or the shape it takes in short maximlike arguments—it everywhere carefully excludes the idea that there is anything wrong in it.

That is the real issue. That is the issue that will continue in this country, when these poor tongues of Judge Douglas and myself shall be silent. It is the eternal struggle between these two principles—right and wrong—throughout the world. They are the two principles that have stood face to face from the beginning of time and will ever continue to struggle. The one is the common right of humanity, and the other the divine right of kings. It is the same principle in whatever shape it develops itself. It is the same spirit that says, "You work and toil and earn bread, and I'll eat it." No matter in what shape it comes, whether from the mouth of a king who seeks to bestride the people of his own nation and live by the fruit of their labor, or from one race of men as an apology for enslaving another race, it is the same tyrannical principle. . . .

I understand I have ten minutes yet. I will employ it in saying something about this argument Judge Douglas uses, while he sustains the *Dred Scott* decision, that the people of the territories can still somehow exclude slavery. The first thing I ask attention to is the fact that Judge Douglas constantly said, before the decision, that whether they could or not, was a question for the Supreme Court. But after the court had made the decision he virtually says it is *not* a question for the Supreme

Court, but for the people. And how is it he tells us they can exclude it? He says it needs "police regulation," and that admits of "unfriendly legislation." Although it is a right established by the Constitution of the United States to take a slave into a territory of the United States and hold him as property, yet unless the territorial legislature will give friendly legislation, and, more especially, if they adopt unfriendly legislation, they can practically exclude him. Now, without meeting this proposition as a matter of fact, I pass to consider the real constitutional obligation. Let me take the gentleman who looks me in the face before me, and let us suppose that he is a member of the territorial legislature. The first thing he will do will be to swear that he will support the Constitution of the United States. His neighbor by his side in the territory has slaves and needs territorial legislation to enable him to enjoy that constitutional right. Can he withhold the legislation which his neighbor needs for the enjoyment of a right which is fixed in his favor in the Constitution of the United States, which he has sworn to support? Can he withhold it without violating his oath? And, more especially, can he pass unfriendly legislation to violate his oath? Why, this is a monstrous sort of talk about the Constitution of the United States! There has never been as outlandish or lawless a doctrine from the mouth of any respectable man on earth. I do not believe it is a constitutional right to hold slaves in a territory of the United States. I believe the decision was improperly made, and I go for reversing it. Judge Douglas is furious against those who go for reversing a decision. But he is for legislating it out of all force while the law itself stands. I repeat that there has never been so monstrous a doctrine uttered from the mouth of a respectable man. . . .

I say that no man can deny his obligation to give the necessary legislation to support slavery in a territory, who believes it is a constitutional right to have it there. No man can, who does not give the abolitionists an argument to deny the obligation enjoined by the Constitution to enact a fugitive slave law. Try it now. It is the strongest abolition argument ever made. I say if that *Dred Scott* decision is correct, then the right to hold slaves in a territory is equally a constitutional right with the right of a slaveholder to have his runaway returned. No one can show the distinction between them. The one is express, so that we cannot deny it. The other is construed to be in the Constitution, so that he who believes the decision to be correct believes in the right. And the man who argues that by unfriendly legislation, in spite of that constitutional right, slavery may be driven from the territories, cannot avoid furnishing an argument by which abolitionists may deny the obligation to return fugitives and claim the power to pass laws unfriendly to the right of the slaveholder to reclaim his fugitive. I do not know how such an argument may strike a popular assembly like this, but I defy anybody to go before a body of men whose minds are educated to estimating evidence and reasoning and show that there is an iota of difference between the constitutional right to reclaim a fugitive, and the constitutional right to hold a slave, in a territory, provided this *Dred Scott* decision is correct. I defy any man to make an argument that will justify unfriendly legislation to deprive a slaveholder of his right to hold a slave in a territory, that will not equally, in all its length, breadth, and thickness, furnish an argument for nullifying the Fugitive Slave law. Why, there is not such an abolitionist in the nation as Douglas, after all.

STEPHEN A. DOUGLAS

— ★ —

Seventh Lincoln-Douglas Debate, Illinois Campaign for the U.S. Senate

ALTON, ILLINOIS; OCTOBER 15, 1858

Stephen Douglas (1813–1861) had represented Illinois in the U.S. House of Representatives from 1843 and in the Senate from 1847. He supported Henry Clay's Compromise of 1850 legislation and in 1854 incorporated the principle of popular sovereignty in the bills that established the territories of Kansas and Nebraska, thus allowing the status of slavery in those areas to be decided by their residents. As the Democratic party's candidate for reelection as U.S. senator, he spoke in the seventh and final debate with Lincoln in support of expansionism and the rights of each state or territory to choose or reject slavery. Predictably, partisan sources chose sides in assessing the outcome of the debates, and in the November election Douglas emerged victorious. Lincoln and Douglas faced each other again in the presidential campaign of 1860.

M r. Lincoln has concluded his remarks by saying that there is not such an abolitionist as I am in all America. If he could make the abolitionists of Illinois believe that, he would not have much show for the Senate. Let him make the abolitionists believe the truth of that statement, and his political back is broken. . . .

Mr. Lincoln tries to avoid the main issue by attacking the truth of my proposition that our fathers made this government divided into free and slave states, recognizing the right of each to decide all its local questions for itself. Did they not thus make it? It is true that they did not establish slavery in any of the states, or abolish it in any of them, but finding thirteen states, twelve of which were slave and one free, they agreed to form a government uniting them together as they stood divided into free and slave states and to guarantee forever to each state the right to do as it pleased on the slavery question. Having thus made the government, and conferred this right upon each state forever, I assert that this government can exist as they made it, divided into free and slave states, if any one state chooses to retain slavery. He says that he looks forward to a time when slavery shall be abolished everywhere. I look forward to a time when each state shall be allowed to do as it pleases. If it chooses to keep slavery forever, it is not my business, but its own; if it chooses to abolish slavery, it is its own business—not mine. I care more for the great principle of self-government, the right of the people to rule, than I do for all the Negroes in Christendom. I would not endanger the perpetuity of this Union, I would not blot out the great inalienable rights of the white men, for all the Negroes that ever existed. Hence, I say, let us maintain this government on the principles that our fathers made it, recognizing the right of each state to keep slavery as long as its people determine, or to abolish it when they please. But Mr. Lincoln says that when our fathers made this government they did not look forward to the state of things now existing, and therefore he thinks the doctrine was wrong; and he quotes Brooks, of South Carolina, to prove that our fathers then thought that probably slavery would be abolished by each state acting for itself before this time. Suppose they did; suppose they did not foresee what has occurred—does that change the principles of our government? They did not probably foresee the telegraph that transmits intelligence by lightning, nor did they foresee the railroads that now form the bonds of union between the different states, or the thousand mechanical inventions that have elevated mankind. But do these things change the principles of the government? Our fathers, I say, made this government on the principle of the right of each state to do as it pleases in its own domestic affairs, subject to the Constitution, and allowed the people of each to apply to every new change of circumstances such remedy as they may see fit to improve their condition. This right they have for all time to come.

Mr. Lincoln went on to tell you that he does not at all desire to interfere with slavery in the states where it exists, nor does his party. I expected him to say that down here. Let me ask him, then, how he expects to put slavery in the course of ultimate extinction everywhere, if he does not intend to interfere with it in the states where it exists? He says that he will prohibit it in all territories, and the inference is, then, that unless they make free states out of them he will keep them out of the Union; for, mark you, he did not say whether or not he would vote to admit Kansas with slavery or not, as her people might apply; he did not say whether or not he was in favor of bringing the territories now in existence into the Union on the principle of Clay's Compromise Measures on the slavery question. I told you that he would not. His idea is that he will prohibit slavery in all the territories and thus force them all to become free states, surrounding the slave states with a cordon of free states, and hemming them in, keeping the slaves confined to their present limits whilst they go on multiplying, until the soil on which they live will no longer feed them, and he will thus be able to put slavery in a course of ultimate extinction by starvation.

He will extinguish slavery in the Southern states as the French general exterminated the Algerines when he smoked them out. He is going to extinguish slavery by surrounding the slave states, hemming in the slaves, and starving them out of existence, as you smoke a fox out of his hole. He intends to do that in the name of humanity and Christianity, in order that we may get rid of the terrible crime and sin entailed upon our fathers of holding slaves. Mr. Lincoln makes out that line of policy and appeals to the moral sense of justice and to the Christian feeling of the community to sustain him. He says that any man who holds to the contrary doctrine is in the position of the king who claimed to govern by divine right. Let us examine for a moment and see what principle it was that overthrew the divine right of George III to govern us. Did not these colonies rebel because the British Parliament had no right to pass laws concerning our property and domestic and private institutions without our consent? We demanded that the British government should not pass such laws unless they gave us representation in the body passing them, and this the British government insisting on doing, we went to war, on the principle that the Home government should not control and govern distant colonies without giving them a representation. Now, Mr. Lincoln proposes to govern the territories without giving them a representation and calls on Congress to pass laws controlling their property and domestic concerns without their consent and against their will. Thus, he asserts for his party the identical principle asserted by George III and the Tories of the Revolution.

I ask you to look into these things and then tell me whether the democracy or the abolitionists are right. I hold that the people of a territory, like those of a state (I use the language of Mr. Buchanan in his letter of acceptance), have the right to decide for themselves whether slavery shall or shall not exist within their limits. The point upon which Chief Justice Taney expresses his opinion is simply this: that slaves, being property, stand on an equal footing with other property, and consequently that the owner has the same right to carry that property into a territory that he has any other, subject to the same conditions. Suppose that one of your merchants was to take fifty or one hundred thousand dollars' worth of liquors to Kansas. He has a right to go there, under that decision, but when he gets there he finds the Maine liquor law in force, and what can he do with his property after he gets it there? He cannot sell it; he cannot use it; it is subject to the local law, and that law is against him; and the best thing he can do with it is to bring it back into Missouri or Illinois and sell it. If you take Negroes to Kansas, as Colonel Jeff Davis said in his Bangor speech, from which I have quoted today, you must take them there subject to the local law. If the people want the institution of slavery, they will protect and encourage it; but if they do not want it they will withhold that protection, and the absence of local legislation protecting slavery excludes it as completely as a positive prohibition. You slaveholders of Missouri might as well understand what you know practically, that you cannot carry slavery where the people do not want it. All you have a right to ask is that the people shall do as they please; if they want slavery, let them have it; if they do not want it, allow them to refuse to encourage it.

My friends, if, as I have said before, we will only live up to this great fundamental principle, there will be peace between the North and the South. Mr. Lincoln admits that under the Constitution, on all domestic questions, except slavery, we ought not to interfere with the people of each state. What right have we to interfere with the people of each state? What right have we to interfere with slavery any more than we have to interfere with any other question? He says that this slavery question is now the bone of contention. Why? Simply because agitators have combined in all the free states to make war upon it. Suppose the agitators in the states should combine in one-half of the Union to make war upon the railroad system of the other half. They would thus be driven to the same sectional strife. Suppose one section makes war upon any other particular institution of the opposite section, and the same strife is produced. The only remedy and safety is that we shall stand by the Constitution as our fathers made it, obey the laws as they are passed, while they stand the proper test, and sustain the decisions of the Supreme Court and the constituted authorities.

JOHN BROWN

——— ★ ———

Speech Before the Court

COURTROOM, CHARLESTOWN, VIRGINIA
(NOW WEST VIRGINIA); NOVEMBER 2, 1859

In his efforts to incite a general slave revolt, the fanatical aboli-
tionist John Brown (1800–1859) murdered proslavery settlers in
Kansas and raided Missouri plantations to free their slaves. His
final strike was an armed occupation of the U.S. armory in
Harpers Ferry, Virginia, on October 16, 1859. An assault by
marines, under the command of Colonel Robert E. Lee, resulted
in the death of most of Brown's followers and the capture of
Brown himself and four others. At his trial, a jury found the
abolitionist guilty of murder, treason, and conspiracy with slaves
to create insurrection. John Brown gave his last speech, a defense
of his moral crusade to free slaves, prior to receiving his sentence
of death by hanging.

I have, may it please the court, a few words to say. In the first
place, I deny everything but what I have all along admitted—of a design on my part to free slaves. I intended certainly
to have made a clean thing of that matter, as I did last winter,
when I went into Missouri and there took slaves without the
snapping of a gun on either side, moving them through the
country, and finally leaving them in Canada. I designed to have
done the same thing again, on a larger scale. That was all I
intended. I never did intend murder, or treason, or the destruction of property, or to excite or incite slaves to rebellion, or to
make insurrection.

I have another objection, and that is that it is unjust that
I should suffer such a penalty. Had I interfered in the manner
which I admit, and which I admit has been fairly proved (for

I admire the truthfulness and candor of the greater portion of the witnesses who have testified in this case)—had I so interfered in behalf of the rich, the powerful, the intelligent, the so-called great, or in behalf of any of their friends, either father, mother, brother, sister, wife, or children, or any of that class, and suffered and sacrificed what I have in this interference, it would have been all right. Every man in this court would have deemed it an act worthy of reward rather than punishment.

This court acknowledges, too, as I suppose, the validity of the law of God. I see a book kissed, which I suppose to be the Bible, or at least the New Testament, which teaches me that all things whatsoever I would that men should do to me, I should do even so to them. It teaches me, further, to remember them that are in bonds, as bound with them. I endeavored to act up to that instruction. I say, I am yet too young to understand that God is any respecter of persons. I believe that to have interfered as I have done, as I have always freely admitted I have done, in behalf of His despised poor, was no wrong, but right. Now if it is deemed necessary that I should forfeit my life for the furtherance of the ends of justice, and mingle my blood further with the blood of my children and with the blood of millions in this slave country whose rights are disregarded by wicked, cruel, and unjust enactments—I say, let it be done!

Let me say one word further.

I feel entirely satisfied with the treatment I have received on my trial. Considering all the circumstances, it has been more generous than I expected. But I feel no consciousness of guilt. I have stated from the first what was my intention and what was not. I never had any design against the liberty of any person, nor any disposition to commit treason, or excite slaves to rebel, or make any general insurrection. I never encouraged any man to do so but always discouraged any idea of that kind.

Let me say, also, a word in regard to the statements made

by some of those who were connected with me. I hear it has been stated by some of them that I have induced them to join me. But the contrary is true. I do not say this to injure them, but as regretting their weakness. No one but joined me of his own accord, and the greater part at their own expense. A number of them I never saw, and never had a word of conversation with, till the day they came to me, and that was for the purpose I have stated.

Now I have done.

ABRAHAM LINCOLN

★

First Inaugural Address

CAPITOL, WASHINGTON, D.C.; MARCH 4, 1861

In the presidential election of 1860, Abraham Lincoln defeated three other candidates, John C. Breckinridge, Stephen A. Douglas, and John Bell. President James Buchanan escorted Lincoln to the Capitol, where he took the oath of office from Chief Justice Roger Taney, the man who wrote the majority opinion in the Dred Scott *case. Lincoln's inaugural speech was an attempt to reassure the Southern states of his hands-off policy in regard to slavery while reaffirming his strong opposition to any act of secession. He stated that he had no plan to "interfere with the institution of slavery in the states where it exists" and that "in contemplation of universal law, and of the Constitution, the Union of these states is perpetual." At the time of the address, however, seven states had already seceded, and the Civil War began the next month, when the Confederates fired on Fort Sumter.*

Fellow Citizens of the United States: In compliance with a custom as old as the government itself, I appear before you to address you briefly and to take, in your presence, the oath prescribed by the Constitution of the United States, to be taken by the president "before he enters on the execution of his office."

I do not consider it necessary, at present, for me to discuss those matters of administration about which there is no special anxiety or excitement.

Apprehension seems to exist among the people of the Southern states, that by the accession of a Republican administration, their property, and their peace, and personal security, are to be endangered. There has never been any reasonable cause for such apprehension. Indeed, the most ample evidence to the contrary has all the while existed and been open to their inspection. It is found in nearly all the published speeches of him who now addresses you. I do but quote from one of those speeches when I declare that "I have no purpose, directly or indirectly, to interfere with the institution of slavery in the states where it exists. I believe I have no lawful right to do so, and I have no inclination to do so."

Those who nominated and elected me did so with full knowledge that I had made this, and many similar declarations, and had never recanted them. And more than this, they placed in the platform, for my acceptance, and as a law to themselves, and to me, the clear and emphatic resolution which I now read:

"*Resolved,* That the maintenance inviolate of the rights of the states, and especially the right of each state to order and control its own domestic institutions according to its own judgment exclusively, is essential to that balance of power on which the perfection and endurance of our political fabric depend; and we denounce the lawless invasion by armed force of the soil of any state or territory, no matter under what pretext, as among the gravest of crimes."

I now reiterate these sentiments, and in doing so, I only press upon the public attention the most conclusive evidence of which the case is susceptible—that the property, peace, and security of no section are to be in any wise endangered by the now incoming administration. I add, too, that all the protection which, consistently with the Constitution and the laws, can be given, will be cheerfully given to all the states when lawfully demanded, for whatever cause—as cheerfully to one section as to another.

There is much controversy about the delivering up of fugitives from service or labor. The clause I now read is as plainly written in the Constitution as any other of its provisions:

"No person held to service or labor in one state, under the laws thereof, escaping into another, shall, in consequence of any law or regulation therein, be discharged from such service or labor, but shall be delivered up on claim of the party to whom such service or labor may be due."

It is scarcely questioned that this provision was intended by those who made it, for the reclaiming of what we call fugitive slaves; and the intention of the lawgiver is the law. All members of Congress swear their support to the whole Constitution—to this provision as much as to any other. To the proposition, then, that slaves whose cases come within the terms of this clause "shall be delivered up," their oaths are unanimous. Now, if they would make the effort in good temper, could they not, with nearly equal unanimity, frame and pass a law, by means of which to keep good that unanimous oath? There is some difference of opinion whether this clause should be enforced by national or by state authority; but surely that difference is not a very material one. If the slave is to be surrendered, it can be of but little consequence to him, or to others, by which authority it is done. And should anyone, in any case, be content that his oath shall go unkept, on a merely unsubstantial controversy as to how it shall be kept?

Again, in any law upon this subject, ought not all the safeguards of liberty known in civilized and humane jurisprudence to be introduced, so that a free man be not, in any case, surrendered as a slave? And might it not be well, at the same time, to provide by law for the enforcement of that clause in the Constitution which guarantees that "the citizens of each state shall be entitled to all privileges and immunities of citizens in the several states"?

I take the official oath today, with no mental reservations, and with no purpose to construe the Constitution or laws, by any hypercritical rules. And while I do not choose now to specify particular acts of Congress as proper to be enforced, I do suggest that it will be much safer for all, both in official and private stations, to conform to, and abide by, all those acts which stand unrepealed, than to violate any of them, trusting to find impunity in having them held to be unconstitutional.

It is seventy-two years since the first inauguration of a president under our national Constitution. During that period fifteen different and greatly distinguished citizens have, in succession, administered the executive branch of the government. They have conducted it through many perils; and, generally, with great success. Yet, with all this scope for precedent, I now enter upon the same task for the brief constitutional term of four years, under great and peculiar difficulty. A disruption of the federal Union, heretofore only menaced, is now formidably attempted.

I hold, that in contemplation of universal law, and of the Constitution, the Union of these states is perpetual. Perpetuity is implied, if not expressed, in the fundamental law of all national governments. It is safe to assert that no government proper ever had a provision in its organic law for its own termination. Continue to execute all the express provisions of our national Constitution, and the Union will endure forever—it being impossible to destroy it, except by some action not provided for in the instrument itself.

Again, if the United States be not a government proper, but an association of states in the nature of contract merely, can it, as a contract, be peaceably unmade, by less than all the parties who made it? One party to a contract may violate it—break it, so to speak; but does it not require all to lawfully rescind it? . . .

It follows from these views that no state, upon its own mere motion, can lawfully get out of the Union, that resolves and ordinances to that effect are legally void; and that acts of violence, within any state or states, against the authority of the United States, are insurrectionary or revolutionary, according to circumstances.

I therefore consider that, in view of the Constitution and the laws, the Union is unbroken; and, to the extent of my ability, I shall take care, as the Constitution itself expressly enjoins upon me, that the laws of the Union be faithfully executed in all the states. . . .

In doing this there needs to be no bloodshed or violence; and there shall be none, unless it be forced upon the national authority. The power confided to me will be used to hold, occupy, and possess the property and places belonging to the government and to collect the duties and imposts; but beyond what may be necessary for these objects, there will be no invasion—no using of force against or among the people anywhere. . . .

Physically speaking, we cannot separate. We cannot remove our respective sections from each other, nor build an impassable wall between them. A husband and wife may be divorced and go out of the presence and beyond the reach of each other; but the different parts of our country cannot do this. They cannot but remain face to face; and intercourse, either amicable or hostile, must continue between them. Is it possible then to make that intercourse more advantageous, or more satisfactory, after separation than before? Can aliens make treaties easier than friends can make laws? Can treaties be more faithfully enforced between aliens, than laws can among friends? Suppose you go to war, you cannot fight always; and when, after much loss on both sides and no gain on either, you cease fighting, the identical old questions, as to terms of intercourse, are again upon you.

This country, with its institutions, belongs to the people who inhabit it. Whenever they shall grow weary of the existing government, they can exercise their constitutional right of amending it, or their revolutionary right to dismember, or overthrow it. I cannot be ignorant of the fact that many worthy and patriotic citizens are desirous of having the national Constitution amended. While I make no recommendation of amendments, I fully recognize the rightful authority of the people over the whole subject, to be exercised in either of the modes prescribed in the instrument itself; and I should, under existing circumstances, favor rather than oppose a fair opportunity being afforded the people to act upon it. . . .

The chief magistrate derives all his authority from the people, and they have conferred none upon him to fix terms for the separation of the states. The people themselves can do this also if they choose; but the executive, as such, has nothing to do with it. His duty is to administer the present government, as it came to his hands, and to transmit it, unimpaired by him, to his successor.

Why should there not be a patient confidence in the ultimate justice of the people? Is there any better, or equal hope, in the world? In our present differences, is either party without faith of being in the right? If the Almighty Ruler of Nations, with His eternal truth and justice, be on your side of the North, or on yours of the South, that truth, and that justice, will surely prevail, by the judgment of this great tribunal, the American people. . . .

In your hands, my dissatisfied fellow countrymen, and not in mine, is the momentous issue of civil war. The government will not assail you. You can have no conflict without being yourselves the aggressors. You have no oath registered in heaven to destroy the government, while I shall have the most solemn one to "preserve, protect, and defend it."

I am loath to close. We are not enemies, but friends. We must not be enemies. Though passion may have strained, it must not break our bonds of affection. The mystic chords of memory, stretching from every battlefield and patriot grave to every living heart and hearthstone, all over this broad land, will yet swell the chorus of the Union, when again touched, as surely they will be, by the better angels of our nature.

JEFFERSON DAVIS

——— ★ ———

Inaugural Address as President of the Confederate States of America

CAPITOL SQUARE, RICHMOND, VIRGINIA;
FEBRUARY 22, 1862

South Carolina seceded from the Union on December 20, 1860. Six other states followed—Mississippi, Florida, Alabama, Georgia, Louisiana, and Texas—and together they formed the Confederate States of America in February 1861. The constitutional convention at Montgomery, Alabama, chose Jefferson Davis (1808–1889) as the Confederacy's first president, and he took the oath of office on February 18. The speed of these events underlined the efforts of the Confederacy to create a functioning government prior to Lincoln's inauguration. The Confederate Congress soon adopted a permanent constitution, which allowed for presidential election by popular vote. On February 22, 1862, Davis took a second oath of office, at Richmond, Virginia, and gave his inaugural address.

Fellow Citizens: On this the birthday of the man most identified with the establishment of American independence, and beneath the monument erected to commemorate his heroic virtues and those of his compatriots, we have assembled to usher into existence the permanent government of the Confederate States. Through this instrumentality, under the favor of Divine Providence, we hope to perpetuate the principles of our Revolutionary fathers. The day, the memory, and the purpose seem fitly associated.

It is with mingled feelings of humility and pride that I appear to take, in the presence of the people and before high heaven, the oath prescribed as a qualification for the exalted station to which the unanimous voice of the people has called me. Deeply sensible of all that is implied by this manifestation of the people's confidence, I am yet more profoundly impressed by the vast responsibility of the office and humbly feel my own unworthiness. . . .

When a long course of class legislation, directed not to the general welfare but to the aggrandizement of the Northern section of the Union, culminated in a warfare on the domestic institutions of the Southern states—when the dogmas of a sectional party, substituted for the provisions of the constitutional compact, threatened to destroy the sovereign rights of the states —six of those states, withdrawing from the Union, confederated together to exercise the right and perform the duty of instituting a government which would better secure the liberties for the preservation of which that Union was established.

Whatever of hope some may have entertained that a returning sense of justice would remove the danger with which our rights were threatened, and render it possible to preserve the Union of the Constitution, must have been dispelled by the malignity and barbarity of the Northern states in the prosecution of the existing war. The confidence of the most hopeful among us must have been destroyed by the disregard they have recently exhibited for all the time-honored bulwarks of civil and religious liberty.

Bastilles filled with prisoners, arrested without civil process or indictment duly found; the writ of habeas corpus suspended by executive mandate; a state legislature controlled by the imprisonment of members whose avowed principles suggested to the federal executive that there might be another added to the list of seceded states; elections held under threats of a military power; civil officers, peaceful citizens, and gentlewomen incarcerated for opinion's sake—proclaimed the incapacity of our late associates to administer a government as free, liberal, and humane as that established for our common use.

For proof of the sincerity of our purpose to maintain our ancient institutions, we may point to the Constitution of the Confederacy and the laws enacted under it, as well as to the fact that through all the necessities of an unequal struggle there has been no act on our part to impair personal liberty or the freedom of speech, of thought, or of the press. The courts have been open, the judicial functions fully executed, and every right of the peaceful citizen maintained as securely as if a war of invasion had not disturbed the land.

The people of the states now confederated became convinced the government of the United States had fallen into the hands of a sectional majority, who would pervert that most sacred of all trusts to the destruction of the rights which it was pledged to protect. They believed that to remain longer in the Union would subject them to a continuance of a disparaging discrimination, submission to which would be inconsistent with their welfare and intolerable to a proud people. They therefore determined to sever its bonds and establish a new confederacy for themselves. . . .

The first year in our history has been the most eventful in the annals of this continent. A new government has been established, and its machinery put in operation over an area exceeding seven hundred thousand square miles. The great principles upon which we have been willing to hazard everything that is dear to man have made conquests for us which could never have been achieved by the sword. Our Confederacy has grown from six to thirteen states; and Maryland, already united to us by hallowed memories and material interests, will, I believe, when able to speak with unstifled voice, connect her destiny with the South.

Our people have rallied with unexampled unanimity to the support of the great principles of constitutional government, with firm resolve to perpetuate by arms the right which they could not peacefully secure. A million of men, it is estimated, are now standing in hostile array and waging war along a frontier of thousands of miles. Battles have been fought, sieges have been conducted, and although the contest is not ended, and the tide for the moment is against us, the final result in our favor is not doubtful. . . .

This great strife has awakened in the people the highest emotions and qualities of the human soul. It is cultivating feelings of patriotism, virtue, and courage. Instances of self-sacrifice and of generous devotion to the noble cause for which we are contending are rife throughout the land. Never has a people evinced a more determined spirit than that now animating men, women, and children in every part of our country. Upon the first call, the men fly to arms; and wives and mothers send their husbands and sons to battle without a murmur of regret. . . .

It is a satisfaction that we have maintained the war by our unaided exertions. We have neither asked nor received assistance from any quarter. Yet the interest involved is not wholly our own. The world at large is concerned in opening our markets to its commerce. When the independence of the Confederate States is recognized by the nations of the earth, and we are free to follow our interests and inclinations by cultivating foreign trade, the Southern states will offer to manufacturing nations the most favorable markets which ever invited their commerce. Cotton, sugar, rice, tobacco, provisions, timber, and naval stores will furnish attractive exchanges. . . .

The tyranny of an unbridled majority, the most odious and least responsible form of despotism, has denied us both the rights and the remedy. Therefore we are in arms to renew such sacrifices as our fathers made to the holy cause of constitutional liberty. At the darkest hour of our struggle the provisional gives place to the permanent government. After a series of successes and victories, which covered our arms with glory, we have recently met with serious disasters. But in the heart of a people resolved to be free, these disasters tend but to stimulate to increased resistance.

To show ourselves worthy of the inheritance bequeathed to us by the patriots of the Revolution, we must emulate that heroic devotion which made reverse to them but the crucible in which their patriotism was refined.

With confidence in the wisdom and virtue of those who will share with me the responsibility and aid me in the conduct of public affairs; securely relying on the patriotism and courage of the people, of which the present war has furnished so many examples, I deeply feel the weight of the responsibilities I now, with unaffected diffidence, am about to assume; and fully realizing the inequality of human power to guide and to sustain, my hope is reverently fixed on Him whose favor is ever vouchsafed to the cause which is just. With humble gratitude and adoration, acknowledging the Providence which has so visibly protected the Confederacy during its brief but eventful career, to Thee, O God! I trustingly commit myself, and prayerfully invoke Thy blessing on my country and its cause.

ABRAHAM LINCOLN

— ★ —

Gettysburg Address

BATTLEFIELD, GETTYSBURG, PENNSYLVANIA;
NOVEMBER 19, 1863

---

*The battles of Gettysburg and Vicksburg were turning points for
the Union cause in the Civil War. With great loss of life on both
sides, General George Meade halted the Confederate invasion of
Pennsylvania at Gettysburg in July 1863. On November 19, 1863,
President Lincoln delivered his immortal address at a dedication
ceremony for a cemetery at Gettysburg for those who fell in
battle.*

Fourscore and seven years ago our fathers brought forth
on this continent a new nation, conceived in liberty and
dedicated to the proposition that all men are created equal.

Now we are engaged in a great civil war, testing whether
that nation, or any nation so conceived and so dedicated, can
long endure. We are met on a great battlefield of that war.
We have come to dedicate a portion of that field, as a final
resting place for those who here gave their lives that that nation might live. It is altogether fitting and proper that we
should do this.

But, in a larger sense, we cannot dedicate—we cannot consecrate—we cannot hallow—this ground. The brave men, living and dead, who struggled here have consecrated it, far above
our poor power to add or detract. The world will little note nor
long remember what we say here, but it can never forget what
they did here. It is for us the living, rather, to be dedicated here
to the unfinished work which they who fought here have thus
far so nobly advanced. It is rather for us to be here dedicated to
the great task remaining before us—that from these honored
dead we take increased devotion to that cause for which they

gave the last full measure of devotion—that we here highly resolve that these dead shall not have died in vain—that this nation, under God, shall have a new birth of freedom—and that government of the people, by the people, for the people, shall not perish from the earth.

MARK TWAIN

———★———

The American Press

MONDAY EVENING CLUB,
HARTFORD, CONNECTICUT; 1873

Samuel Langhorne Clemens (1835–1910) began writing under the pen name Mark Twain in 1863 with articles for the Enterprise, *the Virginia City, Nevada, newspaper. His humorous story "The Celebrated Jumping Frog of Calaveras County," published in the* New York Saturday Press *in 1865, brought him national recognition. There soon followed lectures, a tour of Europe and the Holy Land, and the books* Innocents Abroad *(1869) and* Roughing It *(1872). When he delivered his 1873 speech at the Monday Evening Club that severely castigated the abuses and sensationalism of the American press, Clemens had not yet written* The Adventures of Tom Sawyer, The Prince and the Pauper, Life on the Mississippi, *and* The Adventures of Huckleberry Finn.

T[he press] has scoffed at religion till it has made scoffing popular. It has defended official criminals, on party pretexts, until it has created a United States Senate whose members are incapable of determining what crime against law and the dignity of their own body *is*—they are so morally blind—and it has made light of dishonesty till we have as a result a Congress which contracts to work for a certain sum and then deliberately steals additional wages out of the public pocket and is pained and surprised that anybody should worry about a little thing like that.

I am putting all this odious state of things upon the newspaper, and I believe it belongs there—chiefly, at any rate. It is a free press—a press that is more than free—a press which is licensed to say any infamous thing it chooses about a private or a public man or advocate any outrageous doctrine it pleases. It is tied in no way. The public opinion which *should* hold it in bounds it has itself degraded to its own level. There are laws to protect the freedom of the press's speech, but none that are worth anything to protect the people from the press. A libel suit simply brings the plaintiff before a vast newspaper court to be tried before the law tries him, and reviled and ridiculed without mercy. . . .

It seems to me that just in the ratio that our newspapers increase, our morals decay. The more newspapers the worse morals. Where we have one newspaper that does good, I think we have fifty that do harm. We ought to look upon the establishment of a newspaper of the average pattern in a virtuous village as a calamity.

The difference between the tone and conduct of newspapers today and those of thirty or forty years ago is very noteworthy and very sad—I mean the average newspaper (for they had bad ones then, too). In those days the average newspaper was the champion of right and morals, and it dealt conscientiously in the truth. It is not the case now. The other day a reputable New York daily had an editorial defending the salary steal and justifying it on the grounds that congressmen were not paid enough—as if that were an all-sufficient excuse for stealing. That editorial put the matter in a new and perfectly satisfactory light with many a leather-headed reader, without a doubt. It has become a sarcastic proverb that a thing must be true if you saw it in a newspaper. That is the opinion intelligent people have of that lying vehicle in a nutshell. But the trouble is that the stupid people—who constitute the grand overwhelming majority of this and all other nations—*do* believe and *are* molded and convinced by what they get out of a newspaper, and there is where the harm lies.

Among us, the newspaper is a tremendous power. It can make or mar any man's reputation. It has perfect freedom to call the best man in the land a fraud and a thief, and he is destroyed beyond help. . . .

In the Foster murder case the New York papers made a weak pretense of upholding the hands of the governor and urging the people to sustain him in standing firmly by the law; but they printed a whole page of sickly, maudlin appeals to his clemency as a paid advertisement. And I suppose they would have published enough pages of abuse of the governor to destroy his efficiency as a public official to the end of his term if anybody had come forward and paid them for it—as an advertisement. The newspaper that obstructs the law on a trivial pretext, for money's sake, is a dangerous enemy to the public weal.

That awful power, the public opinion of a nation, is created in America by a horde of ignorant, self-complacent simpletons who failed at ditching and shoemaking and fetched up in journalism on their way to the poorhouse. I am personally acquainted with hundreds of journalists, and the opinion of the majority of them would not be worth tuppence in private, but when they speak in print it is the *newspaper* that is talking (the pygmy scribe is not visible) and *then* their utterances shake the community like the thunders of prophecy. . . .

The license of the press has scorched every individual of us in our time, I make no doubt. Poor Stanley was a very god in England, his praises in every man's mouth. But nobody said anything about his lectures—they were charitably quiet on that head and were content to praise his higher virtues. But our papers tore the poor creature limb from limb and scattered the fragments from Maine to California—merely because he couldn't lecture well. His prodigious achievement in Africa goes for naught—the man is pulled down and utterly destroyed—but *still* the persecution follows him as relentlessly from city to city and from village to village as if he had committed some bloody and detestable crime. Bret Harte was suddenly snatched out of obscurity by our papers and throned in the clouds—all the editors in the land stood out in the inclement weather and adored him through their telescopes and swung their hats till they wore them out and then borrowed more; and the first time his family fell sick, and in his trouble and harassment he ground out a rather flat article, . . . that hurrahing host said, "Why, this man's a fraud," and then they began to reach up there for him. And they got him, too, and fetched him down, and walked over him, and rolled him in the mud, and tarred and feathered him, and then set him up for a target and have been heaving dirt at him ever since. The result is that the man has had only just nineteen engagements to lecture this year, and the audience have been so scattering, too, that he has never discharged a sentence yet that hit two people at the same time. The man is ruined—never can get up again. . . .

In a town in Michigan I declined to dine with an editor who was drunk, and he said, in his paper, that my lecture was profane, indecent, and calculated to encourage intemperance. And yet that man never heard it. It might have reformed him if he had.

A Detroit paper once said that I was in the constant habit of beating my wife and that I still kept this recreation up, although I had crippled her for life and she was no longer able to keep out of my way when I came home in my usual frantic frame of mind. Now scarcely the half of that was true. Perhaps I ought to have sued that man for libel—but I knew better. All the papers in America—with a few creditable exceptions—would have found out then, to *their* satisfaction, that I was a wife beater, and they would have given it a pretty general airing, too. . . .

But I will not continue these remarks. I have a sort of vague general idea that there is too much liberty of the press in this country, and that through the absence of all wholesome restraint the newspaper has become in a large degree a national *curse,* and will probably damn the republic yet.

There *are* some excellent virtues in newspapers, some powers that wield vast influences for good; and I could have told all about these things, and glorified them exhaustively—but that would have left you gentlemen nothing to say.

HENRY WARD BEECHER

— ★ —

The Two Revelations

PLYMOUTH CHURCH, BROOKLYN, NEW YORK; MAY 31, 1885

Henry Ward Beecher (1813–1887) was a renowned preacher and political speaker who vigorously supported the antislavery movement, President Lincoln, the Republican party, and the Union cause during the Civil War. In addition to editing two periodicals, The Independent *and the* Christian Union, *and writing more than twenty books, he served as pastor of Plymouth Church in Brooklyn, New York, from 1847 until his death. Beecher's "Two Revelations" sermon reflects his progressive views, reconciling religion with Darwinian principles of evolution.*

That the whole world and the universe were the creation of God is the testimony of the whole Bible, both Jewish and Christian; but how he made them—whether by the direct force of a creative will or indirectly through a long series of gradual changes—the Scriptures do not declare. The grand truth is that this world was not a chance, a creative fermentation, a self-development, but that it was the product of an Intelligent Being, that the divine will in the continuance of this world manifests itself under the form of what are called natural laws, and that the operations of normal and legitimate laws are the results of divine will.

There are two records of God's creative energy. One is the record of the unfolding of *man* and of the race under the inspiration of God's nature: this is a mere sketch; of the ancient periods of man there is almost nothing known. The other of these records or revelations—if you choose to call them so—pertains to the physical globe and reveals the divine thought through the unfolding history of *matter;* and this is the older. So we have two revelations: God's thought in the evolution of matter and God's thought in the evolution of mind; and these are the Old Testament and the New—not in the usual sense of those terms, but in an appropriate scientific use of them.

In that great book of the Old there is a record of the progress, order, and result of God's thought in regard to the globe as a habitation for man. Though not every stage, yet the chief stages of preparation of this dwelling for man have been discovered and are now being deciphered and read. The crude, primitive material of the world of matter, the igneous condition, the aqueous stages, the dynamic and chemical periods, the gradual formation of the soil, the mountain building, the dawn of life, vegetable and animal, the stages of their progress—are not all these things written in the scientific revelation of God's history of creation? When I reflect upon the range of the invisible and the silent God, with the vast and well-nigh incomprehensible stretch of time, and of his compassionate waiting and working through illimitable ages and periods, compared with which a million years as marked by the clock are but seconds; when I reflect that the silent stones and the buried strata contain the record of God's working, and that the globe itself is a sublime history of God as an engineer and architect and as a master-builder, I cannot but marvel at the indifference with which good men have regarded this stupendous revelation of the ages past, and especially at the assaults made by Christian men upon scientific men who are bringing to light the long-hidden record of God's revelation in the material world.

With what eagerness has the world heard of the discovery in Egypt of the tomb that contained the buried kings of the Pharaophnic dynasty! But what are all these mighty kings, wrapped for these thousand years in the shroud of silence, compared with the discovery of God's method and the results of creation millions of centuries ago, retained in the rocks? Were the two tables of stone, written by the finger of God, a memorial to be revered, and their contents to be written in letters of gold in all men's churches, and yet his ministers and priests turn with indifference or with denunciation, even with scorn, sometimes, from the literature of the rocks written by the hand of God all over the earth? . . . Science is but the deciphering of God's thought as revealed in the structure of this world; it is a mere translation of God's primitive revelation. If to reject God's revelation of the Book is infidelity, what is it to reject God's revelation of himself in the structure of the whole globe? . . .

A vague notion exists with multitudes that science is infidel, and that evolution in particular is revolutionary—that is, revolutionary of the doctrines of the church. Men of such views often say, "I know that religion is true. I do not wish to hear anything that threatens to unsettle my faith." But faith that can be unsettled by the access of light and knowledge had better be unsettled. The intensity of such men's faith in their own thoughts is deemed to be safer than a larger view of God's thoughts. Others speak of evolution as a pseudoscience teaching that man descended from monkeys, or ascended as the case may be. They have no conception of it as the history of the divine process in the building of this world. They dismiss it with jests, mostly ancient jests; or, having a smattering of fragmentary knowledge, they address victorious ridicule to audiences as ignorant as they are themselves.

Now the ascent of man from the anthropoid apes is a mere hypothesis. It has not been proved; and in the broader sense of the word "proved," I see certainly no present means of proving it. It stands in the region of hypothesis, pressed forward by a multitude of probabilities. The probabilities are so many, and the light which this hypothesis throws upon human history and human life and phenomena is such that I quite incline to the supposition that it is, in the order of nature, in analogy with all the rest of God's work, and that in the ascending scale there was a time unknown, and methods not yet discovered, in which man left behind his prior relatives and came upon the spiritual ground which now distinguishes him from the whole brute creation. Of one thing I am certain, that whatever may have been the origin, it does not change either the destiny or the moral grandeur of man as he stands in the full light of civilization today. The theory of the evolution of the human race from an inferior race, not proved and yet probable, throws light upon many obscure points of doctrine and of theology that have most sadly needed light and solution.

First, then, what is evolution, and what does it reveal? The theory of evolution teaches that the creation of this earth was not accomplished in six days of twenty-four hours; that the divine method occupied ages and ages of immense duration; that nothing, of all the treasures of the globe as they now stand, was created at first in its present perfectness; that everything has grown through the lapse of ages into its present condition; that the whole earth, with their development in it, was, as it were, an egg, a germ, a seed; that the forests, the fields, the shrubs, the vineyards, all grasses and flowers, all insects, fishes, and birds, all mammals of every gradation have had a long history, and that they have come to the position in which they now stand through ages and ages of gradual change and unfolding. . . .

Simple religion is the unfolding of the best nature of man toward God, and man has been hindered and embittered by the outrageous complexity of unbearable systems of theology that have existed. If you can change theology, you will emancipate religion; yet men are continually confounding the two terms, religion and theology. They are not alike. Religion is the condition of a man's nature as toward God and toward his fellow men. That is religion—love that breeds truth, love that breeds justice, love that breeds harmonies of intimacy and intercommunication, love that breeds duty, love that breeds conscience, love that carries in its hand the scepter of pain, not to destroy and to torment but to teach and to save. Religion is that state of mind in which a man is related by his emotions, and through his emotions by his will and conduct, to God and to the proper performance of duty in this world. . . .

Evolution will multiply the motives and facilities of righteousness, which was and is the design of the whole Bible. It will not dull the executive doctrines of religion, that is, the forms of them by which an active and reviving ministry arouses men's consciences, by which they inspire faith, repentance, reformation, spiritual communion with God. Not only will those great truths be unharmed, by which men work zealously for the reformation of their fellow men, but they will be developed to a breadth and certainty not possible in their present philosophical condition. At present the sword of the spirit is in the sheath of a false theology. Evolution, applied to religion, will influence it only as the hidden temples are restored, by removing the sands which have drifted in from the arid deserts of scholastic and medieval theologies. It will change theology, but only to bring out the simple temple of God in clearer and more beautiful lines and proportions. . . .

In every view of it, I think we are to expect great practical fruit from the application of the truths that flow now from the interpretation of evolution. It will obliterate the distinction between natural and revealed religion, both of which are the testimony of God; one, God's testimony as to what is best for man in his social and physical relations, and the other, what is best for man in his higher spiritual nature. What is called morality will be no longer dissevered from religion. . . .

In every view, then, it is the duty of the friends of simple and unadulterated Christianity to hail the rising light and to uncover every element of religious teaching to its wholesome beams. Old men may be charitably permitted to die in peace, but young men and men in their prime are by God's providence laid under the most solemn obligation to thus discern the signs of the times, and to make themselves acquainted with the knowledge which science is laying before them. And above all, those zealots of the pulpit—who make faces at a science which they do not understand and who reason from prejudice to ignorance, who not only will not lead their people but hold up to scorn those who strive to take off the burden of ignorance from their shoulders—these men are bound to open their eyes and see God's sun shining in the heavens.

JOHN LA FARGE

———— ★ ————

The Modern Museum and the Teaching of Art

METROPOLITAN MUSEUM OF ART,
NEW YORK, NEW YORK; 1893

John La Farge (1835–1900), an enthusiastic promoter of the visual arts in late nineteenth-century America, was president of the Society of American Artists. Famed for his murals and work in stained glass, he was a leader in the revival of decorative arts and in the use of oriental design. La Farge's lecture at the Metropolitan Museum in 1893 stressed the importance of the museum —over the limited approach of the traditional academies—in teaching art free of rules. Particularly with the "smaller arts . . . the glass, metal work, carvings of wood and stone, fragments of buildings, leather, tapestry," La Farge stated, "if the museum is great enough, . . . whatever rule has been set down for you will find a contradiction—and a triumphant contradiction—in some small treasure, some choice fragment stored in the collections."

The museum, as you know, is a modern institution. It is admirable in one sense; in another, what it replaces was better for the life of art than what it gives today. If it were not so, this age of museums, of collections of general interest in art, of written teaching, of oral explanations, of academies, of government and municipal schools, should have given us the largest and richest development of art which the world has ever seen. . . .

No doubt that with each year the guardians of such vast intellectual property as we detain in museums will feel more and more the responsibility entrusted to them and will aid by many means the diffusion of their knowledge, the appreciation of the manner of their production; and as the position becomes more and more a function of high educational service, men of learning, men of inquiry, will more and more be chosen to make, by their aiding efforts, common intellectual property of this accumulation. . . .

In those smaller divisions of work in art, which I referred to when I spoke of work done in community, we shall probably see for us some return of the past. But the day of such a natural manner of life may be far off. For our art of painting, the nearest approach to it today is still in the schools; but the hold there is a precarious one, and the connection between the greater and smaller is interrupted and dependent upon something else than the necessary progress from first knowledge to full development.

In the older days the master might show his pupils what had been done before them by others than himself, in separate examples, with each of which would go a form of teaching all the more influential from its not being academic. The impression on the younger painter's mind of the great works hung in churches, seen one by one, their colors, their forms distinctly fitted to the place for which they were meant, their meaning emphasized by the circumstances of the place, by the importance attached to the use for which these works of art were meant, must have been far stronger, from its unity, its singleness, than that which students can get today from these very same works, confused upon the walls of a building like a museum, not built to hold them more than others—where light falls with democratic indifference, lighting each one impartially, and none of them as they were meant to be lit.

With this division, then, established in the methods of record, the academy teaching certain things and the museum all things; the one analytical and in sequence, the other as life teaches—in a mass of facts—we come to feel that to bring back the ancient synthesis, the two divisions forced upon us by modern changes must be brought together.

What we need to think of today, and in a certain way I am here to show you, is that the museum knows more than the academy. In the smaller arts, in that innumerable mass of materials made for use, or what we call mere ornament—the glass, metal work, carvings of wood and stone, fragments of buildings, leather, tapestry—the teaching is evident. Every rule has been applied, both those you know and those you have not heard of. It might almost seem at first, if the museum is great enough, that whatever rule has been set down for you will find a contradiction—and a triumphant contradiction—in some small treasure, some choice fragment stored in the collections. In such a case, it will always be that your teaching has been too narrow—probably not narrow so far as any execution may have gone; because that of itself carries its own reasoning, through the use, and sometimes the predominance, of material; but it will have been because some question of practice, quite valid—even very splendid—has been put before you as a principle.

And in no division of the arts of sight has there been more misapplied ingenuity of teaching, more narrowness of reasoning, more individual assertion, more professional incapacity, than in the law making which has been done in our century, for the reasonable production of the work of art that we call decoration. Perhaps there, more than in our art of painting, is this natural—because of the less powerful, human, individual factor and the necessity for the artist of carrying out such forms of art in conjunction with others, his superiors in the social management. For he, individually, does not count so much: his material is more important than in any other form of art—I mean more rebellious, less a creation of his own (compare at the two extremes a drawing in ink and a stained-glass window); and he works already to supply some wish of others; and he is directed, therefore, somewhat by the taste of the day, somewhat by the larger interests, for instance, of architects, some of whose work he supplies. But whenever one wishes to breathe freely again; whenever one wishes to see freedom in the use of material; whenever one wishes to see the man and not the workshop, the artist and not the trader, the poet, not the schoolmaster, then, tired and disgusted with the present incapacity—the present deplored, undoubted incapacity—one shall find in the museums a rest to the mind, and perhaps, as man after all is the same, a hope for the future.

Remember how human the so-called older pieces of little art seem to you, when compared with the modern. Recognize, then, how you come across the result of that same principle which we first recognized, that the man is almost everything, and that anything which does not allow us to feel this is *at once* the imitation and not the reality; be it a piece of machine-made lace, or a regulation stained-glass window, or the nineteenth-century carving of a Renaissance facade, or the fine and silly tooling of a piece of modern silver.

And do not think that even in the slightest way, by drawing your attention to what are called the minor arts, I go outside of what I am teaching you. If I should ask you to come upstairs with me and look at some little piece of Japanese lacquer, for instance, with a surface suggesting the weight, as well as the mystery, of moonlight; with depths of shadow that are typical of the art of varnish glazes; with iridescences like those of living birds or insects; with sparkling recalling the track of the stars in water; with patterns firm like the pattern of a flower; and all so dwelling in unity that you cannot think of their being displaced from the little world of box or tray in which they live, so that to the eye, they give the pleasure of notes of music in accord—if I took you to look at such a thing, as a lesson, it would be, among other things, a lesson of what we divide as color and composition.

That is, as you know, the special line in which the museum has requested me to direct my teaching. And there is but one way of considering such a division: and that is, that it is almost so large as to include *all* that your eye can possibly light on. You know that what you see is translated to you by some effect of colored light, and you know that that effect is placed within certain laws of arrangement which we study out in some cases and call perspective, but which, in other cases, are so obscure, or rather so complicated, that all we can do is to assume that they all must fall within a universal geometry—so that we can feel at ease in the spaces occupied by all the arts that appeal to the sight, and get from each or any what setting right we require.

BOOKER T. WASHINGTON

—— ★ ——

Atlanta Exposition Address

COTTON STATES' EXPOSITION, ATLANTA, GEORGIA;
SEPTEMBER 18, 1895

Born into slavery on a Virginia plantation, Booker Taliaferro Washington (1856–1915) worked as a janitor to pay for his education at Hampton Normal and Agricultural Institute, Virginia, from which he was graduated in 1875. He attended Wayland Seminary in Washington, D.C., and then returned to Hampton as an instructor. He was instrumental in the creation of Tuskegee Institute, a black school in Alabama, serving as its principal from 1881 to 1915. Washington wrote a number of books, including Up from Slavery *(1901), and his many speeches emphasized the importance of education and hard work for the advancement of African Americans. Washington's audience at the Cotton States' Exposition included both white and black Southerners, and his speech received enormous attention throughout the country. The other major African-American leader of the era, W.E.B. DuBois, who stressed the active pursuit of total equality, referred to Washington's address as the "Atlanta Compromise."*

M r. President and Gentlemen of the Board of Directors and Citizens: One-third of the population of the South is of the Negro race. No enterprise seeking the material, civil, or moral welfare of this section can disregard this element of our population and reach the highest success. I but convey to you, Mr. President and directors, the sentiment of the masses of my race when I say that in no way have the value and manhood of the American Negro been more fittingly and generously recognized than by the managers of this magnificent exposition at every stage of its progress. It is a recognition that will do more to cement the friendship of the two races than any occurrence since the dawn of our freedom.

Not only this, but the opportunity here afforded will awaken among us a new era of industrial progress. Ignorant and inexperienced, it is not strange that in the first years of our new life we began at the top instead of at the bottom; that a seat in Congress or the state legislature was more sought than real estate or industrial skill; that the political convention or stump speaking had more attractions than starting a dairy farm or truck garden.

A ship lost at sea for many days suddenly sighted a friendly vessel. From the mast of the unfortunate vessel was seen a signal, "Water, water; we die of thirst!" The answer from the friendly vessel at once came back, "Cast down your bucket where you are." And a third and fourth signal for water was answered, "Cast down your bucket where you are." The captain of the distressed vessel, at last heeding the injunction, cast down his bucket, and it came up full of fresh, sparkling water from the mouth of the Amazon River. To those of my race who depend on bettering their condition in a foreign land or who underestimate the importance of cultivating friendly relations with the Southern white man, who is their next-door neighbor, I would say: "Cast down your bucket where you are"—cast it down in making friends in every manly way of the people of all races by whom we are surrounded.

Cast it down in agriculture, mechanics, in commerce, in domestic service, and in the professions. And in this connection it is well to bear in mind that whatever other sins the

South may be called to bear, when it comes to business, pure and simple, it is in the South that the Negro is given a man's chance in the commercial world, and in nothing is this exposition more eloquent than in emphasizing this chance. Our greatest danger is that in the great leap from slavery to freedom we may overlook the fact that the masses of us are to live by the productions of our hands, and fail to keep in mind that we shall prosper in proportion as we learn to dignify and glorify common labor and put brains and skill into the common occupations of life; shall prosper in proportion as we learn to draw the line between the superficial and the substantial, the ornamental gew-gaws of life and the useful. No race can prosper till it learns that there is as much dignity in tilling a field as in writing a poem. It is at the bottom of life we must begin, and not at the top. Nor should we permit our grievances to overshadow our opportunities.

To those of the white race who look to the incoming of those of foreign birth and strange tongue and habits for the prosperity of the South, were I permitted I would repeat what I say to my own race, "Cast down your bucket where you are." Cast it down among the eight millions of Negroes whose habits you know, whose fidelity and love you have tested in days when to have proved treacherous meant the ruin of your firesides. Cast down your bucket among these people who have, without strikes and labor wars, tilled your fields, cleared your forests, built your railroads and cities, and brought forth treasures from the bowels of the earth, and helped make possible this magnificent representation of the progress of the South. Casting down your bucket among my people, helping and encouraging them as you are doing on these grounds, and to education of head, hand, and heart, you will find that they will buy your surplus land, make blossom the waste places in your fields, and run your factories. While doing this, you can be sure in the future, as in the past, that you and your families will be surrounded by the most patient, faithful, law-abiding, and unresentful people that the world has seen. As we have proved our loyalty to you in the past, in nursing your children, watching by the sick-bed of your mothers and fathers, and often following them with tear-dimmed eyes to their graves, so in the future, in our humble way, we shall stand by you with a devotion that no foreigner can approach, ready to lay down our lives, if need be, in defense of yours, interlacing our industrial, commercial, civil, and religious life with yours in a way that shall make the interests of both races one. In all things that are purely social we can be as separate as the fingers, yet one as the hand in all things essential to mutual progress.

There is no defense or security for any of us except in the highest intelligence and development of all. If anywhere there are efforts tending to curtail the fullest growth of the Negro, let these efforts be turned into stimulating, encouraging, and making him the most useful and intelligent citizen. Effort or means so invested will pay a thousand percent interest. These efforts will be twice blessed—"blessing him that gives and him that takes."

There is no escape through law of man or God from the inevitable:

> The laws of changeless justice bind
>   Oppressor with oppressed;
> And close as sin and suffering joined
>   We march to fate abreast.

Nearly sixteen millions of hands will aid you in pulling the load upward; or they will pull against you the load downward. We shall constitute one-third and more of the ignorance and crime of the South, or one-third its intelligence and progress; we shall contribute one-third to the business and industrial prosperity of the South, or we shall prove a veritable body of death, stagnating, depressing, retarding every effort to advance the body politic.

Gentlemen of the exposition, as we present to you our humble effort at an exhibition of our progress, you must not expect overmuch. Starting thirty years ago with ownership here and there in a few quilts and pumpkins and chickens (gathered from miscellaneous sources), remember the path that has led from these to the inventions and production of agricultural implements, buggies, steam engines, newspapers, books, statuary, carving, paintings, the management of drugstores and banks, has not been trodden without contact with thorns and thistles. While we take pride in what we exhibit as a result of our independent efforts, we do not for a moment forget that our part in this exhibition would fall far short of your expectations but for the constant help that has come to our educational life, not only from the Southern states, but especially from Northern philanthropists, who have made their gifts a constant stream of blessing and encouragement.

The wisest among my race understand that the agitation of questions of social equality is the extremest folly, and that progress in the enjoyment of all the privileges that will come to us must be the result of severe and constant struggle rather than of artificial forcing. No race that has anything to contribute to the markets of the world is long in any degree ostracized. It is important and right that all privileges of the law be ours, but it is vastly more important that we be prepared for the exercises of these privileges. The opportunity to earn a dollar in a factory just now is worth infinitely more than the opportunity to spend a dollar in an opera house.

In conclusion, may I repeat that nothing in thirty years has given us more hope and encouragement, and drawn us so near to you of the white race, as this opportunity offered by the exposition; and here bending, as it were, over the altar that represents the results of the struggles of your race and mine, both starting practically empty-handed three decades ago, I pledge that in your effort to work out the great and intricate problem which God has laid at the doors of the South, you shall have at all times the patient, sympathetic help of my race; only let this be constantly in mind, that, while from representations in these buildings of the product of field, of forest, of mine, of factory, letters, and art, much good will come, yet far above and beyond material benefits will be that higher good, that, let us pray God, will come, in a blotting out of sectional differences and racial animosities and suspicions, in a determination to administer absolute justice, in a willing obedience among all classes to the mandates of law. This, this, coupled with our material prosperity, will bring into our beloved South a new heaven and a new earth.

WILLIAM JENNINGS BRYAN

———— ★ ————

The Cross of Gold Speech

DEMOCRATIC NATIONAL CONVENTION, CHICAGO, ILLINOIS; JULY 8, 1896

William Jennings Bryan's speech in support of the unlimited coinage of silver at the 1896 Democratic Convention not only helped to defeat a platform resolution in favor of the gold standard but catapulted him into his party's nomination for the presidency. One of America's greatest orators, Bryan (1860–1925) used the free-silver issue as a symbol of support for the middle and lower classes and the interests of westerners, in opposition to the conservative eastern monied interests symbolized by the gold standard, which was supported by the Republican candidate, William McKinley. Bryan ran for the presidency three times; he was defeated by McKinley in 1896 and 1900 and by Taft in 1908. He served as secretary of state under Woodrow Wilson and opposed Clarence Darrow in the famous Scopes evolution trial in 1925.

Never before in the history of this country has there been witnessed such a contest as that through which we have just passed. Never before in the history of American politics has a great issue been fought out as this issue has been, by the voters of a great party. On the fourth of March, 1895, a few Democrats, most of them members of Congress, issued an address to the Democrats of the nation, asserting that the money question was the paramount issue of the hour; declaring that a majority of the Democratic party had the right to control the action of the party on this paramount issue; and concluding with the request that the believers in the free coinage of silver in the Democratic party should organize, take charge of, and control the policy of the Democratic party. Three months later, at Memphis, an organization was perfected, and the silver Democrats went forth openly and courageously proclaiming their belief and declaring that, if successful, they would crystallize into a platform the declaration which they had made. Then began the conflict. With a zeal approaching the zeal which inspired the Crusaders who followed Peter the Hermit, our silver Democrats went forth from victory unto victory until they are now assembled, not to discuss, not to debate, but to enter up the judgment already rendered by the plain people of this country. In this contest brother has been arrayed against brother, father against son. The warmest ties of love, acquaintance and association have been disregarded; old leaders have been cast aside when they have refused to give expression to the sentiments of those whom they would lead, and new leaders have sprung up to give direction to this cause of truth. Thus has the contest been waged, and we have assembled here under as binding and solemn instructions as were ever imposed upon representatives of the people. . . .

They tell us that this platform was made to catch votes. We reply to them that changing conditions make new issues, that the principles on which Democracy rests are as everlasting as the hills, but that they must be applied to new conditions as they arise. Conditions have arisen, and we are here to meet those conditions. They tell us that the income tax ought not be brought in here; that it is a new idea. They criticize us for our criticism of the Supreme Court of the United States. My friends, we have not criticized; we have simply called attention to what you already know. If you want criticisms, read the dissenting opinions of the court. There you will find criticisms. They say that we passed an unconstitutional law; we deny it. The income tax law was not unconstitutional when it was passed; it was not unconstitutional when it went before the Supreme Court for the first time; it did not become unconstitutional until one of the judges changed his mind, and we cannot be expected to know when a judge will change his mind. The income tax is just. It simply intends to put the burdens of government upon the backs of the people. I am in favor of an income tax. When I find a man who is not willing to bear his share of the burdens of the government which protects him, I find a man who is unworthy to enjoy the blessings of a government like ours. . . .

We say in our platform that we believe that the right to coin and issue money is a function of government. We believe it. We believe that it is a part of sovereignty and can no more with safety be delegated to private individuals than we could afford to delegate to private individuals the power to make penal statutes or levy taxes. Mr. Jefferson, who was once regarded as good Democratic authority, seems to have differed in opinion from the gentleman who has addressed us on the part of the minority. Those who are opposed to this proposition tell us that the issue of paper money is a function of the bank, and that the government ought to go out of the banking business. I stand with Jefferson rather than with them and tell them, as he did, that the issue of money is a function of government and that banks ought to go out of the governing business. . . .

We go forth confident that we shall win. Why? Because upon the paramount issue of this campaign there is not a spot of ground upon which the enemy will dare to challenge battle. If they tell us that the gold standard is a good thing, we shall point to their platform and tell them that their platform pledges the party to get rid of the gold standard and substitute bimetalism. If the gold standard is a good thing, why try to get rid of it? I call your attention to the fact that some of the very people who are in this convention today and who tell us that we ought to declare in favor of international bimetalism—thereby declaring that the gold standard is wrong and that the principle of bimetalism is better—these very people four months ago were open and avowed advocates of the gold standard, and were then telling us that we could not legislate two metals together, even with the aid of all the world. If the gold standard is a good thing, we ought to declare in favor of its retention and not in favor of abandoning it; and if the gold standard is a bad thing, why should we wait until other nations are willing to help us to let go?

Here is the line of battle, and we care not upon which issue they force the fight; we are prepared to meet them on either issue or on both. If they tell us that the gold standard is the standard of civilization, we reply to them that this, the most enlightened of all the nations of the earth, has never declared for a gold standard and that both the great parties this year are declaring against it. If the gold standard is the standard of civilization, why, my friends, should we not have it? . . .

Mr. Carlisle said in 1878 that this was a struggle between "the idle holders of idle capital" and "the struggling masses, who produce the wealth and pay the taxes of the country"; and, my friends, the question we are to decide is: Upon which side will the Democratic party fight? Upon the side of "the idle holders of idle capital" or upon the side of "the struggling masses"? That is the question which the party must answer first, and then it must be answered by each individual hereafter. The sympathies of the Democratic party, as shown by the platform, are on the side of the struggling masses who have ever been the foundation of the Democratic party. There are two ideas of government. There are those who believe that, if you will only legislate to make the well-to-do prosperous, their prosperity will leak through on those below. The Democratic idea, however, [is] that if you legislate to make the masses prosperous, their prosperity will find its way up through every class which rests upon them. . . .

My friends, we declare that this nation is able to legislate for its own people on every question, without waiting for the aid or consent of any other nation on earth; and upon that issue we expect to carry every state in the Union. I shall not slander the inhabitants of the fair state of Massachusetts nor the inhabitants of the state of New York by saying that, when they are confronted with the proposition, they will declare that this nation is not able to attend to its own business. It is the issue of 1776 over again. Our ancestors, when but three millions in number, had the courage to declare their political independence of every other nation; shall we, their descendants, when we have grown to seventy millions, declare that we are less independent than our forefathers? No, my friends, that will never be the verdict of our people. Therefore we care not upon what lines the battle is fought. If they say bimetalism is good, but that we cannot have it until the other nations help us, we reply that, instead of having a gold standard because England has, we will restore bimetalism and then let England have bimetalism because the United States has it. If they dare to come out in the open field and defend the gold standard as a good thing, we will fight them to the uttermost. Having behind us the producing masses of this nation and the world, supported by the commercial interests, the laboring interests, and the toilers everywhere, we will answer their demand for a gold standard by saying to them: You shall not press down upon the brow of labor this crown of thorns; you shall not crucify mankind upon a cross of gold.

FRANK LLOYD WRIGHT

—— ★ ——

The Art and Craft of the Machine: Democracy and New Forms in Architecture

CHICAGO ARTS AND CRAFTS SOCIETY, HULL HOUSE,
CHICAGO, ILLINOIS; MARCH 6, 1901

Considered by many to be America's greatest architect, Frank Lloyd Wright (1869–1959) championed the use of the geometric, simplified elements that were to become basic components of twentieth-century architecture. Wright's philosophy, however, did not promote a mechanistic and sterile art; rather, he stressed an "organic architecture," believing that buildings should seem to grow from their natural settings—for example, Wright designed the Kaufmann House in Pennsylvania to be built over a waterfall. When he was in his eighties, he completed the plans for a unique spiral building, the Guggenheim Museum in New York City. Wright's lecture at Hull House in Chicago (later repeated to the Western Society of Engineers and the Daughters of the American Revolution) was a pioneering call for the abandonment of overdecorated buildings and for the use of new forms in architecture made possible by the machine age, which he equated with American democracy.

That the machine has dealt art in the grand old sense a death-blow, none will deny—the evidence is too substantial: art in the grand old sense, meaning art in the sense of structural tradition, whose craft is fashioned upon the handicraft ideal, ancient or modern; an art wherein this form and that form as structural parts were laboriously joined in such a way as to beautifully emphasize the manner of the joining . . . craft that will not see that human thought is stripping off one form and donning another, and artists are everywhere, whether catering to the leisure class of old England or ground beneath the heel of commercial abuse here in the great West, the unwilling symptoms of the inevitable, organic nature of the machine they combat, the hell-smoke of the factories they scorn to understand.

And, invincible, triumphant, the machine goes on, gathering force and knitting the material necessities of mankind ever closer into a universal automatic fabric; the engine, the motor, and the battleship, the works of art of the century!

The machine is intellect mastering the drudgery of earth that the plastic art may live; that the margin of leisure and strength by which man's life upon the earth can be made beautiful, may immeasurably widen, its function ultimately to emancipate human expression!

It is a universal educator, surely raising the level of human intelligence, so carrying within itself the power to destroy, by its own momentum, the greed which in [William] Morris's time and still in our own time turns it to a deadly engine of enslavement. The only comfort left the poor artist, sidetracked as he is, seemingly is a mean one: the thought that the very selfishness which man's early art idealized, now reduced to its lowest terms, is swiftly and surely destroying itself through the medium of the machine.

The artist's present plight is a sad one, but may he truthfully say that society is less well off because architecture, or even art, as it was, is dead, and printing, or the machine, lives? Every age has done its work, produced its art with the best tools or contrivances it knew, the tools most successful in saving the most precious thing in the world—human effort. Greece used the chattel slave as the essential tool of its art and civilization. This tool we have discarded, and we would refuse the return of Greek art upon the terms of its restoration, because we insist now upon a basis of democracy.

Is it not more likely that the medium of artistic expression itself has broadened and changed until a new definition and new direction must be given the art activity of the future, and that the machine has finally made for the artist, whether he will yet own it or not, a splendid distinction between the art of old and the art to come?—A distinction made by the tool which frees human labor, lengthens and broadens the life of the simplest man, thereby the basis of the democracy upon which we insist.

To shed some light upon this distinction, let us take an instance in the field naturally ripened first by the machine—the commercial field.

The tall modern office building is the machine pure and simple.

We may here sense an advanced stage of a condition surely entering all art for all time; its already triumphant glare in the deadly struggle taking place here between the machine and the art of structural tradition reveals "art" torn and hung upon the steel frame of commerce, a forlorn head upon a pike, a solemn warning to architects and artists the world over. . . .

The modern tall office building problem is one representative problem of the machine. The only rational solutions it has received in the world may be counted upon the fingers of one hand. . . . We may object to the mannerism of these buildings, but we can take no exception to their manner nor hide from their evident truth. The steel frame has been recognized as a legitimate basis for a simple, sincere clothing of plastic material that idealizes its purpose without structural pretense. This principle has at last been recognized in architecture, and though the masters refuse to accept it as architecture at all, it is a glimmer in a darkened field—the first sane word that has been said in art for the machine. . . .

Let us turn to the decorative arts, the immense middle-ground of all art now mortally sickened by the machine—sickened that it may slough the art ideal of the constructural art for the plasticity of the new art, the art of democracy.

Here we find the most deadly perversion of all—the magnificent prowess of the machine bombarding the civilized world with the mangled corpses of strenuous horrors that once stood for cultivated luxury—standing now for a species of fatty degeneration simply vulgar. . . . The idea of fitness to purpose, harmony between form and use with regard to any of these things, is possessed by very few, and utilized by them as a protest chiefly—a protest against the machine! . . . Artists who feel toward modernity and the machine now as William Morris and Ruskin were justified in feeling then had best distinctly wait and work sociologically where great work may still be done by them. In the field of art activity they will do distinct harm. Already they have wrought much miserable mischief.

If the artist will only open his eyes he will see that the machine he dreads has made it possible to wipe out the mass of meaningless torture to which mankind, in the name of the artistic, has been more or less subjected since time began; for that matter, has made possible a cleanly strength, an ideality and a poetic fire that the art of the world has not yet seen; for the machine, the process now smooths away the necessity for petty structural deceits, soothes this wearisome struggle to make things seem what they are not and can never be; satisfies the simple term of the modern art equation as the ball of clay in the sculptor's hand yields to his desire—comforting forever this realistic, brain-sick masquerade we are wont to suppose art.

William Morris pleaded well for simplicity as the basis of all true art. Let us understand the significance to art of that word—*simplicity*—for it is vital to the art of the machine. . . . Simplicity in art, rightly understood, is a synthetic, positive quality, in which we may see evidence of mind, breadth of scheme, wealth of detail, and withal a sense of completeness found in a tree or a flower. A work may have the delicacies of a rare orchid or the stanch fortitude of the oak, and still be simple. A thing to be simple needs only to be true to itself in organic sense.

Theodore Roosevelt

—— ★ ——

Dealing with the Big Corporations

Music Hall, Cincinnati, Ohio;
September 20, 1902

Active in politics as a Republican from 1880, Theodore Roosevelt (1858–1919) served in the Spanish-American War, leading the Rough Riders in a renowned charge up San Juan Hill in Cuba. He was elected governor of New York in 1898 and vice president in 1900. The following year Roosevelt succeeded President McKinley, who fell victim to an assassin. Reelected as president in 1904, Roosevelt won the 1906 Nobel Peace Prize for helping to end the Russo-Japanese War. In 1912, he again ran for president, as a candidate of the Progressive (Bull Moose) party, but he and the Republican candidate, William Howard Taft, lost to Woodrow Wilson. In an effort to control monopolies and preserve competition, Congress had passed the Sherman (Antitrust) Act in 1890, and Roosevelt vigorously insisted on the enforcement of this law, often speaking publicly on the need to curtail the power of corporate trusts.

The whole subject of the trusts is of vital concern to us, because it presents one, and perhaps the most conspicuous, of the many problems forced upon our attention by the tremendous industrial development which has taken place during the last century, a development which is occurring in all civilized countries, notably in our own. There have been many factors responsible for bringing about these changed conditions. Of these, steam and electricity are the chief. . . . Those are the facts. Because of them have resulted the specialization of industries, and the unexampled opportunities offered for the employment of huge amounts of capital, and therefore for the rise in the business world of those masterminds through whom alone it is possible for such vast amounts of capital to be employed with profit. It matters very little whether we like these new conditions or whether we dislike them, whether we like the creation of these new opportunities or not. Many admirable qualities which were developed in the older, simpler, less progressive life have tended to atrophy under our rather feverish, high-pressure, complex life of today.

But our likes and dislikes have nothing to do with the matter. The new conditions are here. . . . It is foolish to pride ourselves upon our progress and prosperity, upon our commanding position in the international industrial world, and at the same time have nothing but denunciation for the men to whose commanding position we in part owe this very progress and prosperity, this commanding position. . . .

In dealing with the big corporations which we call trusts, we must resolutely purpose to proceed by evolution and not revolution. . . . The evils attendant upon overcapitalization alone are, in my judgment, sufficient to warrant a far closer supervision and control than now exists over the great corporations. Wherever a substantial monopoly can be shown to exist we should certainly try our utmost to devise an expedient by which it can be controlled. . . .

The first thing to remember is that if we are to accomplish any good at all it must be by resolutely keeping in mind the intention to do away with any evils in the conduct of big corporations, while steadfastly refusing to assent to indiscriminate assault upon all forms of corporate capital as such. The line of demarcation we draw must always be on conduct, not upon wealth; our objection to any given corporation must be not that it is big, but that it behaves badly. . . .

Nor can we afford to tolerate any proposal which will strike at the so-called trusts only by striking at the general well-being. We are now enjoying a period of great prosperity. The prosperity is generally diffused through all sections and through all classes. . . . If we are forced to the alternative of choosing either a system under which most of us prosper somewhat, though a few of us prosper too much, or else a system under which no one prospers enough, of course we will choose the former. If the policy advocated is so revolutionary and destructive as to involve the whole community in the crash of common disaster, it is as certain as anything can be that when the disaster has occurred all efforts to regulate the trusts will cease, and that the one aim will be to restore prosperity. . . .

You must face the fact that only harm will come from a proposition to attack the so-called trusts in a vindictive spirit by measures conceived solely with a desire of hurting them, without regard as to whether or not discrimination should be made between the good and evil in them, and without even any regard as to whether a necessary sequence of the action would be the hurting of other interests. The adoption of such a policy would mean temporary damage to the trusts, because it would mean temporary damage to all of our business interests; but the effect would be only temporary, for exactly as the damage affected all alike, good and bad, so the reaction would affect all alike, good and bad. The necessary supervision and control, in which I firmly believe as the only method of eliminating the real evils of the trusts, must come through wisely and cautiously framed legislation, which shall aim in the first place to give definite control to some sovereign over the great corporations, and which shall be followed, when once this power has been conferred, by a system giving to the government the full knowledge which is the essential for satisfactory action. . . .

Without the adoption of a constitutional amendment, my belief is that a good deal can be done by law. It is difficult to say exactly how much, because experience has taught us that in dealing with these subjects, where the lines dividing the rights and duties of the states and of the nation are in doubt, it has sometimes been difficult for Congress to forecast the action of the courts upon its legislation. Such legislation (whether obtainable now or obtainable only after a constitutional amendment) should provide for a reasonable supervision, the most prominent feature of which at first should be publicity—that is, the making public, both to the governmental authorities and to the people at large, the essential facts in which the public is concerned. . . .

I wish to repeat with all emphasis that desirable though it is that the nation should have the power I suggest, it is equally desirable that it should be used with wisdom and self-restraint. . . . We need to keep steadily in mind the fact that besides the tangible property in each corporation there lies behind the spirit which brings it success, and in the case of each very successful corporation this is usually the spirit of some one man or set of men. Under exactly similar conditions one corporation will make a stupendous success where another makes a stupendous failure, simply because one is well managed and the other is not.

While making it clear that we do not intend to allow wrongdoing by one of the captains of industry any more than by the humblest private in the industrial ranks, we must also in the interests of all of us avoid cramping a strength which, if beneficently used, will be for the good of all of us. The marvelous prosperity we have been enjoying for the past few years has been due primarily to the high average of honesty, thrift, and business capacity among our people as a whole; but some of it has also been due to the ability of the men who are the industrial leaders of the nation. In securing just and fair dealing by these men let us remember to do them justice in return, and this not only because it is our duty but because it is our interest—not only for their sakes but for ours. We are neither the friend of the rich man as such nor the friend of the poor man as such; we are the friend of the honest man, rich or poor; and we intend that all men, rich and poor alike, shall obey the law alike and receive its protection alike.

THEODORE ROOSEVELT

—— ★ ——

Preservation of the Forests

LELAND STANFORD JUNIOR UNIVERSITY, PALO ALTO, CALIFORNIA; MAY 12, 1903

Theodore Roosevelt communicated directly with the American people at every possible opportunity. In 1902 and 1903, for example, the president spoke publicly at least once a week—and sometimes twice a day—in cities and towns from Massachusetts to California. Roosevelt continually addressed subjects of concern to himself and the country—Cuba, the Philippines, the large corporations, good citizenship, forest preservation. His speeches were different in each location, and he always conveyed important philosophical ideas and explained government policies in a friendly, clear, and conversational manner. Roosevelt's speech at Leland Stanford Junior University in California reflects his position as a pioneer conservationist.

I want today, here in California, to make a special appeal to all of you, and to California as a whole, for work along a certain line—the line of preserving your great natural advantages alike from the standpoint of use and from the standpoint of beauty. If the students of this institution have not by the mere fact of their surroundings learned to appreciate beauty, then the fault is in you and not in the surroundings. Here in California you have some of the great wonders of the world. You have a singularly beautiful landscape, singularly beautiful and singularly majestic scenery, and it should certainly be your aim to try to preserve for those who are to come after you that beauty, to try to keep unmarred that majesty.

Closely entwined with keeping unmarred the beauty of your scenery, your great natural attractions, is the question of making use of, not for the moment merely, but for future time, of your great natural products. Yesterday I saw for the first time a grove of your great trees, a grove which it has taken the ages several thousands of years to build up; and I feel most emphatically that we should not turn into shingles a tree which was old when the first Egyptian conqueror penetrated to the valley of the Euphrates, which it has taken so many thousands of years to build up, and which can be put to better use.

That, you may say, is not looking at the matter from the practical standpoint. There is nothing more practical in the end than the preservation of beauty, than the preservation of anything that appeals to the higher emotions in mankind. But, furthermore, I appeal to you from the standpoint of use. A few big trees, of unusual size and beauty, should be preserved for their own sake; but the forests as a whole should be used for business purposes, only they should be used in a way that will preserve them as permanent sources of national wealth. In many parts of California the whole future welfare of the state depends upon the way in which you are able to use your water supply; and the preservation of the forests and the preservation of the use of the water are inseparably connected.

I believe we are past the stage of national existence when we could look on complacently at the individual who skinned the land and was content, for the sake of three years' profit for himself, to leave a desert for the children of those who were to inherit the soil. I think we have passed that stage. We should handle, and I think we now do handle, all problems such as those of forestry and of the preservation and use of our waters from the standpoint of the permanent interests of the home maker in any region—the man who comes in not to take what he can out of the soil and leave, having exploited the country, but who comes to dwell therein, to bring up his children, and to leave them a heritage in the country not merely unimpaired, but if possible even improved. That is the sensible view of civic obligation, and the policy of the state and of the nation should be shaped in that direction. It should be shaped in the interest of the home maker, the actual resident, the man who is not only to be benefited himself, but whose children and children's children are to be benefited by what he has done.

California has for years, I am happy to say, taken a more sensible, a more intelligent interest in forest preservation than any other state. It early appointed a forest commission; later on some of the functions of that commission were replaced by the Sierra Club, a club which has done much on the Pacific coast to perpetuate the spirit of the explorer and the pioneer. Then I am happy to say a great business interest showed an intelligent and farsighted spirit which is of happy augury, for the Redwood Manufacturers of San Francisco were first among lumbermen's associations to give assistance to the cause of practical forestry. The study of the redwood which the action of this association made possible was the pioneer study in the cooperative work which is now being carried out between lumbermen all over the United States and the Federal Bureau of Forestry.

All of this kind of work is peculiarly the kind of work in which we have a right to expect not merely hearty cooperation from, but leadership in college men trained in the universities of this Pacific coast state; for the forests of this state stand alone in the world. There are none others like them anywhere. There are no other trees anywhere like the giant sequoias; nowhere else is there a more beautiful forest than that which clothes the western slope of the Sierra. Very early your forests attracted lumbermen from other states, and by the course of timber land investments some of the best of the big tree groves were threatened with destruction. Destruction came upon some of them, but the women of California rose to the emergency through the California Club, and later the Sempervirens Club took vigorous action. But the Calaveras grove is not yet safe, and there should be no rest until that safety is secured, by the action of private individuals, by the action of the state, by the action of the nation. The interest of California in forest protection was shown even more effectively by the purchase of the Big Basin Redwood Park, a superb forest property the possession of which should be a source of just pride to all citizens jealous of California's good name.

I appeal to you, as I say, to protect these mighty trees, these wonderful monuments of beauty. I appeal to you to protect them for the sake of their beauty, but I also make the appeal just as strongly on economic grounds; as I am well aware that in dealing with such questions a farsighted economic policy must be that to which alone in the long run one can safely appeal. The interests of California in forests depend directly of course upon the handling of her wood and water supplies and the supply of material from the lumber woods and the production of agricultural products on irrigated farms. The great valleys which stretch through the state between the Sierra Nevada and coast ranges must owe their future development as they owe their present prosperity to irrigation. Whatever tends to destroy the water supply of the Sacramento, the San Gabriel, and the other valleys strikes vitally at the welfare of California. The welfare of California depends in no small measure upon the preservation of water for the purposes of irrigation in those beautiful and fertile valleys which cannot grow crops by rainfall alone. The forest cover upon the drainage basins of streams used for irrigation purposes is of prime importance to the interests of the entire state.

Now keep in mind that the whole object of forest protection is, as I have said again and again, the making and maintaining of prosperous homes. I am not advocating forest protection from the aesthetic standpoint only. I do advocate the keeping of big trees, the great monarchs of the woods, for the sake of their beauty, but I advocate the preservation and wise use of the forests because I feel it essential to the interests of the actual settlers. I am asking that the forests be used wisely for the sake of the successors of the pioneers, for the sake of the settlers who dwell on the land and by doing so extend the borders of our civilization. I ask it for the sake of the man who makes his farm in the woods or lower down along the sides of the streams which have their rise in the mountains. . . .

Citizenship is the prime test in the welfare of the nation; but we need good laws; and above all we need good land laws throughout the West. We want to see the free farmer own his home. The best of the public lands are already in private hands, and yet the rate of their disposal is steadily increasing. More than six million acres were patented during the first three months of the present year. It is time for us to see that our remaining public lands are saved for the home maker to the utmost limit of his possible use. I say this to you of this university because we have a right to expect that the best-trained, the best-educated men on the Pacific Slope, the Rocky Mountains and Great Plains states will take the lead in the preservation and right use of the forests, in securing the right use of the waters, and in seeing to it that our land policy is not twisted from its original purpose, but is perpetuated by amendment, by change when such change is necessary in the line of that purpose, the purpose being to turn the public domain into farms each to be the property of the man who actually tills it and makes his home on it.

Robert E. Peary

—— ★ ——

Arctic Exploration

Lotos Club, New York, New York;
February 2, 1907

---

*Explorer Robert E. Peary (1856–1920) led expeditions to Green-
land in 1891–1892 and 1893–1895. There, in addition to discovering the Melville meteorite, he determined the exact location of
the polar ice cap. In attempts to reach the North Pole, he arrived
at latitudes 87°17′ N in 1902 and 86°6′ N in 1906. Peary gave his
Lotos Club speech in 1907; the following year he set out on a
third expedition, and in 1909 he announced that he had finally
discovered the North Pole on April 6.*

Many of you are aware of the fact that during the last
eighteen months a new degree has been added, and the
Stars and Stripes have been placed in the lead in the international race for the pole. But that is not the only result of the last
eighteen months of work, for new lands have been discovered
and new and valuable scientific and geographical information
and data have been obtained.

The point of view of Mr. Jesup and his associates in the
Peary Arctic Club has been that arctic work today is a simple
business proposition and should combine in intimate coordina-
tion two objects: the attainment of the pole as a matter of record
and national prestige and the securing of all possible geo-
graphic, hydrographic, and other scientific information from the
unknown regions about the pole. And since the government has
not considered it advisable to undertake the work, the club
gladly assumed it and shares the resulting honor, whatever there
may be, and the scientific material, with the country and its
museums.

The steamer *Roosevelt,* built especially for arctic work,

sailed, in July 1905, on her northern voyage. This ship was built from American timber from Maine, New Hampshire, and other states, built in an American shipyard and fitted with American machinery. The ship, one hundred and eight feet long and thirty-eight feet beam, was fundamentally better fitted for the work than any ship that had ever gone north and was in reality a steamer with auxiliary sail-power.

We followed the ordinary itinerary to Sydney, Cape Breton, and then we beat our way up the west coast to Grantland, where we took on board the Esquimaux. There is a little tribe of Esquimaux who are the most northern people in the world, and they form one of the most important adjuncts in arctic work. I knew their capabilities, and so I was able to select the pick and flower of the entire tribe. These men, with their wives, their children, and their dogs and sledges—in fact, all their belongings—we took on board the ship, to act as drivers and carriers.

Off Cape Sabine we had eighteen days of incessant battle, a battle of a kind many of you cannot understand, using the ship as a huge battering-ram and driving it at the ice. Nobody at this dinner can imagine what that work was. After eighteen days we managed to reach Cape Sabine at last, five hundred statute miles from the pole itself.

Here I followed the routine of every arctic explorer, a routine which is compelled by the sequence of the arctic seasons. A ship goes north one summer in August or September and goes into winter quarters before the months of darkness set in, when nothing can be done; and perhaps I can bring that home clearly to you when I say that the sun set for us on the twelfth of October and rose again on the sixth of March. How many of you can really bring that home to yourselves? What would it be right here in New York if the sun were to set in October and not rise again until March? That winter night is really the only real source of trouble in arctic work. Ninety-nine out of a hundred people have the impression that the cold is the great trouble; but when you are up there, and dressed for it in fur clothing, and properly fed, the cold at seventy-seven degrees below zero is not nearly as disagreeable as is the damp, raw cold that we have in New York every winter.

And the last five hundred miles of that journey of only three thousand miles from New York to the pole must be accomplished with dogs and sledges; that is inevitable. The winter quarters of the *Roosevelt* were farther north than the winter quarters of any other arctic ship except one, the *Fram*.

We went west along the coast, parallel with it for some sixty miles; we made some eighty miles when we came to a break or lead in the ice which was impassable. . . . Then from the northern side of the lead we made three good marches north and were stopped by a blizzard which set the ice in motion. Here we built a hut for shelter, and one night we had to get out in the storm and build another. . . .

We put our best efforts to setting a pace, and the first march of thirty miles was made in ten hours; for the most part, I set the pace in the lead. On the second march we overtook one of the parties I had sent in advance, waiting beside a lead. They immediately hitched up and joined us, and we kept on with our small party of seven men and six teams until the twenty-first of April, when we halted in the middle of the day to take observations, which showed that we had reached latitude 87°6′ N, which at present is the nearest approach to the North Pole. . . . It is true that we had attained a record—we couldn't have come back without it—but the feeling that that record fell so far short of the splendid thing on which I had set my heart for years, and for which I had been almost literally straining my life out, was one of most intense disappointment. But you can possibly imagine where my heart was when I looked at the skeleton figures of the few remaining dogs and remembered the drifting ice and the big lead. I felt that I had cut the margin just as close as it could possibly be done, and from that point we turned back.

Before we turned, however, my flags were hoisted on the highest pinnacle near us, and a little beyond this I erected a cairn and in it I left a bottle containing a brief record and a piece of the silk flag—the flag that hangs over there, gentlemen, and which is the same one I have carried for six years. Had our provisions lasted, and had we been able to keep up a pace of twenty miles a day, in ten to twelve days we should have been at our goal. . . .

I need not speak of the voyage home but may add a few remarks as to arctic work, on points not generally understood. The incentive of the earliest northern voyages was commercial, the desire of the northern European nations to find a navigable northern route to the fabled wealth of the East. When the impracticability of such a route was proven, the adventurous spirit of Anglo-Saxon and Teuton found in the mystery, the danger, the excitement, which crystalized under the name North Pole, a worthy antagonist for their fearless blood. The result of their efforts has been to add millions to the world's wealth, to demonstrate some of the most important scientific propositions, and to develop some of the most splendid examples of manly courage and heroism that adorn the human record.

Let me call your attention to that flag, that tattered and torn and patched flag you see hanging over the mantel there. That is the flag from which I have taken pieces for deposit in the cairns I built. You will notice that three pieces are gone. One is in the cairn at the "farthest north," 87.6 degrees; a second piece I placed in a cairn I built on one of the twin peaks of Columbia, Cape Columbia; and the third in the cairn on the northern point of Jesup Land. . . .

In view of the fact that the work has defined the most northern land in the world, and has fixed the northern limit of the world's largest island, was that work a useless expenditure of time, effort, and money? Neither the club nor I think so. The money was theirs, the time and effort mine.

But the scientific results are the immediate practical ones, and British and foreign commentators do not obscure or overlook them; and these results, together with the expedition's nonloss of a man, entire freedom from scurvy or sickness in any form, and return of the ship, have had their very friendly comments. . . .

The discovery not only of the North, but of the South Pole as well, is not only our privilege, but our duty and destiny, as much as the building of the Panama Canal, and the control of the Pacific. The canal and the control of the Pacific mean wealth, commercial supremacy, and unassailable power; but the discovery of the poles spells just as strongly as the others, national *prestige,* with the moral strength that comes from the feeling that not even century-defying problems can withstand us.

WOODROW WILSON

——— ★ ———

War Message

U.S. HOUSE OF REPRESENTATIVES,
WASHINGTON, D.C.; APRIL 2, 1917

*On March 5, 1917, President Woodrow Wilson delivered his
second inaugural address as the nations of the world engaged in
war. "The tragical events of the thirty months of vital turmoil
through which we have just passed have made us citizens of the
world. There can be no turning back. . . . All nations are equally
interested in the peace of the world and in the political stability
of free peoples, and equally responsible for their maintenance . . . ," said Wilson (1856–1924). Less than a month later, the
president, citing Germany's policy of unlimited submarine warfare against its enemies as well as neutral countries, including the
United States, asked Congress for a declaration of war against
the Imperial German government. The United States entered the
First World War on April 6, 1917.*

I have called the Congress into extraordinary session because
there are serious, very serious, choices of policy to be made,
and made immediately, which it was neither right nor constitu-
tionally permissible that I should assume the responsibility of
making.

On the third of February last, I officially laid before you the
extraordinary announcement of the Imperial German government that on and after the first day of February it was its
purpose to put aside all restraints of law or of humanity and use
its submarines to sink every vessel that sought to approach
either the ports of Great Britain and Ireland, or the western
coasts of Europe, or any of the ports controlled by the enemies
of Germany within the Mediterranean.

That had seemed to be the object of the German submarine

warfare earlier in the war; but since April of last year the Imperial government had somewhat restrained the commanders of its undersea craft in conformity with its promise then given to us that passenger boats should not be sunk and that due warning would be given to all other vessels which its submarines might seek to destroy, when no resistance was offered or escape attempted, and care taken that their crews were given at least a fair chance to save their lives in their open boats. The precautions taken were meager and haphazard enough, as was proved in distressing instance after instance in the progress of the cruel and unmanly business, but a certain degree of restraint was observed.

The new policy has swept every restriction aside. Vessels of every kind, whatever their flag, their character, their cargo, their destination, their errand, have been ruthlessly sent to the bottom without warning and without thought of help or mercy for those on board—the vessels of friendly neutrals along with those of belligerents. Even hospital ships and ships carrying relief to the sorely bereaved and stricken people of Belgium, though the latter were provided with safe conduct through the proscribed areas by the German government itself and were distinguished by unmistakable marks of identity, have been sunk with the same reckless lack of compassion or of principle.

I was for a little while unable to believe that such things would in fact be done by any government that had hitherto subscribed to the humane practices of civilized nations. International law had its origin in the attempt to set up some law which would be respected and observed upon the seas, where no nation had right of dominion and where lay the free highways of the world. By painful stage after stage has that law been built up, with meager enough results, indeed, after all was accomplished that could be accomplished, but always with a clear view, at least, of what the heart and conscience of mankind demanded.

This minimum of right the German government has swept aside under the plea of retaliation and necessity and because it had no weapons which it could use at sea except those which it is impossible to employ as it is employing them without throwing to the winds all scruples of humanity or of respect for the understandings that were supposed to underlie the intercourse of the world. I am not now thinking of the loss of property involved, immense and serious as that is, but only of the wanton and wholesale destruction of the lives of noncombatants, men, women, and children, engaged in pursuits which have always, even in the darkest periods of modern history, been deemed innocent and legitimate. Property can be paid for; the lives of peaceful and innocent people cannot be. The present German submarine warfare against commerce is a warfare against mankind.

It is a war against all nations. American ships have been sunk, American lives taken, in ways which it has stirred us very deeply to learn of, but the ships and people of other neutral and friendly nations have been sunk and overwhelmed in the waters in the same way. There has been no discrimination. The challenge is to all mankind. Each nation must decide for itself how it will meet it. The choice we make for ourselves must be made with a moderation of counsel and a temperateness of judgment befitting our character and our motives as a nation. We must put excited feeling away. Our motive will not be revenge or the victorious assertion of the physical might of the nation, but only the vindication of right, of human right, of which we are only a single champion. . . .

With a profound sense of the solemn and even tragical character of the step I am taking, and of the grave responsibilities which it involves, but in unhesitating obedience to what I deem my constitutional duty, I advise that the Congress declare the recent course of the Imperial German government to be in fact nothing less than war against the government and people of the United States; that it formally accept the status of belligerent which has thus been thrust upon it; and that it take immediate steps not only to put the country in a more thorough state of defense, but also to exert all its power and employ all its resources to bring the government of the German Empire to terms and end the war. . . .

We have no quarrel with the German people. We have no feeling toward them but one of sympathy and friendship. It was not upon their impulse that their government acted in entering this war. It was not with their previous knowledge or approval. It was a war determined upon as wars used to be determined upon in the old, unhappy days when peoples were nowhere consulted by their rulers and wars were provoked and waged in the interest of dynasties or little groups of ambitious men who were accustomed to use their fellow men as pawns and tools. . . .

A steadfast concert for peace can never be maintained except by a partnership of democratic nations. No autocratic government could be trusted to keep faith within it or observe its covenants. It must be a league of honor, a partnership of opinion. Intrigue would eat its vitals away; the plottings of inner circles who could plan what they would and render account to no one would be a corruption seated at its very heart. Only free peoples can hold their purpose and their honor steady to a common end and prefer the interests of mankind to any narrow interest of their own. . . .

One of the things that has served to convince us that the Prussian autocracy was not and could never be our friend is that from the very outset of the present war it has filled our unsuspecting communities and even our offices of government with spies and set criminal intrigues everywhere afoot against our national unity of counsel, our peace within and without, our industries and our commerce. . . .

We are glad, now that we see the facts with no veil of false pretense about them, to fight thus for the ultimate peace of the world and for the liberation of its peoples, the German peoples included: for the rights of nations great and small and the privilege of men everywhere to choose their way of life and of obedience. The world must be made safe for democracy. Its peace must be planted upon the tested foundations of political liberty. We have no selfish ends to serve. We desire no conquest, no dominion. We seek no indemnities for ourselves, no material compensation for the sacrifices we shall freely make. We are but one of the champions of the rights of mankind. We shall be satisfied when those rights have been made as secure as the faith and the freedom of nations can make them. . . .

It will be all the easier for us to conduct ourselves as belligerents in a high spirit of right and fairness because we act without animus, not in enmity toward a people or with the desire to bring any injury or disadvantage upon them, but only in armed opposition to an irresponsible government which has thrown aside all considerations of humanity and of right and is running amuck. We are, let me say again, the sincere friends of the German people, and shall desire nothing so much as the early reestablishment of intimate relations of mutual advantage between us—however hard it may be for them, for the time being, to believe that this is spoken from our hearts.

We have borne with their present government through all these bitter months because of that friendship—exercising a patience and forbearance which would otherwise have been impossible. We shall, happily, still have an opportunity to prove that friendship in our daily attitude and actions toward the millions of men and women of German birth and native sympathy who live amongst us and share our life, and we shall be proud to prove it toward all who are in fact loyal to their neighbors and to the government in the hour of test. They are, most of them, as true and loyal Americans as if they had never known any other fealty or allegiance. They will be prompt to stand with us in rebuking and restraining the few who may be of a different mind and purpose. If there should be disloyalty, it will be dealt with with a firm hand of stern repression; but, if it lifts its head at all, it will lift it only here and there and without countenance except from a lawless and malignant few.

It is a distressing and oppressive duty, gentlemen of the Congress, which I have performed in thus addressing you. There are, it may be, many months of fiery trial and sacrifice ahead of us. It is a fearful thing to lead this great peaceful people into war, into the most terrible and disastrous of all wars, civilization itself seeming to be in the balance. But the right is more precious than peace, and we shall fight for the things which we have always carried nearest our hearts—for democracy, for the right of those who submit to authority to have a voice in their own governments, for the rights and liberties of small nations, for a universal dominion of right by such a concert of free peoples as shall bring peace and safety to all nations and make the world itself at last free. To such a task we can dedicate our lives and our fortunes, everything that we are and everything that we have, with the pride of those who know that the day has come when America is privileged to spend her blood and her might for the principles that gave her birth and happiness and the peace which she has treasured. God helping her, she can do no other.

WOODROW WILSON

——— ★ ———

The Fourteen Points

U.S. HOUSE OF REPRESENTATIVES,
WASHINGTON, D.C.; JANUARY 8, 1918

The Great War ended on November 11, 1918, and President Wilson brought to the Paris Peace Conference an outline for peace composed of fourteen points, which he had presented in an address to Congress eleven months earlier. The speech had met with great enthusiasm on both sides of the Atlantic, and when the Treaty of Versailles was signed on June 28, 1919, Wilson's cornerstone proposal, the establishment of a League of Nations, was included. The president embarked on a cross-country speaking tour to take his case for Senate ratification of the League of Nations Covenant directly to the people. On September 26, in the midst of the tour, Wilson suffered a stroke, from which he never recovered. The Senate rejected the covenant in March 1920, and the United States never joined the League of Nations.

We entered this war because violations of right had occurred which touched us to the quick and made the life of our own people impossible unless they were corrected and the world secured once for all against their recurrence. What we demand in this war, therefore, is nothing peculiar to ourselves. It is that the world be made fit and safe to live in—and particularly that it be made safe for every peace-loving nation which, like our own, wishes to live its own life, determine its own institutions, be assured of justice and fair dealing by the other peoples of the world as against force and selfish aggression. All the peoples of the world are in effect partners in this interest, and for our own part we see very clearly that unless justice be done to others it will not be done to us. The program of the world's peace, therefore, is our program; and that program, the only possible program, as we see it, is this:

1. Open covenants of peace, openly arrived at, after which there shall be no private international understandings of any kind but diplomacy shall proceed always frankly and in the public view.

2. Absolute freedom of navigation upon the seas, outside territorial waters, alike in peace and in war, except as the seas may be closed in whole or in part by international action for the enforcement of international covenants.

3. The removal, so far as possible, of all economic barriers and the establishment of an equality of trade conditions among all the nations consenting to the peace and associating themselves for its maintenance.

4. Adequate guarantees given and taken that national armaments will be reduced to the lowest point consistent with domestic safety.

5. A free, open-minded, and absolutely impartial adjustment of all colonial claims, based upon a strict observance of the principle that in determining all such questions of sovereignty the interests of the populations concerned must have equal weight with the equitable claims of the government whose title is to be determined.

6. The evacuation of all Russian territory and such a settlement of all questions affecting Russia as will secure the best and freest cooperation of the other nations of the world in obtaining for her an unhampered and unembarrassed opportunity for the independent determination of her own political development and national policy and assure her of a sincere welcome into the society of free nations under institutions of her own choosing — and, more than a welcome, assistance also of every kind that she may need and may herself desire. . . .

7. Belgium, the whole world will agree, must be evacuated and restored, without any attempt to limit the sovereignty which she enjoys in common with all other free nations. . . .

8. All French territory should be freed and the invaded portions restored, and the wrong done to France by Prussia in 1871 in the matter of Alsace-Lorraine, which has unsettled the peace of the world for nearly fifty years, should be righted, in order that peace may once more be made secure in the interest of all.

9. A readjustment of the frontiers of Italy should be effected along clearly recognizable lines of nationality.

10. The peoples of Austria-Hungary, whose place among the nations we wish to see safeguarded and assured, should be accorded the freest opportunity of autonomous development.

11. Rumania, Serbia, and Montenegro should be evacuated; occupied territories restored; Serbia accorded free and secure access to the sea; and the relations of the several Balkan states to one another determined by friendly counsel along historically established lines of allegiance and nationality; and international guarantees of the political and economic independence and territorial integrity of the several Balkan states should be entered into.

12. The Turkish portions of the present Ottoman Empire should be assured a secure sovereignty, but the other nationalities which are now under Turkish rule should be assured an undoubted security of life and an absolutely unmolested opportunity of autonomous development, and the Dardanelles should be permanently opened as a free passage to the ships and commerce of all nations under international guarantees.

13. An independent Polish state should be erected which should include the territories inhabited by indisputably Polish populations, which should be assured a free and secure access to the sea, and whose political and economic independence and territorial integrity should be guaranteed by international covenant.

14. A general association of nations must be formed under specific covenants for the purpose of affording mutual guarantees of political independence and territorial integrity to great and small states alike. . . .

For such arrangements and covenants we are willing to fight and to continue to fight until they are achieved; but only because we wish the right to prevail and desire a just and stable peace such as can be secured only by removing the chief provocations to war, which this program does not remove. We have no jealousy of German greatness, and there is nothing in this program that impairs it. . . .

We have spoken now, surely, in terms too concrete to admit of any further doubt or question. An evident principle runs through the whole program I have outlined. It is the principle of justice to all peoples and nationalities, and their right to live on equal terms of liberty and safety with one another, whether they be strong or weak. Unless this principle be made its foundation no part of the structure of international justice can stand. The people of the United States could act upon no other principle; and to the vindication of this principle they are ready to devote their lives, their honor, and everything that they possess. The moral climax of this the culminating and final war for human liberty has come, and they are ready to put their own strength, their own highest purpose, their own integrity and devotion to the test.

SAMUEL GOMPERS

—— ★ ——

Should a Labor Party Be Formed?

CONTINENTAL HOTEL, NEW YORK, NEW YORK; DECEMBER 19, 1918

*Samuel Gompers (1850–1924) was elected the American Federa-
tion of Labor's first president in 1886. Approached by various
committees to consider forming a labor-oriented political party,
Gompers called a labor conference in New York on December 19, 1918. There he stated his position that a labor party
would dilute the power of the labor movement, which should
concentrate on convincing the existing political parties to support laws protecting "the interest and welfare of the workers."*

I have read the fourteen points which have been formulated for
the proposed labor party here. Is there one of them of an
essential character to the interests and welfare of the working
people of the United States which is not contained in the curricu-
lum, the work and the principles of the bona fide labor movement in our country?

Which movement, economic or political, in any country on
the face of the globe has brought more hope and encouragement, more real advantage, to the working people than the trade
union movement of America has brought to the wage-earning
masses of our country?

The organization of a political labor party would simply
mean the dividing of the activities and allegiance of the men and
women of labor between two bodies, such as would often come
in conflict. . . .

Who are we going to have as the leaders of this new political
labor party here? I understand that there is impatience among
our fellows. It is creditable to them that they are impatient.
There is not any man in all America, or in all the world, more

impatient than I with the progress that has been made, with the position we occupy. I want more, more, for labor. I think I have tried and am trying to do my share. My associates of the Executive Council have tried to do their share, but there is such a thing as attempting to overrun, and by overrunning to defeat the object we would gain for the wage-earners and to throw them into the hands of those who do not know the honest aspirations of labor or who would direct them for personal aggrandizement.

I have been the president of the American Federation of Labor for many, many years. I regard that position as the most exalted that I could occupy. I have no aspiration to hold this or that position. It is not that I ask you to follow me. I ask that the trade union movement be given its fullest opportunity for growth and development so that it may be the instrumentality to secure better and better and better and constantly better conditions for the workers of our country. . . .

It is not true, as some carping critics allege, that the American Federation of Labor is a nonpolitical organization. As a matter of fact, the workers of the United States and the organized labor movement act voluntarily in the exercise of their political right and power. We have changed the control of our government from the old-time interest of corporate power and judicial usurpation. We have secured from the government of the United States the labor provision of the Clayton Antitrust Law, the declaration in the law that the labor of a human being is not a commodity or article of commerce. In that law we have secured the right of our men to exercise functions for which, under the old regime, our men were brought before the bar of justice and fined or imprisoned. We have secured the eight-hour workday not only as a basic principle but as a fact. We have secured the Seamen's law giving to the seamen the freedom to leave their vessels when in safe harbor. The seamen of America are now free men and own themselves. We have secured a child labor law, and although it has been declared unconstitutional, we are again at work to secure a law for the protection of our children. Better than all, we have established the concept in law and in administration that the interest and welfare of the workers are paramount, and this not only in the laws of our republic but in the laws of our states and municipalities.

There are other laws in the interest of labor which we have secured, more than I can mention offhand, but far above all these are the improvements brought into the lives and work of the toilers by their own actions as organized workers. We have established unity of spirit; we have brought about the extension of organization among the formerly unorganized, and our organized free existence to function and to express ourselves is now practically unquestioned.

Suppose in 1912 we had had a labor party in existence; do you think for a moment that we could have gone as the American labor movement to the other political parties and said: "We want you to inaugurate in your platform this and this declaration." If one of the parties had refused and the other party consented and took its chance, would the American Federation of Labor have been permitted to exercise that independent political and economic course if the labor party had been in existence? How long would we have had to wait for the passage of a law by Congress declaring law, in practice and in principle that the labor of a human being is not a commodity or an article of commerce—the most far-reaching declaration ever made by any government in the history of the world.

I say this to you. I am sixty-eight years of age. I have been tried and seared as few men have. I have almost had my very soul burned in the trials of life. With my two associates Mr. Mitchell and Mr. Morrison I have suffered the indignity of being brought before the courts of our country and adjudged guilty and sentenced to imprisonment. Our eyes were wide open. I do not think that it is improper for me to say that I led in the thought and activity of that work, of that willingness to suffer, but it was not a very nice thing to have the endeavor made to besmirch our honor by a sentence of imprisonment—Mr. Morrison, six months, Mr. Mitchell, nine months, and I, twelve months. We fought that sentence, fought it and fought it, supported by the activity of the organized labor movement in all the states and towns of our country, until the principle for which we were contending through that action brought about the incorporation of those provisions in the Clayton Antitrust Law which confirmed and legalized the very things for which we were sentenced to imprisonment. They were legalized, not for us alone but for labor. . . .

I wanted to present these thoughts to you. I did not have in mind any particular theme or course to present to you. I know I feel and understand and apprehend the danger which is involved in the project which is now being so very actively agitated in some quarters of the labor movement of our country. I fear no danger, I am just as good a follower, perhaps a better follower, than I am a leader, and I am perfectly willing to occupy either position. I would be recreant to the great labor movement and all it portends now and for the future if I did not take you into my confidence, men and women of labor, and tell you what I have told you. I am apprehensive, justly so, justified by every event in the whole history of labor, that a great mistake may be made, a great injury inflicted upon our fellows, not for a day, not for a year, not for a decade, but perhaps for many, many years to come. I want to present that view to you so that you may understand the situation clearly.

I have spoken calmly and without ceremony or attempt to touch your feelings, but simply to touch the innermost recesses of your minds and to lay before you the responsibility which rests upon you.

CLARENCE DARROW

——— ★ ———

Mercy for Leopold and Loeb

TRIAL OF LEOPOLD AND LOEB,
CHICAGO, ILLINOIS; AUGUST 1924

*Clarence Seward Darrow (1857–1938) was the defense attorney
in many celebrated American trials involving social issues, including those of socialist Eugene V. Debs, for calling a general
strike of rail workers in 1894, and John Thomas Scopes, who was
prosecuted in 1925 by William Jennings Bryan for teaching evolution in Tennessee. Darrow's appeal to the court for mercy at
the murder trial of Nathan Leopold and Richard Loeb—two
teenagers convicted of killing fourteen-year-old Robert Franks
—reflects his lifelong opposition to capital punishment. The
defendants were sentenced to life imprisonment.*

For four long years the civilized world was engaged in killing
men. Christian against Christian, barbarian uniting with
Christians to kill Christians; anything to kill. It was taught in
every school, aye in the Sunday schools. The little children
played at war. The toddling children on the street. Do you
suppose this world has ever been the same since then? How
long, Your Honor, will it take for the world to get back the
humane emotions that were slowly growing before the war?
How long will it take the calloused hearts of men before the
scars of hatred and cruelty shall be removed?

We read of killing one hundred thousand men in a day. We
read about it and we rejoiced in it—if it was the other fellows
who were killed. We were fed on flesh and drank blood. Even
down to the prattling babe. I need not tell Your Honor this,
because you know; I need not tell you how many upright,
honorable young boys have come into this court charged with
murder, some saved and some sent to their death, boys who

fought in this war and learned to place a cheap value on human life. You know it and I know it. These boys were brought up in it. The tales of death were in their homes, their playgrounds, their schools; they were in the newspapers that they read; it was a part of the common frenzy—what was a life? It was nothing. It was the least sacred thing in existence and these boys were trained to this cruelty.

It will take fifty years to wipe it out of the human heart, if ever. I know this, that after the Civil War in 1865, crimes of this sort increased, marvelously. No one needs to tell me that crime has no cause. It has as definite a cause as any other disease, and I know that out of the hatred and bitterness of the Civil War crime increased as America had never known it before. I know that growing out of the Napoleonic wars there was an era of crime such as Europe had never seen before. I know that Europe is going through the same experience today; I know it has followed every war; and I know it has influenced these boys so that life was not the same to them as it would have been if the world had not been made red with blood. I protest against the crimes and mistakes of society being visited upon them. All of us have a share in it. I have mine. I cannot tell and I shall never know how many words of mine might have given birth to cruelty in place of love and kindness and charity.

Your Honor knows that in this very court crimes of violence have increased growing out of the war. Not necessarily by those who fought but by those that learned that blood was cheap, and human life was cheap, and if the state could take it lightly why not the boy? There are causes for this terrible crime. There are causes, as I have said, for everything that happens in the world. War is a part of it; education is a part of it; birth is a part of it; money is a part of it—all these conspired to compass the destruction of these two poor boys.

Has the court any right to consider anything but these two boys? The state says that Your Honor has a right to consider the welfare of the community, as you have. If the welfare of the community would be benefited by taking these lives, well and good. I think it would work evil that no one could measure. Has Your Honor a right to consider the families of these two defendants? I have been sorry, and I am sorry for the bereavement of Mr. and Mrs. Frank, for those broken ties that cannot be healed. All I can hope and wish is that some good may come from it all. But as compared with the families of Leopold and Loeb, the Franks are to be envied—and everyone knows it.

I do not know how much salvage there is in these two boys. I hate to say it in their presence, but what is there to look forward to? I do not know but what Your Honor would be merciful if you tied a rope around their necks and let them die; merciful to them, but not merciful to civilization, and not merciful to those who would be left behind. To spend the balance of their days in prison is mighty little to look forward to, if anything. Is it anything? They may have the hope that as the years roll around they might be released. I do not know. I do not know. I will be honest with this court as I have tried to be from the beginning. I know that these boys are not fit to be at large. . . .

The easy thing and the popular thing to do is to hang my clients. I know it. Men and women who do not think will applaud. The cruel and thoughtless will approve. It will be easy today; but in Chicago, and reaching out over the length and breadth of the land, more and more fathers and mothers, the humane, the kind, and the hopeful, who are gaining an understanding and asking questions not only about these poor boys, but about their own—these will join in no acclaim at the death of my clients. These would ask that the shedding of blood be stopped, and that the normal feelings of man resume their sway. And as the days and the months and the years go on, they will ask it more and more. But, Your Honor, what they shall ask may not count. I know the easy way. I know Your Honor stands between the future and the past. I know the future is with me, and what I stand for here; not merely for the lives of these two unfortunate lads, but for all boys and all girls; for all of the young, and as far as possible, for all of the old. I am pleading for life, understanding, charity, kindness, and the infinite mercy that considers all. I am pleading that we overcome cruelty with kindness and hatred with love. I know the future is on my side. Your Honor stands between the past and the future. You may hang these boys; you may hang them by the neck until they are dead. But in doing it you will turn your face toward the past. In doing it you are making it harder for every other boy who in ignorance and darkness must grope his way through the mazes which only childhood knows. In doing it you will make it harder for unborn children. You may save them and make it easier for every child that sometime may stand where these boys stand. You will make it easier for every human being with an aspiration and a vision and a hope and a fate. I am pleading for the future; I am pleading for a time when hatred and cruelty will not control the hearts of men. When we can learn by reason and judgment and understanding and faith that all life is worth saving, and that mercy is the highest attribute of man.

Franklin Delano Roosevelt

— ★ —

First Inaugural Address

CAPITOL, WASHINGTON, D.C.; MARCH 4, 1933

Franklin Roosevelt (1882–1945) had been the Democratic party's vice-presidential candidate in 1920 and governor of New York until his election as president in 1932. Roosevelt's first inaugural address, broadcast throughout the country, was intended to boost the morale and hopes of a nation under the weight of a terrible economic depression. The speech offered the timeless advice: "The only thing we have to fear is fear itself." Roosevelt went on to reassure the American people that the problems were solvable and that there was indeed much that the government could and would do to end the crisis.

President Hoover, Mr. Chief Justice, My Friends: This is a day of national consecration, and I am certain that my fellow Americans expect that on my induction into the presidency I will address them with a candor and a decision which the present situation of our nation impels.

This is preeminently the time to speak the truth, the whole truth, frankly and boldly. Nor need we shrink from honestly facing conditions in our country today. This great nation will endure as it has endured, will revive, and will prosper.

So first of all let me assert my firm belief that the only thing we have to fear is fear itself—nameless, unreasoning, unjustified terror which paralyzes needed efforts to convert retreat into advance.

In every dark hour of our national life a leadership of frankness and vigor has met with that understanding and support of the people themselves which is essential to victory. I am convinced that you will again give that support to leadership in these critical days.

In such a spirit on my part and on yours we face our common difficulties. They concern, thank God, only material things. Values have shrunken to fantastic levels; taxes have risen; our ability to pay has fallen; government of all kinds is faced by serious curtailment of income; the means of exchange are frozen in the currents of trade; the withered leaves of industrial enterprise lie on every side; farmers find no markets for their produce; the savings of many years in thousands of families are gone.

More important, a host of unemployed citizens face the grim problem of existence, and an equally great number toil with little return. Only a foolish optimist can deny the dark realities of the moment.

Yet our distress comes from no failure of substance. We are stricken by no plague of locusts. Compared with the perils which our forefathers conquered, because they believed and were not afraid, we have still much to be thankful for. Nature still offers her bounty and human efforts have multiplied it. Plenty is at our doorstep, but a generous use of it languishes in the very sight of the supply.

Primarily, this is because the rulers of the exchange of mankind's goods have failed through their own stubbornness and their own incompetence, have admitted their failure and abdicated. Practices of the unscrupulous money changers stand indicted in the court of public opinion, rejected by the hearts and minds of men.

True, they have tried, but their efforts have been cast in the pattern of an outworn tradition. Faced by failure of credit, they have proposed only the lending of more money.

Stripped of the lure of profit by which to induce our people to follow their false leadership, they have resorted to exhortations, pleading tearfully for restored confidence. They know only the rules of a generation of self-seekers.

They have no vision, and when there is no vision the people perish.

The money changers have fled from their high seats in the

temple of our civilization. We may now restore that temple to the ancient truths.

The measure of the restoration lies in the extent to which we apply social values more noble than mere monetary profit.

Happiness lies not in the mere possession of money; it lies in the joy of achievement, in the thrill of creative effort.

The joy and moral stimulation of work no longer must be forgotten in the mad chase of evanescent profits. These dark days will be worth all they cost us if they teach us that our true destiny is not to be ministered unto but to minister to ourselves and to our fellow men.

Recognition of the falsity of material wealth as the standard of success goes hand in hand with the abandonment of the false belief that public office and high political position are to be valued only by the standards of pride of place and personal profit; and there must be an end to a conduct in banking and in business which too often has given to a sacred trust the likeness of callous and selfish wrongdoing.

Small wonder that confidence languishes, for it thrives only on honesty, on honor, on the sacredness of obligations, on faithful protection, on unselfish performance. Without them it cannot live.

Restoration calls, however, not for changes in ethics alone. This nation asks for action, and action now.

Our greatest primary task is to put people to work. This is no unsolvable problem if we face it wisely and courageously.

It can be accomplished in part by direct recruiting by the government itself, treating the task as we would treat the emergency of a war, but at the same time, through this employment, accomplishing greatly needed projects to stimulate and reorganize the use of our natural resources.

Hand in hand with this, we must frankly recognize the overbalance of population in our industrial centers and, by engaging on a national scale in a redistribution, endeavor to provide a better use of the land for those best fitted for the land.

The task can be helped by definite efforts to raise the values of agricultural products and with this the power to purchase the output of our cities.

It can be helped by preventing realistically the tragedy of the growing loss, through foreclosure, of our small homes and our farms.

It can be helped by insistence that the federal, state, and local governments act forthwith on the demand that their cost be drastically reduced.

It can be helped by the unifying of relief activities which today are often scattered, uneconomical and unequal. It can be helped by national planning for and supervision of all forms of transportation and of communications and other utilities which have a definite public character.

There are many ways in which it can be helped, but it can never be helped merely by talking about it. We must act, and act quickly.

Finally, in our progress toward a resumption of work we require two safeguards against a return of the evils of the old order; there must be a strict supervision of all banking and credits and investments; there must be an end to speculation with other people's money, and there must be provision for an adequate but sound currency.

These are the lines of attack. I shall presently urge upon a new Congress in special session detailed measures for their fulfillment, and I shall seek the immediate assistance of the several states.

Through this program of action we address ourselves to putting our own national house in order and making income balance outgo.

Our international trade relations, though vastly important, are, in point of time and necessity, secondary to the establishment of a sound national economy.

I favor as a practical policy the putting of first things first. I shall spare no effort to restore world trade by international economic readjustment, but the emergency at home cannot wait on that accomplishment.

The basic thought that guides these specific means of national recovery is not narrowly nationalistic.

It is the insistence, as a first consideration, upon the interdependence of the various elements in, and parts of, the United States—a recognition of the old and permanently important manifestation of the American spirit of the pioneer.

It is the way to recovery. It is the immediate way. It is the strongest assurance that the recovery will endure.

In the field of world policy I would dedicate this nation to the policy of the good neighbor—the neighbor who resolutely respects himself and, because he does so, respects the rights of others—the neighbor who respects his obligations and respects the sanctity of his agreements in and with a world of neighbors.

If I read the temper of our people correctly, we now realize as we have never before, our interdependence on each other; that we cannot merely take, but we must give as well; that if we are to go forward we must move as a trained and loyal army willing to sacrifice for the good of a common discipline, because, without such discipline, no progress is made, no leadership becomes effective.

We are, I know, ready and willing to submit our lives and property to such discipline because it makes possible a leadership which aims at a larger good.

This I propose to offer, pledging that the larger purposes will bind upon us all as a sacred obligation with a unity of duty hitherto evoked only in time of armed strife.

With this pledge taken, I assume unhesitatingly the leadership of this great army of our people, dedicated to a disciplined attack upon our common problems.

Action in this image and to this end is feasible under the form of government which we have inherited from our ancestors.

Our Constitution is so simple and practical that it is possible always to meet extraordinary needs by changes in emphasis and arrangement without loss of essential form.

That is why our constitutional system has proved itself the

most superbly enduring political mechanism the modern world has produced. It has met every stress of vast expansion of territory, of foreign wars, of bitter internal strife, of world relations.

It is to be hoped that the normal balance of executive and legislative authority may be wholly adequate to meet the unprecedented task before us. But it may be that an unprecedented demand and need for undelayed action may call for temporary departure from that normal balance of public procedure.

I am prepared under my constitutional duty to recommend the measures that a stricken nation in the midst of a stricken world may require.

These measures, or such other measures as the Congress may build out of its experience and wisdom, I shall seek, within my constitutional authority, to bring to speedy adoption.

But in the event that the Congress shall fail to take one of these two courses, and in the event that the national emergency is still critical, I shall not evade the clear course of duty that will then confront me.

I shall ask the Congress for the one remaining instrument to meet the crisis—broad executive power to wage a war against the emergency as great as the power that would be given me if we were in fact invaded by a foreign foe.

For the trust reposed in me I will return the courage and the devotion that befit the time. I can do no less.

We face the arduous days that lie before us in the warm courage of national unity; with the clear consciousness of seeking old and precious moral values; with the clean satisfaction that comes from the stern performance of duty by old and young alike.

We aim at the assurance of a rounded and permanent national life.

We do not distrust the future of essential democracy. The people of the United States have not failed. In their need they have registered a mandate that they want direct, vigorous action.

They have asked for discipline and direction under leadership. They have made me the present instrument of their wishes. In the spirit of the gift I take it.

In this dedication of a nation we humbly ask the blessing of God. May He protect each and every one of us! May He guide me in the days to come!

FRANKLIN DELANO ROOSEVELT

——— ★ ———

The Four Freedoms

U.S. HOUSE OF REPRESENTATIVES, WASHINGTON, D.C.; JANUARY 6, 1941

By 1941 the president's New Deal policies had helped America regain its balance and Roosevelt had been elected to an unprecedented third term. World War II had already commenced, and the United States clearly supported the Allied cause. In his January 6, 1941, state-of-the-union address before Congress, Roosevelt warned that the "democratic way of life is at this moment being directly assailed in every part of the world. . . . The future and the safety of our country and of our democracy are overwhelmingly involved in events far beyond our borders." Essentially, the message was that the country should prepare for war—to ensure a secure world "founded upon four essential freedoms: . . . freedom of speech and expression . . . freedom of every person to worship God in his own way . . . freedom from want . . . freedom from fear."

Every realist knows that the democratic way of life is at this moment being directly assailed in every part of the world —assailed either by arms, or by secret spreading of poisonous propaganda by those who seek to destroy unity and promote discord in nations that are still at peace.

During sixteen long months this assault has blotted out the whole pattern of democratic life in an appalling number of independent nations, great and small. The assailants are still on the march, threatening other nations, great and small.

Therefore, as your president, performing my constitutional duty to "give to the Congress information of the state of the Union," I find it, unhappily, necessary to report that the future and the safety of our country and of our democracy are overwhelmingly involved in events far beyond our borders.

Armed defense of democratic existence is now being gallantly waged in four continents. If that defense fails, all the population and all the resources of Europe, Asia, Africa, and Australasia will be dominated by the conquerors. Let us remember that the total of those populations and their resources in those four continents greatly exceeds the sum total of the population and the resources of the whole of the Western Hemisphere—many times over.

In times like these it is immature—and incidentally, untrue—for anybody to brag that an unprepared America, single-handed, and with one hand tied behind its back, can hold off the whole world.

No realistic American can expect from a dictator's peace international generosity, or return of true independence, or world disarmament, or freedom of expression, or freedom of religion—or even good business.

Such a peace would bring no security for us or for our neighbors. . . .

Just as our national policy in internal affairs has been based upon a decent respect for the rights and the dignity of all our fellow men within our gates, so our national policy in foreign affairs has been based on a decent respect for the rights and dignity of all nations, large and small. And the justice of morality must and will win in the end.

Our national policy is this:

First, by an impressive expression of the public will and

without regard to partisanship, we are committed to all-inclusive national defense.

Second, by an impressive expression of the public will and without regard to partisanship, we are committed to full support of all those resolute peoples, everywhere, who are resisting aggression and are thereby keeping war away from our hemisphere. By this support, we express our determination that the democratic cause shall prevail, and we strengthen the defense and the security of our own nation.

Third, by an impressive expression of the public will and without regard to partisanship, we are committed to the proposition that principles of morality and considerations for our own security will never permit us to acquiesce in a peace dictated by aggressors and sponsored by appeasers. We know that enduring peace cannot be bought at the cost of other people's freedom.

In the recent national election there was no substantial difference between the two great parties in respect to that national policy. No issue was fought out on this line before the American electorate. Today it is abundantly evident that American citizens everywhere are demanding and supporting speedy and complete action in recognition of obvious danger.

Therefore, the immediate need is a swift and driving increase in our armament production. . . .

To change a whole nation from a basis of peacetime production of implements of peace to a basis of wartime production of implements of war is no small task. And the greatest difficulty comes at the beginning of the program when new tools, new plant facilities, new assembly lines, and new shipways must first be constructed before the actual matériel begins to flow steadily and speedily from them. . . .

New circumstances are constantly begetting new needs for our safety. I shall ask this Congress for greatly increased new appropriations and authorizations to carry on what we have begun.

I also ask this Congress for authority and for funds sufficient to manufacture additional munitions and war supplies of many kinds, to be turned over to those nations which are now in actual war with aggressor nations.

Our most useful and immediate role is to act as an arsenal for them as well as for ourselves. They do not need manpower, but they do need billions of dollars worth of the weapons of defense. . . .

Let us say to the democracies: "We Americans are vitally concerned in your defense of freedom. We are putting forth our energies, our resources, and our organizing powers to give you the strength to regain and maintain a free world. We shall send you, in ever increasing numbers, ships, planes, tanks, guns. This is our purpose and our pledge." . . .

As men do not live by bread alone, they do not fight by armaments alone. Those who man our defenses, and those behind them who build our defenses, must have the stamina and the courage which come from unshakable belief in the manner of life which they are defending. The mighty action that we are calling for cannot be based on a disregard of all things worth fighting for. . . .

Certainly this is no time for any of us to stop thinking about the social and economic problems which are the root cause of the social revolution which is today a supreme factor in the world.

For there is nothing mysterious about the foundations of a healthy and strong democracy. The basic things expected by our people of their political and economic systems are simple. They are:

Equality of opportunity for youth and for others.

Jobs for those who can work.

Security for those who need it.

The ending of special privilege for the few.

The preservation of civil liberties for all.

The enjoyment of the fruits of scientific progress in a wider and constantly rising standard of living.

These are the simple, basic things that must never be lost sight of in the turmoil and unbelievable complexity of our modern world. The inner and abiding strength of our economic and political systems is dependent upon the degree to which they fulfill these expectations. . . .

In the future days, which we seek to make secure, we look forward to a world founded upon four essential human freedoms.

The first is freedom of speech and expression—everywhere in the world.

The second is freedom of every person to worship God in his own way—everywhere in the world.

The third is freedom from want—which, translated into world terms, means economic understandings which will secure to every nation a healthy peacetime life for its inhabitants —everywhere in the world.

The fourth is freedom from fear—which, translated into world terms, means a worldwide reduction of armaments to such a point and in such a thorough fashion that no nation will be in a position to commit an act of physical aggression against any neighbor—anywhere in the world.

That is no vision of a distant millennium. It is a definite basis for a kind of world attainable in our own time and generation. That kind of world is the very antithesis of the so-called new order of tyranny which the dictators seek to create with the crash of a bomb.

To that new order we oppose the greater conception—the moral order. A good society is able to face schemes of world domination and foreign revolutions alike without fear.

Since the beginnings of our American history, we have been engaged in change—in a perpetual peaceful revolution—a revolution which goes on steadily, quietly adjusting itself to changing conditions—without the concentration camp or the quicklime in the ditch. The world order which we seek is the cooperation of free countries, working together in a friendly, civilized society.

This nation has placed its destiny in the hands and heads and hearts of its millions of free men and women; and its faith in freedom under the guidance of God. Freedom means the supremacy of human rights everywhere. Our support goes to those who struggle to gain those rights or keep them. Our strength is our unity of purpose.

To that high concept there can be no end save victory.

FRANKLIN DELANO ROOSEVELT

——— ★ ———

Pearl Harbor Address

U.S. HOUSE OF REPRESENTATIVES,
WASHINGTON, D.C.; DECEMBER 8, 1941

On Sunday morning, December 7, 1941, the Japanese military conducted a surprise attack on the U.S. naval base at Pearl Harbor, Hawaii, resulting in the loss of more than two thousand American lives and the destruction of ships and airplanes. The next day, Roosevelt addressed Congress and the nation in a broadcast heard worldwide. He branded December 7 "a date which will live in infamy" and exposed the treachery of Japan in launching surprise raids all over the Pacific at the same time. The speech was a call for a declaration of war against Japan—and therefore against its Axis allies in Europe. By the afternoon of the eighth, Congress had passed the resolution for war.

To the Congress of the United States: Yesterday, December 7, 1941—a date which will live in infamy—the United States of America was suddenly and deliberately attacked by naval and air forces of the Empire of Japan.

The United States was at peace with that nation and, at the solicitation of Japan, was still in conversation with its government and its emperor looking toward the maintenance of peace in the Pacific. Indeed, one hour after Japanese air squadrons had commenced bombing in Oahu, the Japanese ambassador to the United States and his colleague delivered to the secretary of state a formal reply to a recent American message. While this reply stated that it seemed useless to continue the existing diplomatic negotiations, it contained no threat or hint of war or armed attack.

It will be recorded that the distance of Hawaii from Japan makes it obvious that the attack was deliberately planned many days or even weeks ago. During the intervening time the Japanese government had deliberately sought to deceive the United States by false statements and expressions of hope for continued peace.

The attack yesterday on the Hawaiian Islands has caused severe damage to American naval and military forces. Very many American lives have been lost. In addition American ships have been reported torpedoed on the high seas between San Francisco and Honolulu.

Yesterday the Japanese government also launched an attack against Malaya.

Last night Japanese forces attacked Hong Kong.

Last night Japanese forces attacked Guam.

Last night Japanese forces attacked the Philippine Islands.

Last night the Japanese attacked Wake Island.

This morning the Japanese attacked Midway Island.

Japan has, therefore, undertaken a surprise offensive extending throughout the Pacific area. The facts of yesterday speak for themselves. The people of the United States have already formed their opinions and well understand the implications to the very life and safety of our nation.

As commander in chief of the army and navy I have directed that all measures be taken for our defense.

Always will we remember the character of the onslaught against us.

No matter how long it may take us to overcome this premeditated invasion, the American people in their righteous might will win through to absolute victory.

I believe I interpret the will of the Congress and of the people when I assert that we will not only defend ourselves to the uttermost but will make very certain that this form of treachery shall never endanger us again.

Hostilities exist. There is no blinking at the fact that our people, our territory, and our interests are in grave danger.

With confidence in our armed forces—with the unbounded determination of our people—we will gain the inevitable triumph—so help us God.

I ask that the Congress declare that since the unprovoked and dastardly attack by Japan on Sunday, December 7, a state of war has existed between the United States and the Japanese Empire.

HARRY S. TRUMAN

——— ★ ———

Announcement of the
Dropping of the Atomic Bomb

BROADCAST ADDRESS TO THE NATION
(FROM THE SS *AUGUSTA*); AUGUST 6, 1945

---

*Harry S. Truman (1884–1972), a U.S. senator from Missouri,
was a supporter of the New Deal, and he served as vice president
beginning with Roosevelt's fourth term in 1945. Truman became
president when Roosevelt died suddenly on April 12, 1945. Less
than a month later, when World War II in Europe ended with the
surrender of Germany, it was Truman who attended to the details of peace with Soviet and British leaders at the Potsdam
Conference in Germany. To hasten an end to the war in the
Pacific, Truman authorized the dropping of atomic bombs on the
Japanese cities of Hiroshima and Nagasaki on August 6 and 9,
1945. Japan surrendered on August 14. In his radio announcement to the American people from aboard a ship leaving Potsdam, Truman revealed the existence of the powerful weapon that
had been in secret development for five years: the atomic bomb,
which on that day was used for the first time.*

Sixteen hours ago an American airplane dropped one bomb
on Hiroshima, an important Japanese army base. That
bomb had more power than twenty thousand tons of TNT. It
had more than two thousand times the blast power of the British
Grand Slam, which is the largest bomb ever yet used in the
history of warfare.

The Japanese began the war from the air at Pearl Harbor.
They have been repaid manyfold. And the end is not yet.
With this bomb we have now added a new and revolutionary increase in destruction to supplement the growing power of our
armed forces. In their present form these bombs are now in

production, and even more powerful forms are in development.

It is an atomic bomb. It is a harnessing of the basic power of the universe. The force from which the sun draws its power has been loosed against those who brought war to the Far East.

Before 1939, it was the accepted belief of scientists that it was theoretically possible to release atomic energy. But no one knew any practical method of doing it. By 1942, however, we knew that the Germans were working feverishly to find a way to add atomic energy to the other engines of war with which they hoped to enslave the world. But they failed. We may be grateful to Providence that the Germans got the V-Is and V-2s late and in limited quantities and even more grateful that they did not get the atomic bomb at all.

The battle of the laboratories held fateful risks for us as well as the battles of the air, land, and sea, and we have now won the battle of the laboratories as we have won the other battles.

Beginning in 1940, before Pearl Harbor, scientific knowledge useful in war was pooled between the United States and Great Britain, and many priceless helps to our victories have come from that arrangement. Under that general policy the research on the atomic bomb was begun. With American and British scientists working together we entered the race of discovery against the Germans.

The United States had available the large number of scientists of distinction in the many needed areas of knowledge. It had the tremendous industrial and financial resources necessary for the project, and they could be devoted to it without undue impairment of other vital war work. In the United States the laboratory work and the production plants, on which a substantial start had already been made, would be out of reach of enemy bombing, while at that time Britain was exposed to constant air attack and was still threatened with the possibility of invasion. For these reasons Prime Minister Churchill and President Roosevelt agreed that it was wise to carry on the project here.

We now have two great plants and many lesser works devoted to the production of atomic power. Employment during peak construction numbered 125,000 and over 65,000 individuals are even now engaged in operating the plants. Many have worked there for two and a half years. Few know what they have been producing. They see great quantities of material going in and they see nothing coming out of these plants, for the physical size of the explosive charge is exceedingly small. We have spent $2 million on the greatest scientific gamble in history—and won.

But the greatest marvel is not the size of the enterprise, its secrecy, nor its cost, but the achievement of scientific brains in putting together infinitely complex pieces of knowledge held by many men in different fields of science into a workable plan. And hardly less marvelous has been the capacity of industry to design, and of labor to operate, the machines and methods to do things never done before so that the brainchild of many minds came forth in physical shape and performed as it was supposed to do. Both science and industry worked under the direction of the United States Army, which achieved a unique success in managing so diverse a problem in the advancement of knowledge in an amazingly short time. It is doubtful if such another combination could be got together in the world. What has been done is the greatest achievement of organized science in history. It was done under high pressure and without failure.

We are now prepared to obliterate more rapidly and completely every productive enterprise the Japanese have above ground in any city. We shall destroy their docks, their factories, and their communications. Let there be no mistake; we shall completely destroy Japan's power to make war.

It was to spare the Japanese people from utter destruction that the ultimatum of July 26 was issued at Potsdam. Their leaders promptly rejected that ultimatum. If they do not now accept our terms they may expect a rain of ruin from the air, the like of which has never been seen on this earth. Behind this air attack will follow sea and land forces in such numbers and power as they have not yet seen and with the fighting skill of which they are already well aware.

The secretary of war, who has kept in personal touch with all phases of the project, will immediately make public a statement giving further details.

His statement will give facts concerning the sites at Oak Ridge near Knoxville, Tennessee, and at Richland near Pasco, Washington, and an installation near Santa Fe, New Mexico. Although the workers at the sites have been making materials to be used in producing the greatest destructive force in history, they have not themselves been in danger beyond that of many other occupations, for the utmost care has been taken of their safety.

The fact that we can release atomic energy ushers in a new era in man's understanding of nature's forces. Atomic energy may in the future supplement the power that now comes from coal, oil, and falling water, but at present it cannot be produced on a basis to compete with them commercially. Before that comes there must be a long period of intensive research.

It has never been the habit of the scientists of this country or the policy of this government to withhold from the world scientific knowledge. Normally, therefore, everything about the work with atomic energy would be made public.

But under present circumstances it is not intended to divulge the technical processes of production or all the military applications, pending further examination of possible methods of protecting us and the rest of the world from the danger of sudden destruction.

I shall recommend that the Congress of the United States consider promptly the establishment of an appropriate commission to control the production and use of atomic power within the United States. I shall give further consideration and make further recommendations to the Congress as to how atomic power can become a powerful and forceful influence toward the maintenance of world peace.

———— ★ ————

The Marshall Plan

HARVARD UNIVERSITY, CAMBRIDGE, MASSACHUSETTS; JUNE 5, 1947

George Marshall (1880–1959), who had been U.S. Army chief of staff under Roosevelt, was appointed by President Truman as special representative to China in an effort to mediate the civil war there. In January 1947 he became Truman's secretary of state. Marshall was the architect of the European Recovery Program, better known as the Marshall Plan, which provided billions of dollars in U.S. grants and loans, from 1947 to 1951, to help the war-ravaged nations of the new Organization for European Economic Cooperation to regain economic stability. Marshall served as secretary of defense in 1950–1951 and won the Nobel Peace Prize in 1953.

I need not tell you, gentlemen, that the world situation is very serious. That must be apparent to all intelligent people. I think one difficulty is that the problem is one of such enormous complexity that the very mass of facts presented to the public by press and radio make it exceedingly difficult for the man in the street to reach a clear appraisement of the situation. Furthermore, the people of this country are distant from the troubled areas of the earth, and it is hard for them to comprehend the plight and consequent reactions of the long-suffering peoples and the effect of those reactions on their governments in connection with our efforts to promote peace in the world.

In considering the requirements for the rehabilitation of Europe, the physical loss of life, the visible destruction of cities, factories, mines, and railroads was correctly estimated; but it has become obvious during recent months that this visible destruction was probably less serious than the dislocation of the entire fabric of European economy. For the past ten years conditions have been highly abnormal.

The feverish preparation for war and the more feverish maintenance of the war effort engulfed all aspects of national economies. Machinery has fallen into disrepair or is entirely obsolete. Under the arbitrary and destructive Nazi rule, virtually every possible enterprise was geared into the German war machine. Long-standing commercial ties, private institutions, banks, insurance companies, and shipping companies disappeared through loss of capital, absorption through nationalization, or by simple destruction.

In many countries confidence in the local currency has been severely shaken. The breakdown of the business structure of Europe during the war was complete. Recovery has been seriously retarded by the fact that two years after the close of hostilities a peace settlement with Germany and Austria has not been agreed upon. But even given a more prompt solution of these difficult problems, the rehabilitation of the economic structure of Europe quite evidently will require a much longer time and greater effort than had been foreseen.

There is a phase of this matter which is both interesting and serious. The farmer has always produced the foodstuffs to exchange with the city dweller for the other necessities of life. This division of labor is the basis of modern civilization. At the present time it is threatened with breakdown. The town and city industries are not producing adequate goods to exchange with the food-producing farmer. Raw material and fuel are in short supply. Machinery is lacking or worn out.

The farmer or the peasant cannot find the goods for sale which he desires to purchase. So the sale of his farm produce for money which he cannot use seems to him an unprofitable transaction. He, therefore, has withdrawn many fields from crop cultivation and is using them for grazing. He feeds more grain to stock and finds for himself and his family an ample supply of food, however short he may be on clothing and the other ordinary gadgets of civilization. Meanwhile, people in the cities are short of food and fuel. So the governments are forced to use their foreign money and credits to procure these necessities abroad. This process exhausts funds which are urgently needed for reconstruction. Thus a very serious situation is rapidly developing which bodes no good for the world. The modern system of the division of labor upon which the exchange of products is based is in danger of breaking down.

The truth of the matter is that Europe's requirements for the next three or four years of foreign food and other essential products—principally from America—are so much greater than her present ability to pay that she must have substantial additional help, or face economic, social, and political deterioration of a very grave character.

The remedy lies in breaking the vicious circle and restoring the confidence of the European people in the economic future of their own countries, and of Europe as a whole. The manufacturer and the farmer throughout wide areas must be able and willing to exchange their products for currencies, the continuing value of which is not open to question.

Aside from the demoralizing effect on the world at large and the possibilities of disturbances arising as a result of the desperation of the people concerned, the consequences to the economy of the United States should be apparent to all. It is logical that the United States should do whatever it is able to do to assist in the return of normal economic health in the world, without which there can be no political stability and no assured peace.

Our policy is directed not against any country or doctrine but against hunger, poverty, desperation, and chaos. Its purpose should be the revival of a working economy in the world so as to permit the emergence of political and social conditions in which free institutions can exist. Such assistance, I am convinced, must not be on a piecemeal basis as various crises develop. Any assistance that this government may render in the future should provide a cure rather than a mere palliative.

Any government that is willing to assist in the task of recovery will find full cooperation, I am sure, on the part of the

United States government. Any government which maneuvers to block the recovery of other countries cannot expect help from us. Furthermore, governments, political parties, or groups which seek to perpetuate human misery in order to profit therefrom politically or otherwise will encounter the opposition of the United States.

It is already evident that, before the United States government can proceed much further in its efforts to alleviate the situation and help start the European world on its way to recovery, there must be some agreement among the countries of Europe as to the requirements of the situation and the part those countries themselves will take in order to give proper effect to whatever action might be undertaken by this government. It would be neither fitting nor efficacious for this government to undertake to draw up unilaterally a program designed to place Europe on its feet economically. This is the business of the Europeans. The initiative, I think, must come from Europe. The role of this country should consist of friendly aid in the drafting of a European program, and of later support of such a program so far as it may be practical for us to do so. The program should be a joint one, agreed to by a number, if not all, European nations.

An essential part of any successful action on the part of the United States is an understanding on the part of the people of America of the character of the problem and the remedies to be applied. Political passion and prejudice should have no part. With foresight, and a willingness on the part of our people to face up to the vast responsibility which history has clearly placed upon our country, the difficulties I have outlined can and will be overcome.

ALBERT EINSTEIN

———— ★ ————

The Menace of Mass Destruction

SECOND ANNUAL DINNER OF THE FOREIGN PRESS
ASSOCIATION TO THE GENERAL ASSEMBLY
AND SECURITY COUNCIL OF THE UNITED NATIONS,
WALDORF-ASTORIA HOTEL, NEW YORK, NEW YORK;
NOVEMBER 11, 1947

*By the 1920s, Albert Einstein (1879–1955) was internationally
revered as a great intellect and scientist. His revolutionary concepts of photoelectric effect, molecule measurement, and relativity—the interdependence of space and time and the equivalence
of gravity and inertia—were verified within decades of their
publication. Although a great humanitarian and pacifist, the Ger-
man-born Einstein—who had become an American citizen and
had taught at Princeton University since 1933—encouraged the
United States to develop an atomic weapon (using his famous
equation $E = mc^2$) before the Nazis could create their own. After
the war, Einstein often spoke on science, on social and moral
concerns, and on world disarmament. His speech to the Foreign
Press Association in 1947 decried the danger of a divided world,
with the potential for mass destruction.*

Everyone is aware of the difficult and menacing situation in
which human society—shrunk into one community with a
common fate—finds itself, but only a few act accordingly. Most
people go on living their everyday life: half frightened, half
indifferent, they behold the ghostly tragicomedy that is being
performed on the international stage before the eyes and ears of
the world. But on that stage, on which the actors under the
floodlights play their ordained parts, our fate of tomorrow, life
or death of the nations, is being decided.

It would be different if the problem were not one of things

made by man himself, such as the atomic bomb and other means of mass destruction equally menacing all peoples. It would be different, for instance, if an epidemic of bubonic plague were threatening the entire world. In such a case conscientious and expert persons would be brought together and they would work out an intelligent plan to combat the plague. After having reached agreement upon the right ways and means, they would submit their plan to the governments. Those would hardly raise serious objections but rather agree speedily on the measures to be taken. They certainly would never think of trying to handle the matter in such a way that their own nation would be spared whereas the next one would be decimated.

But could not our situation be compared to one of a menacing epidemic? People are unable to view this situation in its true light, for their eyes are blinded by passion. General fear and anxiety create hatred and aggressiveness. The adaptation to warlike aims and activities has corrupted the mentality of man; as a result, intelligent, objective, and humane thinking has hardly any effect and is even suspected and persecuted as unpatriotic.

There are, no doubt, in the opposite camps enough people of sound judgment and sense of justice who would be capable and eager to work out together a solution for the factual difficulties. But the efforts of such people are hampered by the fact that it is made impossible for them to come together for informal discussions. I am thinking of persons who are accustomed to the objective approach to a problem and who will not be confused by exaggerated nationalism or other passions. This forced separation of the people of both camps I consider one of the major obstacles to the achievement of an acceptable solution of the burning problem of international security.

As long as contact between the two camps is limited to the official negotiations I can see little prospect for an intelligent agreement being reached, especially since considerations of national prestige as well as the attempt to talk out of the window for the benefit of the masses are bound to make reasonable progress almost impossible. What one party suggests officially is for that reason alone suspected and even made unacceptable to the other. Also behind all official negotiations stands—though veiled—the threat of naked power. The official method can lead to success only after spade-work of an informal nature has prepared the ground; the conviction that a mutually satisfactory solution can be reached must be gained first; then the actual negotiations can get under way with a fair promise of success.

We scientists believe that what we and our fellow men do or fail to do within the next few years will determine the fate of our civilization. And we consider it our task untiringly to explain this truth, to help people realize all that is at stake, and to work, not for appeasement, but for understanding and ultimate agreement between peoples and nations of different views.

HUBERT HUMPHREY

—— ★ ——

In Support of Civil Rights

DEMOCRATIC NATIONAL CONVENTION,
PHILADELPHIA, PENNSYLVANIA; JULY 14, 1948

Hubert Horatio Humphrey (1911–1978) came to the Democratic National Convention of 1948 as the mayor of Minneapolis, Minnesota, and a candidate for U.S. senator. Humphrey sponsored a civil rights plank in the party platform that caused Southern Democrats, the Dixiecrats, to abandon the party. In the general election, J. Strom Thurmond ran as a States' Rights Democrat and won thirty-nine electoral votes, and the Republican candidate, Thomas E. Dewey, nearly defeated the incumbent president, Harry Truman. Senator Humphrey, thereafter a leader in the prolabor and civil rights wing of his party, became Lyndon Johnson's vice president in 1965. He was defeated by Richard Nixon in the 1968 presidential election.

I realize that I am dealing with a charged issue—with an issue which has been confused by emotionalism on all sides. I realize that there are those here—friends and colleagues of mine, many of them—who feel as deeply as I do about this issue and who are yet in complete disagreement with me.

My respect and admiration for these men and their views was great when I came here.

It is now far greater because of the sincerity, the courtesy, and the forthrightness with which they have argued in our discussions.

Because of this very respect—because of my profound belief that we have a challenging task to do here, because good conscience demands it—I feel I must rise at this time to support this report, a report that spells out our democracy, a report that the people will understand and enthusiastically acclaim.

Let me say at the outset that this proposal is made with no single region, no single class, no single racial or religious group in mind.

All regions and all states have shared in the precious heritage of American freedom. All states and all regions have at least some infringements of that freedom—all people, all groups have been the victims of discrimination.

The masterly statement of our keynote speaker, the distinguished United States senator from Kentucky, Alben Barkley, made that point with great force. Speaking of the founder of our party, Thomas Jefferson, he said:

"He did not proclaim that all white, or black, or red, or yellow men are equal; that all Christian or Jewish men are equal; that all Protestant and Catholic men are equal; that all rich or poor men are equal; that all good or bad men are equal.

"What he declared was that all men are equal; and the equality which he proclaimed was equality in the right to enjoy the blessings of free government in which they may participate and to which they have given their consent."

We are here as Democrats. But more important, as Americans—and I firmly believe that as men concerned with our country's future, we must specify in our platform the guarantees which I have mentioned.

Yes, this is far more than a party matter. Every citizen has a stake in the emergence of the United States as the leader of the free world. That world is being challenged by the world of slavery. For us to play our part effectively, we must be in a morally sound position.

We cannot use a double standard for measuring our own and other people's policies. Our demands for democratic practices in other lands will be no more effective than the guarantees of those practiced in our own country.

We are God-fearing men and women. We place our faith in the brotherhood of man under the fatherhood of God.

I do not believe that there can be any compromise of the guarantees of civil rights which I have mentioned.

In spite of my desire for unanimous agreement on the platform there are some matters which I think must be stated without qualification. There can be no hedging—no watering down.

There are those who say to you, "We are rushing this issue of civil rights." I say we are 172 years late.

There are those who say this issue of civil rights is an infringement on states' rights. The time has arrived for the Democratic party to get out of the shadow of states' rights and walk forthrightly into the bright sunshine of human rights.

People, human beings: this is the issue of the twentieth century. People—all kinds and all sorts of people—look to America for leadership, for help, for guidance.

My friends—my fellow Democrats—I ask you for a calm consideration of our historic opportunity. Let us forget the evil passions, the blindness of the past. In these times of world economic, political, and spiritual—above all, spiritual—crisis, we cannot, we must not, turn from the path so plainly before us.

That path has already led us through many valleys of the shadow of death. Now is the time to recall those who were left on that path of American freedom.

For all of us here, for the millions who have sent us, for the whole two billion members of the human family—our land is now, more than ever, the last best hope on earth. I know that we can—I know that we shall—begin here the fuller and richer realization of that hope, that promise of a land where all men are free and equal, and each man uses his freedom and equality wisely and well.

——— ★ ———

On Behalf of a
Declaration of Conscience

U.S. SENATE, WASHINGTON, D.C.;
JUNE 1, 1950

Margaret Chase Smith (1897–   ) was the only woman in the
Senate when she signed and spoke in favor of a declaration by
seven Republican senators denouncing the tactics of Senator
Joseph R. McCarthy of Wisconsin, who had initiated a crusade
to weed out "subversives" in all prominent areas of American
life. "McCarthyism" destroyed many careers and reputations be-
fore its leader was officially condemned by the Senate in Decem-
ber 1954.

M r. President, I would like to speak briefly and simply
about a serious national condition. It is a national
feeling of fear and frustration that could result in national su-
icide and the end of everything that we Americans hold dear.
It is a condition that comes from the lack of effective leadership either in the legislative branch or the executive branch of
our government. That leadership is so lacking that serious
and responsible proposals are being made that national advis-
ory commissions be appointed to provide such critically
needed leadership.

I speak as briefly as possible because too much harm has
already been done with irresponsible words of bitterness and
selfish political opportunism. I speak as simply as possible because the issue is too great to be obscured by eloquence. I speak
simply and briefly in the hope that my words will be taken to
heart.

Mr. President, I speak as a Republican. I speak as a woman. I speak as a United States senator. I speak as an American.

The United States Senate has long enjoyed worldwide respect as the greatest deliberative body in the world. But recently that deliberative character has too often been debased to the level of a forum of hate and character assassination sheltered by the shield of congressional immunity.

It is ironical that we senators can in debate in the Senate, directly or indirectly, by any form of words, impute to any American who is not a senator any conduct or motive unworthy or unbecoming an American—and without that nonsenator American having any legal redress against us—yet if we say the same thing in the Senate about our colleagues we can be stopped on the grounds of being out of order.

It is strange that we can verbally attack anyone else without restraint and with full protection, and yet we hold ourselves above the same type of criticism here on the Senate floor. Surely the United States Senate is big enough to take self-criticism and self-appraisal. Surely we should be able to take the same kind of character attacks that we dish out to outsiders.

I think that it is high time for the United States Senate and its members to do some real soul searching and to weigh our consciences as to the manner in which we are performing our duty to the people of America and the manner in which we are using or abusing our individual powers and privileges.

I think it is high time that we remembered that we have sworn to uphold and defend the Constitution. I think it is high time that we remembered that the Constitution, as amended, speaks not only of the freedom of speech but also of trial by jury instead of trial by accusation.

Whether it be a criminal prosecution in court or a character prosecution in the Senate, there is little practical distinction when the life of a person has been ruined.

Those of us who shout the loudest about Americanism in making character assassinations are all too frequently those who, by our own words and acts, ignore some of the basic principles of Americanism: the right to criticize; the right to hold unpopular beliefs; the right to protest; the right of independent thought.

The exercise of these rights should not cost one single American citizen his reputation or his right to a livelihood nor should he be in danger of losing his reputation or livelihood merely because he happens to know someone who holds unpopular beliefs. Who of us does not? Otherwise none of us could call our souls our own. Otherwise thought control would have set in.

The American people are sick and tired of being afraid to speak their minds lest they be politically smeared as communists or fascists by their opponents. Freedom of speech is not what it used to be in America. It has been so abused by some that it is not exercised by others.

The American people are sick and tired of seeing innocent people smeared and guilty people whitewashed. But there have been enough proved cases . . . to cause nationwide distrust and strong suspicion that there may be something to the unproved, sensational accusations. . . .

Today our country is being psychologically divided by the confusion and the suspicions that are bred in the United States Senate to spread like cancerous tentacles of "know nothing, suspect everything" attitudes. . . .

The record of the present Democratic administration has provided us with sufficient campaign issues without the necessity of resorting to political smears. America is rapidly losing its position as leader of the world simply because the Democratic administration has pitifully failed to provide effective leadership. . . .

The Democratic administration has greatly lost the confidence of the American people by its complacency to the threat of communism here at home and the leak of vital secrets to Russia through key officials of the Democratic administration.

There are enough proved cases to make this point without diluting our criticism with unproved charges. . . .

Surely it is clear that this nation will continue to suffer so long as it is governed by the present ineffective Democratic administration. Yet to displace it with a Republican regime embracing a philosophy that lacks political integrity or intellectual honesty would prove equally disastrous to the nation. The nation sorely needs a Republican victory. But I do not want to see the Republican party ride to political victory on the Four Horsemen of Calumny—fear, ignorance, bigotry, and smear.

Harry S. Truman

——— ★ ———

The Recall of
General Douglas MacArthur

Broadcast Address to the Nation;
April 16, 1951

On June 25, 1950, North Korean forces invaded South Korea, taking the capital of Seoul three days later. On June 27 the United Nations Security Council called for military action against North Korea, and President Truman immediately ordered American forces to the defense of the South Koreans. This U.N.-sponsored "police action" was joined by other nations, including Australia, Belgium, Canada, France, Great Britain, New Zealand, and South Korea; their forces were placed under a United Nations unified command headed by General Douglas MacArthur. The gains made by this army were reversed when Communist China entered the conflict in October 1950. For nearly a year, occupied positions seesawed between the opponents. With a further escalation due to Chinese jet-aircraft strikes originating in Manchuria, the decision had to be made to limit the conflict to Korea or to widen the war into China. MacArthur publicly advocated attacking Manchuria, in opposition to the administration's limited objectives, and the president was forced to remove him from command.

I want to talk plainly to you tonight about what we are doing in Korea and about our policy in the Far East. In the simplest terms, what we are doing in Korea is this: We are trying to prevent a third world war.

I think most people in this country recognized that fact last June. And they warmly supported the decision of the government to help the Republic of Korea against the Communist aggressors. Now, many persons, even some who applauded our decision to defend Korea, have forgotten the basic reason for our action.

It is right for us to be in Korea. It was right last June. It is right today.

I want to remind you why this is true.

The Communists in the Kremlin are engaged in a monstrous conspiracy to stamp out freedom all over the world. If they were to succeed, the United States would be numbered among their principal victims. It must be clear to everyone that the United States cannot—and will not—sit idly by and await foreign conquest. The only question is: When is the best time to meet the threat and how?

The best time to meet the threat is in the beginning. It is easier to put out a fire in the beginning when it is small than after it has become a roaring blaze.

And the best way to meet the threat of aggression is for the peace-loving nations to act together. . . . This is the basic reason why we joined in creating the United Nations. And since the end of World War II we have been putting that lesson into practice—we have been working with other free nations to check the aggressive designs of the Soviet Union before they can result in a third world war.

The question we have had to face is whether the Communist plan of conquest can be stopped without general war. Our government and other countries associated with us in the United Nations believe that the best chance of stopping it without general war is to meet the attack in Korea and defeat it there.

That is what we have been doing. It is a difficult and bitter task.

But so far it has been successful.

So far, we have prevented World War III.

So far, by fighting a limited war in Korea, we have prevented aggression from succeeding and bringing on a general war. And the ability of the whole free world to resist Communist aggression has been greatly improved. . . .

But you may ask: Why can't we take other steps to punish

the aggressor? Why don't we bomb Manchuria and China itself? Why don't we assist Chinese Nationalist troops to land on the mainland of China?

If we were to do these things we would be running a very grave risk of starting a general war. If that were to happen, we would have brought about the exact situation we are trying to prevent. . . .

I have thought long and hard about this question of extending the war in Asia. I have discussed it many times with the ablest military advisers in the country. I believe with all my heart that the course we are following is the best course.

I believe that we must try to limit war to Korea for these vital reasons: to make sure that the precious lives of our fighting men are not wasted; to see that the security of our country and the free world is not needlessly jeopardized; and to prevent a third world war.

A number of events have made it evident that General MacArthur did not agree with that policy. I have therefore considered it essential to relieve General MacArthur so that there would be no doubt or confusion as to the real purpose and aim of our policy.

It was with the deepest personal regret that I found myself compelled to take this action. General MacArthur is one of our greatest military commanders. But the cause of world peace is more important than any individual.

The change in commands in the Far East means no change whatever in the policy of the United States. We will carry on the fight in Korea with vigor and determination in an effort to bring the war to a speedy and successful conclusion.

The new commander, Lieutenant General Matthew Ridgway, has already demonstrated that he has the great qualities of military leadership needed for this task.

We are ready, at any time, to negotiate for a restoration of peace in the area. But we will not engage in appeasement. We are only interested in real peace.

Real peace can be achieved through a settlement based on the following factors:

1. The fighting must stop.

2. Concrete steps must be taken to insure that the fighting will not break out again.

3. There must be an end to the aggression.

A settlement founded upon these elements would open the way for the unification of Korea and the withdrawal of all foreign forces.

In the meantime, I want to be clear about our military objective. We are fighting to resist an outrageous aggression in Korea. We are trying to keep the Korean conflict from spreading to other areas. But at the same time we must conduct our military activities so as to insure the security of our forces. This is essential if they are to continue the fight until the enemy abandons its ruthless attempt to destroy the Republic of Korea.

That is our military objective—to repel attack and to restore peace.

In the hard fighting in Korea, we are proving that collective action among nations is not only a high principle but a workable means of resisting aggression. Defeat of aggression in Korea may be the turning point in the world's search for a practical way of achieving peace and security. . . .

We do not want to widen the conflict. We will use every effort to prevent that disaster. And in so doing we know that we are following the great principles of peace, freedom, and justice.

Douglas MacArthur

———— ★ ————

American Policy in the Pacific

U.S. House of Representatives,
Washington, D.C.; April 19, 1951

Douglas MacArthur (1880–1964) was appointed chief of staff of the U.S. Army with the rank of general in 1930. After the Japanese attack on Pearl Harbor, General MacArthur was made commander in chief of U.S. armed forces in the Far East and, soon afterward, supreme commander of Allied Forces in the Southwest Pacific. MacArthur's Pacific offensive resulted in victory in the battles of Midway, the Coral Sea, and Guadalcanal and the liberation of New Guinea and the Philippines. On September 3, 1945, MacArthur accepted the Japanese surrender. When hostilities broke out in Korea, President Truman named MacArthur commander of the United Nations forces. MacArthur's insistence, in opposition to Truman's policies, on the need to attack Communist bases in Manchuria—and thus possibly risk war with China and the Soviets—caused the president to remove him from command on April 11, 1951. The Korean conflict continued to the advantage of neither side; on July 10, 1951, truce negotiations began, but an armistice agreement was not signed until July 27, 1953.

While I was not consulted prior to the president's decision to intervene in the support of the Republic of Korea, that decision from a military standpoint proved a sound one. As I say, a brief and sound one as we hurled back the invaders and decimated his forces. Our victory was complete and our objectives within reach when Red China intervened with numerically superior ground forces. This created a new war and an entirely new situation, a situation not contemplated when our forces were committed against the North Korean invaders, a situation which called for new decisions in the diplomatic sphere to permit the realistic adjustment of military strategy. Such decisions have not been forthcoming.

While no man in his right mind would advocate sending our ground forces into continental China—and such was never given a thought—the new situation did urgently demand a drastic revision of strategic planning if our political aim was to defeat this new enemy as we had defeated the old.

Apart from the military need as I saw it to neutralize sanctuary, protection given to the enemy north of the Yalu, I felt that military necessity in the conduct of the war made necessary:

First, the intensification of our economic blockade against China.

Second, the imposition of a naval blockade against the China coast.

Third, removal of restrictions on air reconnaissance of China's coastal areas and of Manchuria.

Fourth, removal of restrictions on the forces of the Republic of China on Formosa with logistical support to contribute to their effective operation against the Chinese mainland.

For entertaining these views, all professionally designed to support our forces committed to Korea and bring hostilities to an end with the least possible delay and at a saving of countless American and Allied lives, I have been severely criticized in lay circles, principally abroad, despite my understanding that from a military standpoint the above views have been fully shared in past by practically every military leader concerned with the Korean campaign, including our own Joint Chief of Staff.

I called for reinforcements, but was informed that reinforcements were not available. I made clear that if not permitted to utilize the friendly Chinese force of some six hundred thousand men on Formosa; if not permitted to blockade the China coast to prevent the Chinese Reds from getting succor from without; and if there were to be no hope of major reinforcements, the position of the command from the military standpoint forbade victory. We could hold in Korea by constant maneuver and at an approximate area where our supply line advantages were in balance with the supply line disadvantages of the enemy, but we could hope at best for only an indecisive campaign, with its terrible and constant attrition upon our forces if the enemy utilized his full military potential.

I have constantly called for the new political decisions essential to a solution. Efforts have been made to distort my position. It has been said in effect that I was a warmonger. Nothing could be further from the truth. I know war as few other men now living know it, and nothing to me is more revolting. I have long advocated its complete abolition as its very destructiveness on both friend and foe has rendered it useless as a means of settling international disputes. Indeed, on the second of September, 1945, just following the surrender of the Japanese nation on the battleship *Missouri,* I formally cautioned as follows:

"Men since the beginning of time have sought peace. Various methods through the ages have been attempted to devise an international process to prevent or settle disputes between nations. From the very start, workable methods were found insofar as individual citizens were concerned, but the mechanics of an instrumentality of larger international scope have never been successful. Military alliances, balances of power, leagues of nations, all in turn failed, leaving the only path to be by way of the crucible of war. The utter destructiveness of war now blots out this alternative. We have had our last chance. If we will not devise some greater and more equitable system, Armageddon will be at our door. The problem basically is theological and involves a spiritual recrudescence and improvement of human character that will synchronize with our almost matchless advances in science, art, literature, and all material and cultural developments of the past two thousand years. It must be of the spirit if we are to save the flesh."

But once war is forced upon us, there is no other alternative than to apply every available means to bring it to a swift end. War's very object is victory—not prolonged indecision. In war, indeed, there can be no substitute for victory.

There are some who for varying reasons would appease Red

China. They are blind to history's clear lesson. For history teaches with unmistakable emphasis that appeasement but begets new and bloodier war. It points to no single instance where the end has justified that means—where appeasement has led to more than a sham peace. Like blackmail, it lays the basis for new and successively greater demands, until, as in blackmail, violence becomes the only other alternative. Why, my soldiers asked of me, surrender military advantages to an enemy in the field? I could not answer. Some may say to avoid spread of the conflict into an all-out war with China; others, to avoid Soviet intervention. Neither explanation seems valid. For China is already engaging with the maximum power it can commit and the Soviet will not necessarily mesh its actions with our moves. Like a cobra, any new enemy will more likely strike whenever it feels that the relativity in military or other potential is in its favor on a worldwide basis.

The tragedy of Korea is further heightened by the fact that as military action is confined to its territorial limits, it condemns that nation, which it is our purpose to save, to suffer the devastating impact of full naval and air bombardment, while the enemy's sanctuaries are fully protected from such attack and devastation. Of the nations of the world, Korea alone, up to now, is the sole one which has risked its all against communism. The magnificence of the courage and fortitude of the Korean people defies description. They have chosen to risk death rather than slavery. Their last words to me were: "Don't scuttle the Pacific."

I have just left your fighting sons in Korea. They have met all tests there and I can report to you without reservation they are splendid in every way. It was my constant effort to preserve them and end this savage conflict honorably and with the least loss of time and a minimum sacrifice of life. Its growing bloodshed has caused me the deepest anguish and anxiety. Those gallant men will remain often in my thoughts and in my prayers always.

I am closing my fifty-two years of military service. When I

joined the army even before the turn of the century, it was the fulfillment of all my boyish hopes and dreams. The world has turned over many times since I took the oath on the plain at West Point, and the hopes and dreams have long since vanished. But I still remember the refrain of one of the most popular barrack ballads of that day which proclaimed most proudly that "old soldiers never die; they just fade away." And like the old soldier of that ballad, I now close my military career and just fade away—an old soldier who tried to do his duty as God gave him the light to see that duty.

Goodbye.

ADLAI STEVENSON

———— ★ ————

Presidential Nomination
Acceptance Speech

DEMOCRATIC NATIONAL CONVENTION,
CHICAGO, ILLINOIS; JULY 26, 1952

Adlai Stevenson (1900–1965) was a U.S. delegation adviser and delegate at United Nations sessions from 1945 to 1947. He was elected governor of Illinois in 1948. At the 1952 Democratic National Convention, Stevenson, who had been mentioned as a presidential candidate but had not campaigned, was drafted as the Democratic nominee for president. He was defeated by Eisenhower in November, a scenario that was repeated in the election of 1956. Stevenson returned to the United Nations as U.S. ambassador in 1960. In his 1952 acceptance speech, Stevenson, known as an intellectual, stressed basic philosophical concepts: in the struggle against war, poverty, tyranny, and the assaults on human dignity, he stated, the "walls . . . must be directly stormed by the hosts of courage, of mortality, and of vision, standing shoulder to shoulder, unafraid of ugly truth, contemptuous of lies, half-truths, circuses, and demogoguery."

M r. President, Ladies and Gentlemen of the Convention, My Fellow Citizens: I accept your nomination—and your program.

I should have·preferred to hear those words uttered by a stronger, a wiser, a better man than myself. But after listening to the president's speech I even feel better about myself.

None of you, my friends, can wholly appreciate what is in my heart. I can only hope that you understand my words. They will be few.

I have not sought the honor you have done me. I could not seek it because I aspired to another office, which was the full measure of my ambition. And one does not treat the highest office within the gift of the people of Illinois as an alternative or as a consolation prize.

I would not seek your nomination for the presidency, because the burdens of that office stagger the imagination. Its potential for good or evil now and in the years of our lives smothers exultation and converts vanity to prayer.

I have asked the Merciful Father, the Father of us all, to let this cup pass from me. But from such dread responsibility one does not shrink in fear, in self-interest, or in false humility. . . .

You have summoned me to the highest mission within the gift of any people. I could not be more proud. Better men than I were at hand for this mighty task, and I owe to you and to them every resource of mind and of strength that I possess to make your deed today a good one for our country and for our party. I am confident, too, that your selection of a candidate for vice president will strengthen me and our party immeasurably in the hard, the implacable work that lies ahead of all of us.

I know you join me in gratitude and in respect for the great Democrats and the leaders of our generation whose names you have considered here in this convention, whose vigor, whose character and devotion to the republic we love so well have won the respect of countless Americans and enriched our party. . . .

Let me say, too, that I have been heartened by the conduct of this convention. You have argued and disagreed because as Democrats you care and you care deeply. But you have disagreed and argued without calling each other liars and thieves, without despoiling our best traditions in any naked struggles for power.

And you have written a platform that neither equivocates, contradicts, nor evades.

You have restated our party's record, its principles and its purposes in language that none can mistake, and with a firm confidence in justice, freedom, and peace on earth that will raise the hearts and the hopes of mankind for that distant day when no one rattles a saber and no one drags a chain.

For all these things I am grateful to you. But I feel no exultation, no sense of triumph. Our troubles are all ahead of us.

Some will call us appeasers; others will say that we are the war party.

Some will say we are reactionary; others will say that we stand for socialism.

There will be the inevitable cries of "throw the rascals out"; "it's time for a change"; and so on and so on.

We'll hear all those things and many more besides. But we will hear nothing that we have not heard before. I am not too much concerned with partisan denunciation, with epithets and abuse, because the working man, the farmer, the thoughtful businessman, all know that they are better off than ever before and they all know that the greatest danger to free enterprise in this country died with the great depression under the hammer blows of the Democratic party. . . .

You will hear many sincere and thoughtful people express concern about the continuation of one party in power for twenty years. I don't belittle this attitude. But change for the sake of change has no absolute merit in itself.

If our greatest hazard is preservation of the values of Western civilization, in our self-interest alone, if you please, is it the part of wisdom to change for the sake of change to a party with a split personality; to a leader, whom we all respect, but who has been called upon to minister to a hopeless case of political schizophrenia? . . .

I hope and pray that we Democrats, win or lose, can campaign not as a crusade to exterminate the opposing party, as our opponents seem to prefer, but as a great opportunity to educate and elevate a people whose destiny is leadership, not alone of a rich and prosperous, contented country as in the past, but of a world in ferment.

And, my friends, more important than winning the election is governing the nation. That is the test of a political party—the acid, final test. When the tumult and the shouting die, when the bands are gone and the lights are dimmed, there is the stark reality of responsibility in an hour of history haunted with those gaunt, grim specters of strife, dissension and materialism at home, and ruthless, inscrutable and hostile power abroad.

The ordeal of the twentieth century—the bloodiest, most turbulent era of the Christian age—is far from over. Sacrifice, patience, understanding, and implacable purpose may be our lot for years to come.

Let's face it. Let's talk sense to the American people. Let's tell them the truth, that there are no gains without pains, that we are now on the eve of great decisions, not easy decisions, like resistance when you're attacked, but a long, patient, costly struggle which alone can assure triumph over the great enemies of man—war, poverty, and tyranny—and the assaults upon human dignity which are the most grievous consequences of each.

Let's tell them that the victory to be won in the twentieth century, this portal to the golden age, mocks the pretensions of individual acumen and ingenuity. For it is a citadel guarded by thick walls of ignorance and of mistrust which do not fall before the trumpets' blast or the politicians' imprecations or even a general's baton. They are, my friends, walls that must be directly stormed by the hosts of courage, of mortality and of vision, standing shoulder to shoulder, unafraid of ugly truth, contemptuous of lies, half-truths, circuses, and demagoguery.

The people are wise—wiser than the Republicans think. And the Democratic party is the people's party, not the labor party, not the farmers' party, not the employers' party—it is the party of no one because it is the party of everyone.

That, I think, is our ancient mission. Where we have deserted it we have failed. With your help there will be no desertion now. Better, we lose the election than mislead the people, and better we lose than misgovern the people.

Help me do the job in this autumn of conflict and of campaign; help me do the job in these years of darkness, of doubt and of crisis which stretch beyond the horizon of tonight's happy vision, and we will justify our glorious past and the loyalty of silent millions who look to us for compassion, for understanding, and for honest purpose. Thus we will serve our great tradition greatly.

I ask of you all you have; I will give to you all I have, even as he who came here tonight and honored me, as he has honored you—the Democratic party—by a lifetime of service and bravery that will find him an imperishable page in the history of the republic and of the Democratic party—President Harry S. Truman.

And finally, my friends, in the staggering task that you have assigned me, I shall always try "to do justly, to love mercy, and to walk humbly with my God."

DWIGHT D. EISENHOWER

—— ★ ——

The Korean Armistice

BROADCAST ADDRESS TO THE NATION;
JULY 26, 1953

Dwight David Eisenhower (1890–1969), supreme allied commander for the invasion of Europe in World War II, army chief of staff from 1945 to 1948, president of Columbia University, and, from November 1950, commander of NATO forces in Europe, was the Republicans' choice for president in 1952. He defeated Adlai Stevenson in two successive elections. An economic moderate, he presided over a difficult cold war period and the beginnings of space exploration; in the area of civil rights, he sent federal troops to Little Rock, Arkansas, to enforce court-ordered school integration. During the election of 1952, Eisenhower had pledged to end the war in Korea, and the suspended armistice negotiations were resumed in April 1953, followed by a truce agreement in July.

M y Fellow Citizens: Tonight we greet, with prayers of thanksgiving, the official news that an armistice was signed almost an hour ago in Korea. It will quickly bring to an end the fighting between the United Nations forces and the Communist armies. For this nation the cost of repelling aggression has been high. In thousands of homes it has been incalculable. It has been paid in terms of tragedy.

With special feelings of sorrow—and of solemn gratitude—we think of those who were called upon to lay down their lives in that far-off land to prove once again that only courage and sacrifice can keep freedom alive upon the earth. To the widows and orphans of this war, and to those veterans who bear disabling wounds, America renews tonight her pledge of lasting devotion and care.

Our thoughts turn also to those other Americans wearied by many months of imprisonment behind the enemy lines. The swift return of all of them will bring joy to thousands of families. It will be evidence of good faith on the part of those with whom we have signed this armistice.

Soldiers, sailors, and airmen of sixteen different countries have stood as partners beside us throughout these long and bitter months. America's thanks go to each. In this struggle we have seen the United Nations meet the challenge of aggression—not with pathetic words of protest, but with deeds of decisive purpose. It is proper that we salute particularly the valorous armies of the Republic of Korea, for they have done even more than prove their right to freedom. Inspired by President Syngman Rhee, they have given an example of courage and patriotism which again demonstrates that men of the West and men of the East can fight and work and live together side by side in pursuit of a just and noble cause.

And so at long last the carnage of war is to cease and the negotiation of the conference table is to begin. On this Sabbath evening each of us devoutly prays that all nations may come to see the wisdom of composing differences in this fashion before, rather than after, there is resort to brutal and futile battle.

Now as we strive to bring about that wisdom, there is, in this moment of sober satisfaction, one thought that must discipline our emotions and steady our resolution. It is this: We have won an armistice on a single battleground—not peace in the world. We may not now relax our guard nor cease our quest.

Throughout the coming months, during the period of prisoner screening and exchange, and during the possibly longer period of the political conference which looks toward the unification of Korea, we and our United Nations allies must be vigilant against the possibility of untoward developments.

And, as we do so, we shall fervently strive to insure that this armistice will, in fact, bring free peoples one step nearer to a goal of a world of peace.

My fellow citizens, almost ninety years ago, Abraham Lincoln, at the end of the war, delivered his second inaugural address. At the end of that speech he spoke some words that I think more nearly would express the true feelings of America tonight than would any other words ever spoken or written. You recall them:

> With malice toward none, with charity for all, with firmness in the right as God gives us to see the right, let us strive on to finish the work we are in . . . to do all which may achieve and cherish a just and lasting peace among ourselves and with all nations.

This is our resolve and our dedication.

GEORGE MEANY

—— ★ ——

Labor Day Message

BROADCAST ADDRESS TO THE NATION;
SEPTEMBER 7, 1953

Elected president of the American Federation of Labor the previous year, George Meany (1894–1980) broadcast an address to the nation on Labor Day 1953, highlighting six "glaring weaknesses in our national life which require immediate attention." Meany discussed inflation, housing, social security, health care, education, and the perceived antilabor Taft-Hartley Act. His comments would remain pertinent in the coming years: "Even families with moderate incomes cannot buy the homes they need at prices they can afford. . . . [There is a] growing need for a national program to insure the American people against the high cost of medical care." Meany became president of the newly consolidated AFL-CIO in December 1955 and served as a U.S. delegate to the United Nations in 1957 and 1959.

Labor Day is the one national holiday which does not commemorate famous heroes or historic events. It is dedicated to the millions of men and women who work for wages, the people who have built America's towns and cities, the skilled and unskilled laborers who are responsible, in large measure, for the miracle of American industrial progress.

As the representative of nine million of these working men and women, it is my purpose to report to you on the issues which are of supreme importance on this Labor Day.

First comes the issue of war or peace. It was not resolved by the truce negotiated in Korea. That event has failed to ease the growing international tension caused by Soviet Russia's relentless determination to dominate and control the entire world.

Since the death of Stalin, sweet words have been broadcast by his successors in the Kremlin, but they mean absolutely nothing in the way of concrete assurance of peace. The grim facts are clear. The Russian dictators may change their tactics, but they have not changed their objective. They still refuse to enter into any enforceable agreement for disarmament. They still refuse to give up the use of war of aggression. They even refuse to work out reasonable peace treaties necessary to end chaotic conditions left over from the last World War.

To these ominous factors, something new had been added. The Communists have proved they now possess the secret of the hydrogen bomb—the world's most dreaded weapon.

What does atomic war mean? It means that a million people—men, women, and children—can be wiped out of existence in a few seconds by a single bomb blast. It means that whole cities, with most of their population, can be reduced to ashes overnight.

To us that kind of warfare is unthinkable. Labor builds. It does not destroy. The thought of having our entire civilization go up in smoke appears to us nothing short of madness.

How can we prevent such a war? Our national leaders have explored every conceivable way to induce the Communists to listen to reason and used every possible approach to bring about peace by negotiation without concrete results. It would be folly to suppose that appeasement would provide a solution. No dictator in history has ever been converted to human decency by appeasement. Partial surrender to the insatiable demands of the Communists can only lead eventually to total surrender.

The only thing they fear or respect is superior power. The only factor that will deter them from plunging the world into another war is the knowledge that they will have to contend against superior power.

How does America stand? Do we possess greater power than the Soviet empire? If not, how can we achieve it? . . .

Some of our military strategists believe that the production problem of greatest concern is access to raw materials. I disagree. All the materials in the world and all the machines in the world put together would produce nothing without a capable, a loyal, and a willing work force.

Thus the human element is obviously the main element in the national defense picture. And that is why, by all means, we should concentrate on strengthening the status and the security of the working men and women who serve in the front lines of our defense production program.

On this Labor Day, the American worker stands head and shoulders above the workers of any other land. His wages and working conditions are better. He and his family have better homes to live in, better food to eat, and better clothing. These advances did not come to the workers of our country automatically. They were won by organizing into trade unions and by struggle against stubborn opposition.

Because they are better off, the workers of America produce more than workers in other countries, who do not possess the skill, the training, nor the incentive to get ahead. By the same token, the high standards enjoyed by American workers create the mass purchasing power which has made it possible for industry to grow and expand to a productive capacity unmatched anywhere on earth.

This is the bright side of the picture. But there is another side. There are glaring weaknesses in our national life which require immediate action, vulnerable spots which demand correction if we hope to muster our total strength for the long-drawn-out struggle ahead.

Let's get down to cases. First is the basic problem of inflation. Higher wages don't buy any more groceries when the cost of living keeps climbing to record heights. . . . The working people of this country, and the farmers as well, are being victimized by unjustifiable profiteering. It must be stopped. It is up to

Congress to halt inflation if the nation is to be kept strong.

The second problem is housing. At least eight million of our people are still living in the worst kind of slums—slums that breed disease, juvenile delinquency, and crime. Yet the Eighty-third Congress cut off the low-cost, public housing program which is the only effective method of replacing slums with decent housing for those in the lowest income brackets.

Even families with moderate incomes cannot buy the homes they need at prices they can afford. The government increased interest rates to the bankers on home loans, but it took no action to meet the housing shortage. . . .

Another field, in which we have gone backward instead of forward, is social security. This is the self-insurance program through which our country has sought to protect the American people from fear of unemployment and fear of destitute old age. It has served also as a powerful bulwark to economic stability and the security of the free enterprise system itself.

But what has happened to social security? Millions of Americans are still left unprotected. Inflation, with its fifty-cent dollar, has cut benefits below the minimum subsistence level. Almost 10 percent of our people have now reached the legal retirement age of sixty-five. Millions more are approaching old age in fear of poverty.

To afford them the security which they were promised and for which they paid insurance, through payroll taxes, Congress is duty-bound to improve the social security program. Yet it has done nothing but to postpone action.

The record of the Eighty-third Congress on health problems is even worse. It refused to give any consideration whatsoever to the growing need for a national program to insure the American people against the high cost of medical care. It took no action on bipartisan appeals for aid to medical schools so that the alarming shortage of doctors, nurses, and hospital facilities could be overcome. . . .

When it comes to the need for education, there can be no

controversy. The facts speak for themselves. The federal commissioner of education only a few days ago reported shocking conditions in American schools due to reopen this month, after summer vacations. There is a tremendous shortage of school space for our children. One out of every five will be exposed to the danger of fire-traps. There are not enough teachers to go around. The shortage of seventy-two thousand teachers is due to the fact that teachers' salaries have been allowed to sink shamefully low.

This is the official record. Congress knows all the facts. The members of Congress understand, as well as you or I, the prime importance to our national vitality and safety of good education for the nation's children. Yet what has it done about this basic problem of federal aid to education? Absolutely nothing. Surely, in the field of education, our nation must be greatly strengthened.

Finally, we are still faced with the serious problems arising from the manifest unfairness of the Taft-Hartley Act to the nation's workers. Because it is weighted against labor, this law can—at any time—throw production schedules out of balance. This fact is clear to the responsible leaders of our nation. . . . Unless Congress fulfills its responsibility to act constructively on this issue at its next session, our nation will not be able to achieve its maximum production strength for survival against the threat of Communist dictatorship.

Let me make one thing clear. Congress will not act on any or all of these problems until and unless the people of this country demand action. Your Congress represents you. Under our democracy, you can make your government carry out your wishes or you can vote it out of office. The power to give America the power it needs is in your hands.

This is not the situation behind the Iron Curtain. Under the Soviet dictatorship, the people of Russia and its satellites have no will of their own. They must obey orders or die. . . .

We, in the American Federation of Labor, want no part of

communism. Experience has taught us that free labor can exist and make progress only in a free land. There is no stronger enemy of communism in the world than the nine million men and women who make up the AFL.

Our hopes and objectives on this Labor Day can be summed up briefly. We want to make America strong so that it can continue to be free. We want to build up the whole fabric of our national life, so that the freedoms which all of us cherish can survive and endure.

Dwight D. Eisenhower

——— ★ ———

Atoms for Peace

United Nations General Assembly,
New York, New York; December 8, 1953

A threat of mass destruction so concerned Albert Einstein and others in the years following World War II because of the ever-increasing stockpiling of atomic weapons and the numerous atomic tests conducted by the United States, Great Britain, and the Soviet Union. The U.S. had tested an experimental hydrogen bomb on November 1, 1952; the Soviet Union exploded its version of this superbomb on August 20, 1953. President Eisenhower, in his December 1953 speech before the U.N. General Assembly, daringly acknowledged that there was a need to stop the insanity of this buildup, to "move out of the dark chamber of horrors into the light." Eisenhower proposed that the world's bomb-making potential be reduced by the contribution of various nations' uranium and fissionable materials to an International Atomic Energy Agency, "which would devise methods whereby this fissionable material would be allocated to serve the peaceful pursuits of mankind."

I feel impelled to speak today in a language that in a sense is new—one which I, who have spent so much of my life in the military profession, would have preferred never to use.

That new language is the language of atomic warfare.

The atomic age has moved forward at such a pace that every citizen of the world should have some comprehension, at least in comparative terms, of the extent of this development, of the utmost significance to every one of us. Clearly, if the peoples of the world are to conduct an intelligent search for peace, they must be armed with the significant facts of today's existence.

My recital of atomic danger and power is necessarily stated in United States terms, for these are the only incontrovertible facts that I know. I need hardly point out to this assembly, however, that this subject is global, not merely national in character.

On July 16, 1945, the United States set off the world's first atomic explosion.

Since that date in 1945, the United States of America has conducted forty-two test explosions.

Atomic bombs today are more than twenty-five times as powerful as the weapons with which the atomic age dawned, while hydrogen weapons are in the ranges of millions of tons of TNT equivalent.

Today, the United States' stockpile of atomic weapons, which, of course, increases daily, exceeds by many times the explosive equivalent of the total of all bombs and all shells that came from every plane and every gun in every theatre of war in all of the years of World War II.

A single air group, whether afloat or land-based, can now deliver to any reachable target a destructive cargo exceeding in power all the bombs that fell on Britain in all of World War II.

In size and variety, the development of atomic weapons has been no less remarkable. The development has been such that atomic weapons have virtually achieved conventional status within our armed services. In the United States, the army, the navy, the air force, and the Marine Corps are all capable of putting this weapon to military use.

But the dread secret, and the fearful engines of atomic might, are not ours alone.

In the first place, the secret is possessed by our friends and allies, Great Britain and Canada, whose scientific genius made a tremendous contribution to our original discoveries, and the designs of atomic bombs.

The secret is also known by the Soviet Union.

The Soviet Union has informed us that, over recent years, it has devoted extensive resources to atomic weapons. During this period, the Soviet Union has exploded a series of atomic devices, including at least one involving thermonuclear reactions.

If at one time the United States possessed what might have been called a monopoly of atomic power, that monopoly ceased to exist several years ago. Therefore, although our earlier start has permitted us to accumulate what is today a great quantitative advantage, the atomic realities of today comprehend two facts of even greater significance.

First, the knowledge now possessed by several nations will eventually be shared by others—possibly all others.

Second, even a vast superiority in numbers of weapons, and a consequent capability of devastating retaliation, is no preventive, of itself, against the fearful material damage and toll of human lives that would be inflicted by surprise aggression.

The free world, at least dimly aware of these facts, has naturally embarked on a large program of warning and defense systems. That program will be accelerated and expanded.

But let no one think that the expenditure of vast sums for weapons and systems of defense can guarantee absolute safety for the cities and citizens of any nation. The awful arithmetic of the atomic bomb does not permit of any such easy solution. Even against the most powerful defense, an aggressor in possession of the effective minimum number of atomic bombs for a surprise attack could probably place a sufficient number of his bombs on the chosen targets to cause hideous damage.

Should such an atomic attack be launched against the United States, our reactions would be swift and resolute. But for me to say that the defense capabilities of the United States are such that they could inflict terrible losses upon an aggressor— for me to say that the retaliation capabilities of the United States are so great that such an aggressor's land would be laid waste —all this, while fact, is not the true expression of the purpose and the hope of the United States.

To pause there would be to confirm the hopeless finality of a belief that two atomic colossi are doomed malevolently to eye each other indefinitely across a trembling world. To stop there would be to accept helplessly the probability of civilization destroyed—the annihilation of the irreplaceable heritage of mankind handed down to us generation from generation—and the condemnation of mankind to begin all over again the age-old struggle upward from savagery toward decency, and right, and justice. . . .

It is with the book of history, and not with isolated pages, that the United States will ever wish to be identified. My country wants to be constructive, not destructive. It wants agreements, not wars, among nations. It wants itself to live in freedom and in the confidence that the people of every other nation enjoy equally the right of choosing their own way of life.

So my country's purpose is to help us move out of the dark chamber of horrors into the light, to find a way by which the minds of men, the hopes of men, the souls of men everywhere can move forward toward peace and happiness and well-being. . . .

In its resolution of November 18, 1953, this General Assembly suggested, and I quote:

> that the Disarmament Commission study the desirability of establishing a subcommittee consisting of representatives of the powers principally involved, which should seek in private an acceptable solution . . . and report on such a solution to the General Assembly and to the Security Council not later than 1 September 1954.

The United States, heeding the suggestion of the General Assembly of the United Nations, is instantly prepared to meet privately with such other countries as may be "principally involved," to seek "an acceptable solution" to the atomic armaments race which overshadows not only the peace but the very life of the world.

We shall carry into these private or diplomatic talks a new conception.

The United States would seek more than the mere reduction or elimination of atomic materials for military purposes. . . .

The United States knows that if the fearful trend of atomic military buildup can be reversed, this greatest of destructive forces can be developed into a great boon, for the benefit of all mankind.

The United States knows that peaceful power from atomic energy is no dream of the future. That capability, already proved, is here—now—today. Who can doubt, if the entire body of the world's scientists and engineers had adequate amounts of fissionable material with which to test and develop their ideas, that this capability would rapidly be transformed into universal, efficient, and economic usage.

To hasten the day when fear of the atom will begin to disappear from the minds of people, and the governments of the East and West, there are certain steps that can be taken now.

I therefore make the following proposals:

The governments principally involved, to the extent permitted by elementary prudence, to begin now and continue to make joint contributions from their stockpiles of normal uranium and fissionable materials to an International Atomic Energy Agency. We would expect that such an agency would be set up under the aegis of the United Nations. . . .

The Atomic Energy Agency could be made responsible for the impounding, storage, and protection of the contributed fissionable and other materials. The ingenuity of our scientists will provide special safe conditions under which such a bank of fissionable material can be made essentially immune to surprise seizure.

The more important responsibility of this Atomic Energy Agency would be to devise methods whereby this fissionable material would be allocated to serve the peaceful pursuits of mankind. Experts would be mobilized to apply atomic energy to the needs of agriculture, medicine, and other peaceful activities. A special purpose would be to provide abundant electrical energy in the power-starved areas of the world. Thus the contributing powers would be dedicating some of their strength to serve the needs rather than the fears of mankind.

The United States would be more than willing—it would be proud to take up with others "principally involved" the development of plans whereby such peaceful use of atomic energy would be expedited.

Of those "principally involved" the Soviet Union must, of course, be one. . . .

The coming months will be fraught with fateful decisions. In this assembly, in the capitals and military headquarters of the world, in the hearts of men everywhere, be they governors or governed—may they be the decisions which will lead this world out of fear and into peace.

To the making of these fateful decisions, the United States pledges before you—and therefore before the world—its determination to help solve the fearful atomic dilemma, to devote its entire heart and mind to find the way by which the miraculous inventiveness of man shall not be dedicated to his death but consecrated to his life.

I again thank the delegates for the great honor they have done me, in inviting me to appear before them, and in listening to me so courteously. Thank you.

JOHN F. KENNEDY

—— ★ ——

Inaugural Address

CAPITOL, WASHINGTON, D.C.; JANUARY 20, 1961

John F. Kennedy (1917–1963), U.S. senator from Massachusetts, faced Vice President Richard M. Nixon in the 1960 presidential election. Kennedy, a Democrat, won by a narrow margin of the popular vote. His administration, cut short by his assassination on November 22, 1963, was marked by several cold war crises and the active pursuit of major civil rights legislation and a nuclear-test-ban treaty. Kennedy's inaugural address outlined his priorities: helping poorer citizens, an "alliance for progress" with the Latin American nations, and a new "quest for peace, before the dark powers of destruction unleashed by science engulf all humanity in planned or accidental self-destruction." In closing, Kennedy challenged his fellow citizens with these words: "Ask not what your country can do for you—ask what you can do for your country."

We observe today not a victory of party but a celebration of freedom—symbolizing an end as well as a beginning, signifying renewal as well as change. For I have sworn before you and Almighty God the same solemn oath our forebears prescribed nearly a century and three-quarters ago.

The world is very different now. For man holds in his mortal hands the power to abolish all forms of human poverty and all forms of human life. And yet the same revolutionary beliefs for which our forebears fought are still at issue around the globe: the belief that the rights of man come not from the generosity of the state but from the hand of God.

We dare not forget today that we are the heirs of that first revolution. Let the word go forth from this time and place, to friend and foe alike, that the torch has been passed to a new generation of Americans—born in this century, tempered by war, disciplined by a hard and bitter peace, proud of our ancient heritage—and unwilling to witness or permit the slow undoing of those human rights to which this nation has always been committed, and to which we are committed today at home and around the world.

Let every nation know, whether it wishes us well or ill, that we shall pay any price, bear any burden, meet any hardship, support any friend, oppose any foe to assure the survival and the success of liberty.

This much we pledge—and more.

To those old allies whose cultural and spiritual origins we share, we pledge the loyalty of faithful friends. United, there is little we cannot do in a host of cooperative ventures. Divided, there is little we can do—for we dare not meet a powerful challenge at odds and split asunder.

To those new states whom we welcome to the ranks of the free, we pledge our word that one form of colonial control shall not have passed away merely to be replaced by a far more iron tyranny. We shall not always expect to find them supporting our view. But we shall always hope to find them strongly supporting their own freedom—and to remember that, in the past, those who foolishly sought power by riding the back of the tiger ended up inside.

To those people in the huts and villages of half the globe struggling to break the bonds of mass misery, we pledge our best efforts to help them help themselves, for whatever period is required—not because the Communists may be doing it, not because we seek their votes, but because it is right. If a free society cannot help the many who are poor, it cannot save the few who are rich.

To our sister republics south of the border, we offer a special pledge: to convert our good words into good deeds—in a new alliance for progress—to assist free men and free governments in casting off the chains of poverty. But this peaceful revolution of hope cannot become the prey of hostile powers.

Let all our neighbors know that we shall join with them to oppose aggression or subversion anywhere in the Americas. And let every other power know that this hemisphere intends to remain the master of its own house.

To that world assembly of sovereign states, the United Nations, our last best hope in an age where the instruments of war have far outpaced the instruments of peace, we renew our pledge of support—to prevent it from becoming merely a forum for invective, to strengthen its shield of the new and the weak, and to enlarge the area in which its writ may run.

Finally, to those nations who would make themselves our adversary, we offer not a pledge but a request: that both sides begin anew the quest for peace, before the dark powers of destruction unleashed by science engulf all humanity in planned or accidental self-destruction.

We dare not tempt them with weakness. For only when our arms are sufficient beyond doubt can we be certain beyond doubt that they will never be employed.

But neither can two great and powerful groups of nations take comfort from our present course—both sides overburdened by the cost of modern weapons, both rightly alarmed by the steady spread of the deadly atom, yet both racing to alter that uncertain balance of terror that stays the hand of mankind's final war.

So let us begin anew, remembering on both sides that civility is not a sign of weakness, and sincerity is always subject to proof. Let us never negotiate out of fear. But let us never fear to negotiate.

Let both sides explore what problems unite us instead of belaboring those problems which divide us.

Let both sides, for the first time, formulate serious and precise proposals for the inspection and control of arms—and bring the absolute power to destroy other nations under the absolute control of all nations.

Let both sides seek to invoke the wonders of science instead of its terrors. Together let us explore the stars, conquer the deserts, eradicate disease, tap the ocean depths, and encourage the arts and commerce.

Let both sides unite to heed in all corners of the earth the command of Isaiah—to "undo the heavy burdens . . . [and] let the oppressed go free."

And if a beachhead of cooperation may push back the jungle of suspicion, let both sides join in creating a new endeavor, not a new balance of power, but a new world of law, where the strong are just and the weak secure and the peace preserved.

All this will not be finished in the first one hundred days. Nor will it be finished in the first one thousand days, nor in the life of this administration, nor even perhaps in our lifetime on this planet. But let us begin.

In your hands, my fellow citizens, more than mine, will rest the final success or failure of our course. Since this country was founded, each generation of Americans has been summoned to give testimony to its national loyalty. The graves of young Americans who answered the call to service surround the globe.

Now the trumpet summons us again—not as a call to bear arms, though arms we need; not as a call to battle, though embattled we are—but a call to bear the burden of a long twilight struggle, year in and year out, "rejoicing in hope, patient in tribulation," a struggle against the common enemies of man: tyranny, poverty, disease, and war itself.

Can we forge against these enemies a grand and global alliance, north and south, east and west, that can assure a more fruitful life for all mankind? Will you join in that historic effort?

In the long history of the world, only a few generations have been granted the role of defending freedom in its hour of maximum danger. I do not shrink from this responsibility—I welcome it. I do not believe that any of us would exchange places with any other people or any other generation. The energy, the faith, the devotion which we bring to this endeavor will light our country and all who serve it—and the glow from that fire can truly light the world.

And so, my fellow Americans: Ask not what your country

can do for you—ask what you can do for your country.

My fellow citizens of the world: Ask not what America will do for you, but what together we can do for the freedom of man.

Finally, whether you are citizens of America or citizens of the world, ask of us here the same high standards of strength and sacrifice which we ask of you. With a good conscience our only sure reward, with history the final judge of our deeds, let us go forth to lead the land we love, asking His blessing and His help, but knowing that here on earth God's work must truly be our own.

Newton N. Minow

── ★ ──

Television and the Public Interest

THIRTY-NINTH ANNUAL CONVENTION OF
THE NATIONAL ASSOCIATION OF BROADCASTERS,
WASHINGTON, D.C.; MAY 9, 1961

Newton Minow's 1961 speech before the National Association of Broadcasters introduced the infamous description of television as "a vast wasteland." Minow (1926–) was chairman of the Federal Communications Commission during the Kennedy administration. His speech was an acknowledgment from Washington of television's influence and inferior fare. Asking the question "Why is so much of television so bad?" Newton challenged broadcasters to raise the level of programming. He spoke of "the people's airwaves" and indicated unconditional support for educational television.

Ours has been called the jet age, the atomic age, the space age. It is also, I submit, the television age. And just as history will decide whether the leaders of today's world employed the atom to destroy the world or rebuild it for mankind's benefit, so will history decide whether today's broadcasters employed their powerful voice to enrich the people or debase them. . . .

Like everybody, I wear more than one hat. I am the chairman of the FCC. I am also a television viewer and the husband and father of other television viewers. I have seen a great many television programs that seemed to me eminently worthwhile and I am not talking about the much bemoaned good old days of "Playhouse 90" and "Studio One."

I am talking about this past season. Some were wonderfully entertaining, such as "The Fabulous Fifties," "The Fred Astaire Show," and "The Bing Crosby Special"; some were dramatic and moving, such as Conrad's "Victory" and "Twilight Zone"; some were marvelously informative, such as "The Nation's Future," "CBS Reports," and "The Valiant Years." I could list many more—programs that I am sure everyone here felt enriched his own life and that of his family. When television is good, nothing—not the theater, not the magazines or newspapers—nothing is better.

But when television is bad, nothing is worse. I invite you to sit down in front of your television set when your station goes on the air and stay there without a book, magazine, newspaper, profit and loss sheet, or rating book to distract you—and keep your eyes glued to that set until the station signs off. I can assure you that you will observe a vast wasteland.

You will see a procession of game shows, violence, audience-participation shows, formula comedies about totally unbelievable families, blood and thunder, mayhem, violence, sadism, murder, western badmen, western good men, private eyes, gangsters, more violence, and cartoons. And, endlessly, commercials—many screaming, cajoling, and offending. And most of all, boredom. True, you will see a few things you will enjoy. But they will be very, very few. And if you think I exaggerate, try it. . . .

Why is so much of television so bad? I have heard many

answers: demands of your advertisers; competition for ever higher ratings; the need always to attract a mass audience; the high cost of television programs; the insatiable appetite for programming material—these are some of them. Unquestionably, these are tough problems not susceptible to easy answers. But I am not convinced that you have tried hard enough to solve them.

I do not accept the idea that the present overall programming is aimed accurately at the public taste. The ratings tell us only that some people have their television sets turned on and of that number, so many are tuned to one channel and so many to another. They don't tell us what the public might watch if they were offered half a dozen additional choices. A rating, at best, is an indication of how many people saw what you gave them. Unfortunately, it does not reveal the depth of the penetration, or the intensity of reaction, and it never reveals what the acceptance would have been if what you gave them had been better—if all the forces of art and creativity and daring and imagination had been unleashed. I believe in the people's good sense and good taste, and I am not convinced that the people's taste is as low as some of you assume. . . .

Certainly, I hope you will agree that ratings should have little influence where children are concerned. . . . If parents, teachers, and ministers conducted their responsibilities by following the ratings, children would have a steady diet of ice cream, school holidays, and no Sunday school. What about your responsibilities? Is there no room on television to teach, to inform, to uplift, to stretch, to enlarge the capacities of our children? Is there no room for programs deepening their understanding of children in other lands? Is there no room for a children's news show explaining something about the world to them at their level of understanding? Is there no room for reading the great literature of the past, teaching them the great traditions of freedom? There are some fine children's shows, but they are drowned out in the massive doses of cartoons, violence, and more violence. Must these be your trademarks? Search your consciences and see if you cannot offer more to your young beneficiaries whose future you guide so many hours each and every day.

What about adult programming and ratings? You know, newspaper publishers take popularity ratings too. The answers are pretty clear: it is almost always the comics, followed by the advice-to-the-lovelorn columns. But, ladies and gentlemen, the news is still on the front page of all newspapers, the editorials are not replaced by more comics, the newspapers have not become one long collection of advice to the lovelorn. Yet newspapers do not need a license from the government to be in business—they do not use public property. But in television—where your responsibilities as public trustees are so plain, the moment that the ratings indicate that westerns are popular there are new imitations of westerns on the air faster than the old coaxial cable could take us from Hollywood to New York. Broadcasting cannot continue to live by the numbers. . . .

Let me make clear that what I am talking about is balance. I believe that the public interest is made up of many interests. There are many people in this great country and you must serve all of us. You will get no argument from me if you say that, given a choice between a western and a symphony, more people will watch the western. I like westerns and private eyes too—but a steady diet for the whole country is obviously not in the public interest. We all know that people would more often prefer to be entertained than stimulated or informed. But your obligations are not satisfied if you look only to popularity as a test of what to broadcast. You are not only in show business; you are free to communicate ideas as well as relaxation. You must provide a wider range of choices, more diversity, more alternatives. It is not enough to cater to the nation's whims; you must also serve the nation's needs. . . .

Let me address myself now to my role not as a viewer but as chairman of the FCC. . . . I want to make clear some of the fundamental principles which guide me.

First, the people own the air. They own it as much in prime

evening time as they do at six o'clock Sunday morning. For every hour that the people give you, you owe them something. I intend to see that your debt is paid with service.

Second, I think it would be foolish and wasteful for us to continue any worn-out wrangle over the problems of payola, rigged quiz shows, and other mistakes of the past. There are laws on the books which we will enforce. But there is no chip on my shoulder. We live together in perilous, uncertain times; we face together staggering problems; and we must not waste much time now by rehashing the clichés of past controversy. To quarrel over the past is to lose the future.

Third, I believe in the free enterprise system. I want to see broadcasting improved and I want you to do the job. I am proud to champion your cause. It is not rare for American businessmen to serve a public trust. Yours is a special trust because it is imposed by law.

Fourth, I will do all I can to help educational television. There are still not enough educational stations, and major centers of the country still lack usable educational channels. If there were a limited number of printing presses in this country, you may be sure that a fair porportion of them would be put to educational use. Educational television has an enormous contribution to make to the future, and I intend to give it a hand along the way. If there is not a nationwide educational television system in this country, it will not be the fault of the FCC.

Fifth, I am unalterably opposed to governmental censorship. There will be no suppression of programming which does not meet with bureaucratic tastes. Censorship strikes at the tap root of our free society.

Sixth, I did not come to Washington to idly observe the squandering of the public's airwaves. The squandering of our airwaves is no less important than the lavish waste of any precious natural resource. I intend to take the job of chairman of the FCC very seriously. I believe in the gravity of my own particular sector of the New Frontier. . . .

Now, how will these principles be applied? Clearly, at the

heart of the FCC's authority lies its power to license, to renew or fail to renew, or to revoke a license. As you know, when your license comes up for renewal, your performance is compared with your promises. I understand that many people feel that in the past licenses were often renewed pro forma. I say to you now: Renewal will not be pro forma in the future. There is nothing permanent or sacred about a broadcast license.

But simply matching promises and performance is not enough. I intend to do more. I intend to find out whether the people care. I intend to find out whether the community which each broadcaster serves believes he has been serving the public interest. When a renewal is set down for hearing, I intend—wherever possible—to hold a well-advertised public hearing, right in the community you have promised to serve. I want the people who own the air and the homes that television enters to tell you and the FCC what's been going on. . . .

What I've been saying applies to broadcast stations. Now a station break for the networks:

You know your importance in this great industry. Today, more than one half of all hours of television station programming comes from the networks; in prime time, this rises to more than three quarters of the available hours.

You know that the FCC has been studying network operations for some time. I intend to press this to a speedy conclusion with useful results. I can tell you right now, however, that I am deeply concerned with concentration of power in the hands of the networks. As a result, too many local stations have foregone any efforts at local programming, with little use of live talent and local service. Too many local stations operate with one hand on the network switch and the other on a projector loaded with old movies. We want the individual stations to be free to meet their legal responsibilities to serve their communities. . . .

Tell your sponsors to be less concerned with costs per thousand and more concerned with understanding per millions. And remind your stockholders that an investment in broadcasting is buying a share in public responsibility.

The networks can start this industry on the road to freedom from the dictatorship of numbers. . . .

Television will rapidly join the parade into space. International television will be with us soon. No one knows how long it will be until a broadcast from a studio in New York will be viewed in India as well as in Indiana, will be seen in the Congo as it is seen in Chicago. But as surely as we are meeting here today, that day will come—and once again our world will shrink.

What will the people of other countries think of us when they see our western badmen and good men punching each other in the jaw in between the shooting? What will the Latin American or African child learn of America from our great communications industry? We cannot permit television in its present form to be our voice overseas. . . .

What you gentlemen broadcast through the people's air affects the people's taste, their knowledge, their opinions, their understanding of themselves and of their world—and their future.

The power of instantaneous sight and sound is without precedent in mankind's history. This is an awesome power. It has limitless capabilities for good—and for evil. And it carries with it awesome responsibilities, responsibilities which you and I cannot escape.

In his stirring inaugural address our president said, "And so, my fellow Americans: Ask not what your country can do for you—ask what you can do for your country."

Ladies and gentlemen: Ask not what broadcasting can do for you. Ask what you can do for broadcasting.

I urge you to put the people's airwaves to the service of the people and the cause of freedom. You must help prepare a generation for great decisions. You must help a great nation fulfill its future.

Do this, and I pledge you our help.

JOHN F. KENNEDY

—— ★ ——

The Berlin Crisis

BROADCAST ADDRESS TO THE NATION;
JULY 25, 1961

Amid the heightened tensions of the cold war during the early 1960s, the Kennedy administration faced several serious crises involving Cuba and the Soviet Union. Kennedy's speech to the nation on July 25, 1961, addressed one potentially serious confrontation: Soviet Premier Nikita Khrushchev's threat to sign a treaty with East Germany that would unilaterally end the West's occupation of its half of Berlin—a city divided between the Western allies and the Communists since World War II and lying within the borders of East Germany. West Berlin subsequently remained non-Communist, but on August 13, 1961, the Berlin Wall was erected to keep East Germans from escaping their country through West Berlin.

S even weeks ago tonight I returned from Europe to report on my meeting with Premier Khrushchev and the others. His grim warnings about the future of the world, his aide-mémoire on Berlin, his subsequent speeches and threats which he and his agents have launched, and the increase in the Soviet military budget that he has announced have all prompted a series of decisions by the administration and a series of consultations with the members of the NATO organization. In Berlin, as you recall, he intends to bring to an end, through a stroke of the pen, first our legal rights to be in West Berlin and secondly our ability to make good on our commitment to the two million free people of that city. That we cannot permit. . . .

West Berlin is 110 miles within the area which the Soviets now dominate—which is immediately controlled by the so-called East German regime. . . . We are there as a result of our victory over

Nazi Germany—and our basic rights to be there deriving from that victory include both our presence in West Berlin and the enjoyment of access across East Germany. These rights have been repeatedly confirmed and recognized in special agreements with the Soviet Union. Berlin is not a part of East Germany but a separate territory under the control of the allied powers. Thus our rights there are clear and deep-rooted. But in addition to those rights is our commitment to sustain—and defend, if need be—the opportunity for more than two million people to determine their own future and choose their own way of life.

Thus, our presence in West Berlin, and our access thereto, cannot be ended by any act of the Soviet government. The NATO shield was long ago extended to cover West Berlin —and we have given our word that an attack in that city will be regarded as an attack upon us all.

For West Berlin—lying exposed 110 miles inside East Germany, surrounded by Soviet troops and close to Soviet supply lines—has many roles. It is more than a showcase of liberty, a symbol, an island of freedom in a Communist sea. It is even more than a link with the Free World, a beacon of hope behind the Iron Curtain, an escape hatch for refugees.

West Berlin is all of that. But above all it has now become—as never before—the great testing place of Western courage and will, a focal point where our solemn commitments stretching back over the years since 1945 and Soviet ambitions now meet in basic confrontation.

It would be a mistake for others to look upon Berlin, because of its location, as a tempting target. The United States is there; the United Kingdom and France are there; the pledge of NATO is there—and the people of Berlin are there. It is as secure, in that sense, as the rest of us—for we cannot separate its safety from our own. . . .

We do not want to fight, but we have fought before. And others in earlier times have made the same dangerous mistake of assuming that the West was too selfish and too soft and too divided to resist invasions of freedom in other lands. Those who threaten to unleash the forces of war on a dispute over West Berlin should recall the words of the ancient philosopher: "A man who causes fear cannot be free from fear." . . .

So long as the Communists insist that they are preparing to end by themselves unilaterally our rights in West Berlin and our commitments to its people, we must be prepared to defend those rights and those commitments. We will at all times be ready to talk, if talk will help. But we must also be ready to resist with force, if force is used upon us. Either alone would fail. Together, they can serve the cause of freedom and peace. . . .

Thus, in the days and months ahead, I shall not hesitate to ask the Congress for additional measures or exercise any of the executive powers that I possess to meet this threat to peace. Everything essential to the security of freedom must be done; and if that should require more men, or more taxes, or more controls, or other new powers, I shall not hesitate to ask them. The measures proposed today will be constantly studied and altered as necessary. But while we will not let panic shape our policy, neither will we permit timidity to direct our program.

Accordingly, I am now taking the following steps:

1. I am tomorrow requesting the Congress for the current fiscal year an additional $3.247 billion of appropriations for the armed forces.

2. To fill out our present army divisions, and to make more men available for prompt deployment, I am requesting an increase in the army's total authorized strength from 875,000 to approximately one million men.

3. I am requesting an increase of 29,000 and 63,000 men respectively in the active duty strength of the navy and the air force.

4. To fulfill these manpower needs, I am ordering that our draft calls be doubled and tripled in the coming months; I am asking the Congress for authority to order to active duty certain ready reserve units and individual reservists, and to extend tours of duty; and, under that authority, I am planning to order to active duty a number of air transport squadrons and Air Na-

tional Guard tactical air squadrons, to give us the air-lift capacity and protection that we need. Other reserve forces will be called up when needed.

5. Many ships and planes once headed for retirement are to be retained or reactivated, increasing our air power tactically and our sea-lift, air-lift, and antisubmarine warfare capability. In addition, our strategic air power will be increased by delaying the deactivation of B-47 bombers.

6. Finally, some $1.8 billion—about half of the total sum—is needed for the procurement of nonnuclear weapons, ammunition, and equipment. . . .

To recognize the possibilities of nuclear war in the missile age, without our citizens knowing what they should do and where they should go if bombs begin to fall, would be a failure of responsibility. In May, I pledged a new start on civil defense. Last week, I assigned, on the recommendation of the civil defense director, basic responsibility for this program to the secretary of defense, to make certain it is administered and coordinated with our continental defense efforts at the highest civilian level. Tomorrow, I am requesting of the Congress new funds for the following immediate objectives: to identify and mark space in existing structures—public and private—that could be used for fallout shelters in case of attack; to stock those shelters with food, water, first-aid kits, and other minimum essentials for survival; to increase their capacity; to improve our air-raid warning and fallout detection systems, including a new household warning system which is now under development; and to take other measures that will be effective at an early date to save millions of lives if needed.

In the event of an attack, the lives of those families which are not hit in a nuclear blast and fire can still be saved—if they can be warned to take shelter and if that shelter is available. We owe that kind of insurance to our families—and to our country. In contrast to our friends in Europe, the need for this kind of protection is new to our shores. But the time to start is now. In the coming months, I hope to let every citizen know what steps he can take without delay to protect his family in case of attack. I know that you will want to do no less. . . .

But I must emphasize again that the choice is not merely between resistance and retreat, between atomic holocaust and surrender. Our peacetime military posture is traditionally defensive; but our diplomatic posture need not be. Our response to the Berlin crisis will not be merely military or negative. It will be more than merely standing firm. For we do not intend to leave it to others to choose and monopolize the forum and the framework of discussion. We do not intend to abandon our duty to mankind to seek a peaceful solution. . . .

We recognize the Soviet Union's historical concerns about their security in Central and Eastern Europe, after a series of ravaging invasions—and we believe arrangements can be worked out which will help to meet those concerns and make it possible for both security and freedom to exist in this troubled area.

For it is not the freedom of West Berlin which is "abnormal" in Germany today, but the situation in that entire divided country. If anyone doubts the legality of our rights in Berlin, we are ready to have it submitted to international adjudication. If anyone doubts the extent to which our presence is desired by the people of West Berlin, compared to East German feelings about their regime, we are ready to have that question submitted to a free vote in Berlin and, if possible, among all the German people. And let us hear at that time from the two and one-half million refugees who have fled the Communist regime in East Germany—voting for Western-type freedom with their feet. . . .

The solemn vow each of us gave to West Berlin in time of peace will not be broken in time of danger. If we do not meet our commitments to Berlin, where will we later stand? If we are not true to our word there, all that we have achieved in collective security, which relies on these words, will mean nothing. And if there is one path above all others to war, it is the path of weakness and disunity.

Today, the endangered frontier of freedom runs through

divided Berlin. We want it to remain a frontier of peace. This is the hope of every citizen of the Atlantic Community; every citizen of Eastern Europe; and, I am confident, every citizen of the Soviet Union. For I cannot believe that the Russian people—who bravely suffered enormous losses in the Second World War—would now wish to see the peace upset once more in Germany. The Soviet government alone can convert Berlin's frontier of peace into a pretext for war.

The steps I have indicated tonight are aimed at avoiding that war. To sum it all up: we seek peace—but we shall not surrender. That is the central meaning of this crisis—and the meaning of your government's policy.

With your help, and the help of other free men, this crisis can be surmounted. Freedom can prevail—and peace can endure.

John Glenn, Jr.

— ★ —

The Flight of Friendship 7 and the Space Program

U.S. House of Representatives,
Washington, D.C.; February 26, 1962

*In 1962, Lieutenant Colonel John H. Glenn, Jr., became a symbol
of the television-news age and the space age. The astronaut's
orbit of the earth—the first American to do so—on February 20
as well as his speech before Congress six days later were watched
and heard by a broadcast audience of many millions. Glenn
described the flight and what it was like to travel in space and
view the earth from such an altitude. He made a simple, direct
case for the importance of the U.S. space program, pointing to a
future schedule that would include "additional rendezvous experiments in space, technical and scientific observations—then,
Apollo orbital, circumlunar, and finally, lunar landing flights."
Glenn (1921–   ), an American hero, became a United States
senator from Ohio in 1975.*

Mr. Speaker, Mr. President, Members of the Congress: I
am only too aware of the tremendous honor that is being
shown us at this joint meeting of the Congress today. When I
think of past meetings that involved heads of state and equally
notable persons, I can only say I am most humble to know that
you consider our efforts to be in the same class.

This has been a great experience for all of us present and for
all Americans, of course, and I am certainly glad to see that
pride in our country and its accomplishments is not a thing of
the past.

I still get a hard-to-define feeling inside when the flag goes by—and I know that all of you do, too. Today as we rode up Pennsylvania Avenue from the White House and saw the tremendous outpouring of feeling on the part of so many thousands of our people I got this same feeling all over again. Let us hope that none of us ever loses it.

The flight of *Friendship 7* on February 20 involved much more than one man in the spacecraft in orbit. I would like to have my parents stand up, please . . . my wife's mother and Dr. Castor . . . my son and daughter, David and Carolyn . . . and the real rock in my family, my wife Annie.

There are many more people, of course, involved in our flight in *Friendship 7*, many more things involved, as well as people. There was the vision of Congress that established this national program of space exploration. Beyond that, many thousands of people were involved, civilian contractors and many subcontractors in many different fields, many elements—civilian, civil service, and military, all blending their efforts toward a common goal.

To even attempt to give proper credit to all the individuals on this team effort would be impossible. But let me say that I have never seen a more sincere, dedicated, and hard-working group of people in my life.

From the original vision of the Congress to consummation of this orbital flight has been just over three years. This, in itself, states eloquently the case for the hard work and devotion of the entire Mercury team. This has not been just another job. It has been a dedicated labor such as I have not seen before. It has involved a crosscut of American endeavor with many different disciplines cooperating toward a common objective.

Friendship 7 is just a beginning, a successful experiment. It is another plateau in our step-by-step program of increasingly ambitious flights. The earlier flights of Alan Shepard and Gus Grissom were steppingstones toward *Friendship 7*. My flight in the *Friendship 7* spacecraft will, in turn, provide additional information for use in striving toward future flights that some of the other gentlemen you see here will take part in.

Scott Carpenter here, who was my backup on this flight; Walt Schirra, Deke Slayton, and one missing member, who is still on his way back from Australia, where he was on the tracking station, Gordon Cooper. A lot of direction is necessary for a project such as this, and the director of Project Mercury since its inception has been Dr. Robert Gilruth, who certainly deserves a hand here.

I have been trying to introduce Walt Williams. I do not see him here. There he is up in the corner.

And the associate director of Mercury, who was in the unenviable position of being operational director. He is a character, no matter how you look at him. He says hold the count-foul, and one thing and another.

With all the experience we have had so far, where does this leave us?

There are the building blocks upon which we shall build much more ambitious and more productive portions of the program.

As was to be expected, not everything worked perfectly on my flight. We may well need to make changes—and these will be tried out on subsequent three-orbit flights, later this year, to be followed by eighteen-orbit, twenty-four-hour missions.

Beyond that, we look forward to Project Gemini—a two-man orbital vehicle with greatly increased capability for advanced experiments. There will be additional rendezvous experiments in space, technical and scientific observations—then, Apollo orbital, circumlunar, and finally, lunar landing flights.

What did we learn from the *Friendship 7* flight that will help us attain these objectives?

Some specific items have already been covered briefly in the news reports. And I think it is of more than passing interest to all of us that information attained from these flights is readily available to all nations of the world.

The launch itself was conducted openly and with the news media representatives from around the world in attendance.

Complete information is released as it is evaluated and validated. This is certainly in sharp contrast with similar programs conducted elsewhere in the world and elevates the peaceful intent of our program.

Data from the *Friendship 7* flight is still being analyzed. Certainly, much more information will be added to our storehouse of knowledge.

But these things we know. The Mercury spacecraft and systems design concepts are sound and have now been verified during manned flight. We also proved that man can operate intelligently in space and can adapt rapidly to this new environment.

Zero G or weightlessness—at least for this period of time—appears to be no problem. As a matter of fact, lack of gravity is a rather fascinating thing.

Objects within the cockpit can be parked in midair. For example, at one time during the flight, I was using a hand-held camera. Another system needed attention; so it seemed quite natural to let go of the camera, take care of the other chore in the spacecraft, then reach out, grasp the camera and go back about my business.

It is a real fascinating feeling, needless to say.

There seemed to be little sensation of speed although the craft was traveling at about five miles per second—a speed that I too find difficult to comprehend.

In addition to closely monitoring onboard systems, we were able to make numerous outside observations.

The view from that altitude defies description.

The horizon colors are brilliant and sunsets are spectacular. It is hard to beat a day in which you are permitted the luxury of seeing four sunsets.

I think after all of our talk of space, this morning coming up from Florida on the plane with President Kennedy, we had the opportunity to meet Mrs. Kennedy and Caroline before we took off. I think Caroline really cut us down to size and put us back in the proper position. She looked up, upon being introduced, and said, "Where is the monkey?"

And I did not get a banana pellet on the whole ride.

Our efforts today and what we have done so far are but small building blocks in a huge pyramid to come.

But questions are sometimes raised regarding the immediate payoffs from our efforts. What benefits are we gaining from the money spent? The real benefits we probably cannot even detail. They are probably not even known to man today. But exploration and the pursuit of knowledge have always paid dividends in the long run—usually far greater than anything expected at the outset.

Experimenters with common, green mold little dreamed what effect their discovery of penicillin would have.

The story has been told of Disraeli, prime minister of England at the time, visiting the laboratory of Faraday, one of the early experimenters with basic electrical principles. After viewing various demonstrations of electrical phenomena, Disraeli asked, "But of what possible use is it?" Faraday replied, "Mr. Prime Minister, what good is a baby?"

That is the stage of development in our program today—in its infancy. And it indicates a much broader potential impact, of course, than even the discovery of electricity did. We are just probing the surface of the greatest advancements in man's knowledge of his surroundings that has ever been made, I feel. There are benefits to science across the board. Any major effort such as this results in research by so many different specialties that it is hard to even envision the benefits that will accrue in many fields.

Knowledge begets knowledge. The more I see, the more impressed I am—not with how much we know, but with how tremendous the areas are that are as yet unexplored.

Exploration, knowledge, and achievement are good only insofar as we apply them to our future actions. Progress never stops. We are now on the verge of a new era, I feel.

Today, I know that I seem to be standing alone on this great platform—just as I seemed to be alone in the cockpit of the *Friendship 7* spacecraft. But I am not. There were with me then—and with me now—thousands of Americans and many hundreds of citizens of many countries around the world who contributed to this truly international undertaking voluntarily and in a spirit of cooperation and understanding.

On behalf of all of those people, I would like to express my and their heartfelt thanks for the honors you have bestowed upon us here today.

We are all proud to have been privileged to be part of this effort, to represent our country as we have. As our knowledge of the universe in which we live increases, may God grant us the wisdom and guidance to use it wisely.

MARTIN LUTHER KING, JR.

———— ★ ————

The March on Washington Address

THE MALL, WASHINGTON, D.C.; AUGUST 28, 1963

The Reverend Martin Luther King, Jr. (1929–1968), came to national attention in 1956 as the leader of the Montgomery, Alabama, bus boycott. As president of the Southern Christian Leadership Conference since its inception in 1957, he initiated a path of nonviolent demonstrations against racial segregation. King stirred the hearts of more than two hundred thousand civil rights demonstrators assembled on the Washington, D.C., Mall when he uttered the evocative phrase that would echo for decades—"I have a dream."

Fivescore years ago, a great American, in whose symbolic shadow we stand, signed the Emancipation Proclamation. This momentous decree came as a great beacon light of hope to millions of Negro slaves who had been seared in the flames of withering injustice. It came as a joyous daybreak to end the long night of captivity.

But one hundred years later, we must face the tragic fact that the Negro is still not free. One hundred years later, the life of the Negro is still sadly crippled by the manacles of segregation and the chains of discrimination. One hundred years later, the Negro lives on a lonely island of poverty in the midst of a vast ocean of material prosperity. One hundred years later, the Negro is still languished in the corners of American society and finds himself an exile in his own land. So we have come here today to dramatize an appalling condition.

In a sense we have come to our nation's capital to cash a check. When the architects of our republic wrote the magnificent words of the Constitution and the Declaration of Independence, they were signing a promissory note to which every

239

American was to fall heir. This note was a promise that all men would be guaranteed the unalienable rights of life, liberty, and the pursuit of happiness.

It is obvious today that America has defaulted on this promissory note insofar as her citizens of color are concerned. Instead of honoring this sacred obligation, America has given the Negro people a bad check; a check which has come back marked "insufficient funds." But we refuse to believe that the bank of justice is bankrupt. We refuse to believe that there are insufficient funds in the great vaults of opportunity of this nation. So we have come to cash this check—a check that will give us upon demand the riches of freedom and the security of justice.

We have also come to this hallowed spot to remind America of the fierce urgency of *now*. This is not the time to engage in the luxury of cooling off or to take the tranquilizing drug of gradualism. *Now* is the time to make real the promises of democracy. *Now* is the time to rise from the dark and desolate valley of segregation to the sunlit path of racial justice. *Now* is the time to open the doors of opportunity to all of God's children. *Now* is the time to lift our nation from the quicksands of racial injustice to the solid rock of brotherhood.

It would be fatal for the nation to overlook the urgency of the moment and to underestimate the determination of the Negro. This sweltering summer of the Negro's legitimate discontent will not pass until there is an invigorating autumn of freedom and equality. Nineteen sixty-three is not an end, but a beginning. Those who hope that the Negro needed to blow off steam and will now be content will have a rude awakening if the nation returns to business as usual. There will be neither rest nor tranquillity in America until the Negro is granted his citizenship rights. The whirlwinds of revolt will continue to shake the foundations of our nation until the bright day of justice emerges.

But there is something that I must say to my people who stand on the warm threshold which leads into the palace of justice. In the process of gaining our rightful place we must not be guilty of wrongful deeds. Let us not seek to satisfy our thirst for freedom by drinking from the cup of bitterness and hatred. We must forever conduct our struggle on the high plane of dignity and discipline. We must not allow our creative protest to degenerate into physical violence. Again and again we must rise to the majestic heights of meeting physical force with soul force.

The marvelous new militancy which has engulfed the Negro community must not lead us to a distrust of all white people, for many of our white brothers, as evidenced by their presence here today, have come to realize that their freedom is inextricably bound to our freedom. We cannot walk alone.

And as we walk, we must make the pledge that we shall march ahead. We cannot turn back. There are those who are asking the devotees of civil rights, "When will you be satisfied?"

We can never be satisfied as long as the Negro is the victim of the unspeakable horrors of police brutality.

We can never be satisfied as long as our bodies, heavy with fatigue of travel, cannot gain lodging in the motels of the highways and the cities.

We cannot be satisfied as long as the Negro's basic mobility is from a smaller ghetto to a larger one.

We can never be satisfied as long as a Negro in Mississippi cannot vote and a Negro in New York believes he has nothing for which to vote.

No, no, we are not satisfied, and we will not be satisfied until justice rolls down like waters and righteousness like a mighty stream.

I am not unmindful that some of you have come here out of great trials and tribulations. Some of you have come fresh from narrow jail cells. Some of you have come from areas where your quest for freedom left you battered by the storms of persecution and staggered by the winds of police brutality. You have been the veterans of creative suffering. Continue to work with the faith that unearned suffering is redemptive.

Go back to Mississippi, go back to Alabama, go back to

South Carolina, go back to Georgia, go back to Louisiana, go back to the slums and ghettos of our Northern cities, knowing that somehow this situation can and will be changed. Let us not wallow in the valley of despair.

I say to you today, my friends, that in spite of the difficulties and frustrations of the moment I still have a dream. It is a dream deeply rooted in the American dream.

I have a dream that one day this nation will rise up and live out the true meaning of its creed: "We hold these truths to be self-evident; that all men are created equal."

I have a dream that one day on the red hills of Georgia the sons of former slaves and the sons of former slaveowners will be able to sit down together at the table of brotherhood.

I have a dream that one day even the state of Mississippi, a desert state sweltering with the heat of injustice and oppression, will be transformed into an oasis of freedom and justice.

I have a dream that my four little children will one day live in a nation where they will not be judged by the color of their skin but by the content of their character.

I have a dream today.

I have a dream that one day the state of Alabama, whose governor's lips are presently dripping with the words of interposition and nullification, will be transformed into a situation where little black boys and black girls will be able to join hands with little white boys and girls and walk together as sisters and brothers.

I have a dream today.

I have a dream that one day every valley shall be exalted, every hill and mountain shall be made low, the rough places will be made plain, and the crooked places will be made straight, and the glory of the Lord shall be revealed, and all flesh shall see it together.

This is our hope. This is the faith with which I return to the South. With this faith we will be able to hew out of the mountain of despair a stone of hope. With this faith we will be able to transform the jangling discords of our nation into a beautiful symphony of brotherhood.

With this faith we will be able to work together, to pray together, to struggle together, to go to jail together, to stand up for freedom together, knowing that we will be free one day.

This will be the day when all of God's children will be able to sing with new meaning, "My country 'tis of thee, sweet land of liberty, of thee I sing. Land where my father died, land of the Pilgrims' pride, from every mountainside, let freedom ring."

And if America is to be a great nation, this must become true. So let freedom ring from the prodigious hilltops of New Hampshire. Let freedom ring from the mighty mountains of New York. Let freedom ring from the heightening Alleghenies of Pennsylvania!

Let freedom ring from the snowcapped Rockies of Colorado! Let freedom ring from the curvaceous peaks of California! But not only that; let freedom ring from Stone Mountain of Georgia! Let freedom ring from Lookout Mountain of Tennessee!

Let freedom ring from every hill and molehill of Mississippi. From every mountainside, let freedom ring.

When we let freedom ring, when we let it ring from every village and every hamlet, from every state and every city, we will be able to speed up that day when all of God's children, black men and white men, Jews and Gentiles, Protestants and Catholics, will be able to join hands and sing in the words of the old Negro spiritual, "Free at last! Free at last! Thank God Almighty, we are free at last!"

EUGENE McCARTHY

——— ★ ———

An Indefensible War

CONFERENCE OF CONCERNED DEMOCRATS,
CONRAD HILTON HOTEL,
CHICAGO, ILLINOIS; DECEMBER 2, 1967

As the war in Vietnam escalated and the public outcry grew, Minnesota Senator Eugene McCarthy, an outspoken critic of the administration's Vietnam policy, began to test political and popular support for a presidential candidacy opposed to the war. McCarthy (1916–   ) announced his candidacy for the Democratic party's nomination on November 30, 1967, in Washington, D.C., and on December 2 gave a major antiwar address at the Conference of Concerned Democrats in Chicago. McCarthy's strong showing in the New Hampshire primary in early March was a key factor in President Johnson's decision not to seek a second term.

In 1952, in this city of Chicago, the Democratic party nominated as its candidate for the presidency Adlai Stevenson.

His promise to his party and to the people of the country then was that he would talk sense to them. And he did in the clearest tones. He did not speak above the people, as his enemies charged, but he raised the hard and difficult questions and proposed the difficult answers. His voice became the voice of America. He lifted the spirit of this land. The country, in his language, was purified and given direction.

Before most other men, he recognized the problem of our cities and called for action.

Before other men, he measured the threat of nuclear war and called for a test-ban treaty.

Before other men, he anticipated the problem of conscience which he saw must come with maintaining a peacetime army and a limited draft and urged the political leaders of this country to put their wisdom to the task.

In all of these things he was heard by many but not followed, until under the presidency of John F. Kennedy his ideas were revived in new language and in a new spirit. To the clear sound of the horn was added the beat of a steady and certain drum.

John Kennedy set free the spirit of America. The honest optimism was released. Quiet courage and civility became the mark of American government, and new programs of promise and of dedication were presented: the Peace Corps, the Alliance for Progress, the promise of equal rights for all Americans —and not just the promise, but the beginning of the achievement of that promise.

All the world looked to the United States with new hope, for here was youth and confidence and an openness to the future. Here was a country not being held by the dead hand of the past, nor frightened by the violent hand of the future which was grasping at the world.

This was the spirit of 1963.

What is the spirit of 1967? What is the mood of America and of the world toward America today?

It is a joyless spirit—a mood of frustration, of anxiety, of uncertainty.

In place of the enthusiasm of the Peace Corps among the young people of America, we have protests and demonstrations.

In place of the enthusiasm of the Alliance for Progress, we have distrust and disappointment.

Instead of the language of promise and of hope, we have in politics today a new vocabulary in which the critical word is *war:* war on poverty, war on ignorance, war on crime, war on pollution. None of these problems can be solved by war but only by persistent, dedicated, and thoughtful attention.

But we do have one war which is properly called a war—the war in Vietnam, which is central to all of the problems of America.

A war of questionable legality and questionable constitutionality.

A war which is diplomatically indefensible; the first war in this century in which the United States, which at its founding made an appeal to the decent opinion of mankind in the Declaration of Independence, finds itself without the support of the decent opinion of mankind.

A war which cannot be defended in the context of the judgment of history. It is being presented in the context of an historical judgment of an era which is past. Munich appears to be the starting point of history for the secretary of state and for those who attempt to support his policies. What is necessary is a realization that the United States is a part of the movement of history itself; that it cannot stand apart, attempting to control the world by imposing covenants and treaties and by violent military intervention; that our role is not to police the planet but to use military strength with restraint and within limits, while at the same time we make available to the world the great power of our economy, of our knowledge, and of our good will.

A war which is not defensible even in military terms; which runs contrary to the advice of our greatest generals—Eisenhower, Ridgway, Bradley, and MacArthur—all of whom admonished us against becoming involved in a land war in Asia. Events have proved them right, as estimate after estimate as to the time of success and the military commitment necessary to success has had to be revised—always upward: more troops, more extensive bombing, a widening and intensification of the war. Extension and intensification have been the rule, and projection after projection of success have been proved wrong.

With the escalation of our military commitment has come a parallel of overleaping of objectives: from protecting South Vietnam, to nation building in South Vietnam, to protecting all of Southeast Asia, and ultimately to suggesting that the safety and security of the United States itself is at stake.

Finally, it is a war which is morally wrong. The most recent statement of objectives cannot be accepted as an honest judgment as to why we are in Vietnam. It has become increasingly difficult to justify the methods we are using and the instruments of war which we are using as we have moved from limited targets and somewhat restricted weapons to greater variety and more destructive instruments of war, and also have extended the area of operations almost to the heart of North Vietnam.

Even assuming that both objectives and methods can be defended, the war cannot stand the test of proportion and of prudent judgment. It is no longer possible to prove that the good that may come with what is called victory, or projected as victory, is proportionate to the loss of life and property and to other disorders that follow from this war. . . .

Those of us who are gathered here tonight are not advocating peace at any price. We are willing to pay a high price for peace—for an honorable, rational, and political solution to this war, a solution which will enhance our world position, which will permit us to give the necessary attention to our other commitments abroad, both military and nonmilitary, and leave us with both human and physical resources and with moral energy to deal effectively with the pressing domestic problems of the United States itself.

I see little evidence that the administration has set any limits on the price which it will pay for a military victory which becomes less and less sure and more hollow and empty in promise.

The scriptural promise of the good life is one in which the old men see visions and the young men dream dreams. In the context of this war and all of its implications, the young men of America do not dream dreams, but many live in the nightmare of moral anxiety, of concern and great apprehension; and the old men, instead of visions which they can offer to the young, are projecting, in the language of the secretary of state, a specter of one billion Chinese threatening the peace and safety of the world—a frightening and intimidating future.

The message from the administration today is a message of apprehension, a message of fear, yes—even a message of fear of fear.

This is not the real spirit of America. I do not believe that it is. This is a time to test the mood and spirit:

To offer in place of doubt—trust.

In place of expediency—right judgment.

In place of ghettos, let us have neighborhoods and communities.

In place of incredibility—integrity.

In place of murmuring, let us have clear speech; let us again hear America singing.

In place of disunity, let us have dedication of purpose.

In place of near despair, let us have hope.

This is the promise of greatness which was stated for us by Adlai Stevenson and which was brought to form and positive action in the words and actions of John Kennedy.

Let us pick up again these lost strands and weave them again into the fabric of America.

Let us sort out the music from the sounds and again respond to the trumpet and the steady drum.

Lyndon B. Johnson

—— ★ ——

Leaving the Presidency

Broadcast Address to the Nation; March 31, 1968

By the end of March 1968, Lyndon Johnson (1908–1973) was an unpopular president criticized from many sides for his handling of the Vietnam War. Senator Eugene McCarthy had just made a surprisingly strong showing in the New Hampshire Democratic primary, and Senator Robert F. Kennedy had entered the race for president. With more than a half-million American troops overseas, Johnson announced to the nation on March 31 that the bombing of much of North Vietnam would end and, startlingly, that he would neither seek nor accept the Democratic party's nomination for president. The address underlined the tragedy of the Johnson administration, which had been successful in its ambitious Great Society programs but had failed miserably in pursuing the war in Southeast Asia.

Good evening, my fellow Americans. Tonight I want to speak to you of peace in Vietnam and Southeast Asia.

No other question so preoccupies our people. No other dream so absorbs the 250 million human beings who live in that part of the world. No other goal motivates American policy in Southeast Asia.

For years, representatives of our government and others have traveled the world seeking to find a basis for peace talks. Since last September, they have carried the offer that I made public at San Antonio.

That offer was this: That the United States would stop its bombardment of North Vietnam when that would lead promptly to productive discussions, and that we would assume that North Vietnam would not take military advantage of our restraint.

Hanoi denounced this offer, both privately and publicly. Even while the search for peace was going on, North Vietnam rushed their preparations for a savage assault on the people, the government, and the allies of South Vietnam.

Their attack—during the Tet holidays—failed to achieve its principal objectives. It did not collapse the elected government of South Vietnam or shatter its army, as the Communists had hoped. It did not produce a "general uprising" among the people of the cities as they had predicted.

The Communists were unable to maintain control of any of the more than thirty cities that they attacked. And they took very heavy casualties. But they did compel the South Vietnamese and their allies to move certain forces from the countryside into the cities. They caused widespread disruption and suffering. Their attacks, and the battles that followed, made refugees of half a million human beings. The Communists may renew their attack any day.

They are, it appears, trying to make 1968 the year of decision in South Vietnam—the year that brings, if not final victory or defeat, at least a turning point in the struggle.

This much is clear:

If they do mount another round of heavy attacks, they will not succeed in destroying the fighting power of South Vietnam and its allies.

But tragically, this is also clear: many men—on both sides of the struggle—will be lost. A nation that has already suffered twenty years of warfare will suffer once again. Armies on both sides will take new casualties. And the war will go on.

There is no need for this to be so. There is no need to delay the talks that could bring an end to this long and this bloody war.

Tonight, I renew the offer I made last August—to stop the bombardment of North Vietnam. We ask that talks begin promptly, that they be serious talks on the substance of peace. We assume that during those talks Hanoi will not take advantage of our restraint.

We are prepared to move immediately toward peace through negotiations. So, tonight, in the hope that this action will lead to early talks, I am taking the first step to deescalate the conflict. We are reducing—substantially reducing—the present level of hostilities. And we are doing so unilaterally, and at once.

Tonight, I have ordered our aircraft and our naval vessels to make no attacks on North Vietnam, except in the area north of the Demilitarized Zone where the continuing enemy buildup directly threatens allied forward positions and where the movements of their troops and supplies are clearly related to that threat.

The area in which we are stopping our attacks includes almost 90 percent of North Vietnam's population and most of its territory. Thus there will be no attacks around the principal populated areas or in the food-producing areas of North Vietnam. . . .

Now, as in the past, the United States is ready to send its representatives to any forum, at any time, to discuss the means of bringing this ugly war to an end. . . . I call upon President Ho Chi Minh to respond positively, and favorably, to this new step toward peace. . . .

The main burden of preserving their freedom must be carried out by . . . the South Vietnamese themselves. . . . There has been substantial progress, I think, in building a durable government during these last three years. The South Vietnam of 1965 could not have survived the enemy's Tet offensive of 1968. The elected government of South Vietnam survived that attack— and is rapidly repairing the devastation that it wrought. . . .

We shall accelerate the reequipment of South Vietnam's armed forces in order to meet the enemy's increased firepower. This will enable them progressively to undertake a larger share of combat operations against the Communist invaders.

On many occasions I have told the American people that we would send to Vietnam those forces that are required to accomplish our mission there. So, with that as our guide, we have previously authorized a force level of approximately 525,000.

Some weeks ago—to help meet the enemy's new offensive—we sent to Vietnam about eleven thousand additional marine and airborne troops. They were deployed by air in forty-eight hours, on an emergency basis. But the artillery, tank, aircraft, and other units that were needed to work with and support these infantry troops in combat could not accompany them on that short notice.

In order that these forces may reach maximum combat effectiveness, the Joint Chiefs of Staff have recommended to me that we should prepare to send—during the next five months—support troops totaling approximately 13,500 men. . . .

I cannot promise that the initiative that I have announced tonight will be completely successful in achieving peace any more than the thirty others that we have undertaken and agreed to in recent years.

But it is our fervent hope that North Vietnam, after years of fighting that has left the issue unresolved, will now cease its efforts to achieve a military victory and will join with us in moving toward the peace table. . . .

During the past four and a half years, it has been my fate and my responsibility to be commander in chief. I have lived—daily and nightly—with the cost of this war. I know the pain that it has inflicted. I know perhaps better than anyone the misgivings that it has aroused.

Throughout this entire, long period, I have been sustained by a single principle: that what we are doing now, in Vietnam, is vital not only to the security of Southeast Asia, but it is vital to the security of every American. . . .

I believe that a peaceful Asia is far nearer to reality because of what America has done in Vietnam. I believe that the men who endure the dangers of battle—fighting there for us tonight—are helping the entire world avoid far greater conflicts, far wider wars, far more destruction, than this one. . . .

Finally, my fellow Americans, let me say this: . . .

Throughout my entire public career I have followed the

personal philosophy that I am a free man, an American, a public servant and a member of my party, in that order always and only.

For thirty-seven years in the service of our nation, first as a congressman, as a senator, and as vice president and now as your president, I have put the unity of the people first. I have put it ahead of any divisive partisanship.

And in these times as in times before, it is true that a house divided against itself—by the spirit of faction, of party, of region, of religion, of race—is a house that cannot stand.

There is division in the American house now. There is divisiveness among us all tonight. And holding the trust that is mine, as president of all the people, I cannot disregard the peril to the progress of the American people and the hope and the prospect of peace for all peoples.

So, I would ask all Americans, whatever their personal interests or concern, to guard against divisiveness and all its ugly consequences.

Fifty-two months and ten days ago, in a moment of tragedy and trauma, the duties of this office fell upon me. I asked then for your help and God's, that we might continue America on its course, binding up our wounds, healing our history, moving forward in new unity, to clear the American agenda and to keep the American commitment for all of our people.

United we have kept that commitment. United we have enlarged that commitment.

Through all time to come, I think America will be a stronger nation, a more just society, and a land of greater opportunity and fulfillment because of what we have all done together in these years of unparalleled achievement.

Our reward will come in the life of freedom, peace, and hope that our children will enjoy through ages ahead.

What we won when all of our people united just must not now be lost in suspicion, distrust, selfishness, and politics among any of our people.

Believing this as I do, I have concluded that I should not

permit the presidency to become involved in the partisan divisions that are developing in this political year.

With America's sons in the fields far away, with America's future under challenge right here at home, with our hopes and the world's hopes for peace in the balance every day, I do not believe that I should devote an hour or a day of my time to any personal partisan causes or to any duties other than the awesome duties of this office—the presidency of your country.

Accordingly, I shall not seek, and I will not accept, the nomination of my party for another term as your president.

But let men everywhere know, however, that a strong, a confident, and a vigilant America stands ready tonight to seek an honorable peace—and stands ready tonight to defend an honored cause—whatever the price, whatever the burden, whatever the sacrifices that duty may require.

Thank you for listening.

Good night and God bless all of you.

RALPH NADER

—— ★ ——

The Legal Profession and Service to Society

HARVARD LAW SCHOOL, CAMBRIDGE, MASSACHUSETTS;
FEBRUARY 26, 1972

Ralph Nader's name has been virtually synonymous with consumer protection since the 1960s. Nader (1934–), a lawyer and university lecturer, wrote a ground-breaking indictment of the auto industry in 1965, Unsafe at Any Speed. *He is the founder of numerous public-interest organizations, including the Center for Responsive Law, the Center for Auto Safety, Public Citizen, the Disability Rights Center, and the Project for Corporate Responsibility. In 1972, Nader spoke to Harvard Law School students, urging them to avoid the "materialism syndrome" and generate "political and other persuasive power so that millions of dollars will start flowing into public-interest law work."*

It's much more difficult to discuss the present scene than it was three years ago, when I was here last. Then a great deal of attention was given to portraying the realities of the legal system and the injustice committed by it. A few years ago, and when I was at law school, we were full of innocence, even though what was going on was intolerable, insupportable, and often inscrutable. We don't have that innocence now. . . .

A degree of the intellectual arrogance at the Law School is based on technical competence. Some of the brightest minds in the country go through *Harvard Law Review*. They are not only bright, but they are self-disciplined in study and are confident about their futures.

I've looked into the way the *Law Review* editors and officers of the class of '58 have deployed themselves. The latest figures

255

are that out of thirty-three, four are in business, one is in government foreign service, fifteen are in law firms, nine are law professors, one is in solo practice, one is writing a book in Maine, and two are not accounted for. Is that a set of statistics subject to normative evaluation? It can be assumed that these people are doing honest work, applying their integrity, trying to improve what is being done in their organizations and firms. And we can still evaluate them the same way that we would evaluate, for example, all doctors who decide to practice in a place like Gross Points and who do a very good job by all their patients—while the rest of the country, where the people of lesser means are, do not have doctors.

In short, the evaluation of a professional role is not only internal, based on day-to-day activities, it must also take into account the far broader context—namely, how it is deployed to meet the legitimate claims upon the profession. The deployment is of course the key issue. Evaluation is no longer a description of all the grievances, evils, and injustices. The question now is not even what kind of society we must grope toward. The question is even more basic than that. It is: Are we up to it? Are we cowards, purely biological beings, who have to have two cars, split-level homes, money in the bank, and the comfort of a steady job—the kind of life whose trajectory is well known if we follow the tried steps of getting along by going along?

In many areas we know where we should go and what the problems are. We know that the Uniform Commercial Code is not all honey and milk. We know that the tax system is not all equity. We know that housing is not all in good shape. We know that the courts are among the most demonically inefficient and inaccessible as well as forbidding institutions in the country. We know the state of our mental-retardation and mental institutions, of our schools for criminal behavior, called prisons. We know the bureaucratic paralysis that comes under the mantle of government administration, the enormously varied forms of silent violence that the law has yet to recognize, especially from corporate pollution, product and job hazards, and the impact of poverty and disease. We know there is widespread hunger in this country and terrible discrimination—not just by race and sex, but by age and attractiveness, as these two value-standards are manipulated by industry, particularly Madison Avenue. We know there is discrimination against youth, that the discrimination has become institutionalized and is called adolescence. We have the most prolonged adolescence in the history of mankind. There is no other society that requires so many years to pass before people are grown up, although finally we are allowing eighteen-year-olds to vote. Adolescence is nurtured and prolonged by educational processes and by industry that has found a bonanza in embracing the adolescent population and fortifying "adolescent values." This prolongation of adolescence robs the country of the population group having the most risk takers and the highest ideals.

It is very tempting to talk about how administrative law is taught, what it leaves out, what the situations in Washington and state capitals are. We could probably even agree that the injustice, incompetence, and lack of foresight that pervade are challenges to intellectual endeavor. It is also very tempting to talk about the "solutions" that we have that we are not using—institutional and technical solutions, and legal solutions used as a catalyst for the foregoing two. . . .

These days we are told that many people deployed on a case-by-case tax-law situation don't take advantage of the leverage that is possible. But is it possible for free lawyers to overthrow the corrupt administration of a major city? That would be a nice soap opera, a nice fiction, a nice challenge to the imagination. As a matter of fact, it would also make a nice Law School examination. The problem is that we live in a very intricately meshed society, which means that we can develop a much more repercussive impact with creative litigation, lawmaking, and coalition support for such strategies than we could with less communication, transportation, and technology.

One of the most difficult things to discern is that the most boring subject at a given time can be crucial. Ten or fifteen years ago the subject of food regulation was considered a very boring subject. And it was very low on the academic totem pole. One didn't specialize in it at law school. Auto safety probably produced more yawns than any six subjects: it wasn't considered much of a challenge. . . .

Why are the most important problems so often treated in such a boring way, or so often believed to lack intellectual challenge? If you look, for example, at the written work done at the Law School a dozen years ago, you will see that the concentration was not in the areas where most people can be afflicted, affected, or helped by the legal system—areas like torts, medical-legal, urban development, housing, pollution, and industrial health and safety.

When you study labor law, exactly what do you study? Look at the textbooks and case books. What determines what gets into a case book? What you see is basically what gets appealed. Now and then there are snatches of documentary material, excerpts from articles. And so the question is: What determines what gets appealed? The answer is: What gets tried, or what gets heard. The next question is: What determines what gets tried and who gets heard? And then you start talking about power and its distribution, wealth and its distribution, access and its distribution, lawyers and their distribution. As you can see, from textbooks you get exposure to a narrow spectrum of legal material, and raw material, compared with the rest of the legal society. If you consider all the complaints—consumer, tenant, citizen complaints, etcetera—of Americans that are subject to legal resolution, you find that most Americans are shut out of the legal system. That can be statistically shown, even with very sloppy sampling methods like your memory.

Our legal system has been priced out of the reach, delayed out of the reach, politicized out of the reach and mystified out of the reach of most Americans. And of course the last is especially true in the administrative law area, where so much of the action is at the local, state, and federal agency levels.

Now it would seem that one of the principal subjects to be

studied in law school is who uses the legal system. Who can use the legal system, who wants to use the legal system, and who does not want to use the legal system—all very distinct and self-supporting studies. And I doubt whether that is being given, even in a preliminary way, and any integrated attention. . . .

It boils down to how students are going to use their time in trying to understand, create, and experience these rules—even if they have to shake the profession to its foundations or develop a completely new paralegal dimension. Now there is one problem that you have to face: that is, some of the things that need to be done are not considered to require high technical ability or experience. For instance, there are some law students on campus right now trying to develop a students' public interest research group for eastern Massachusetts, based on a student assessment or contribution, which would hire lawyers, scientists, and other professionals to work full-time for students in the social arena and be directed and controlled by students. This is an attempt to create new opportunities and could open the way for hundreds or thousands of similar jobs across the country, wherever students similarly organize. They are already organized in Oregon and Minnesota, and probably more states will come in with over a million students by next year.

That is something good happening in terms of extracurricular activities at the Law School. This kind of thing is no longer as off-limits as it was. But it does suffer, because it doesn't get the status recognition that it is marketable, and so many students don't gravitate toward it. In short, there is a very sensitive weighing of how students use their time in law school, in terms of what will pay off and what won't. I suppose that one of the most difficult problems to face is what people are willing to sacrifice, what totems to question and what taboos to jettison. I use the word *sacrifice*, but not in its historical sense. Historically, *sacrifice* had a more critical meaning—people died, were injured, thrown out of their professions, jailed, exiled.

Sacrifice today is that of time, and quite frankly, fewer people are willing to engage in it. In fact, the changes in recent years which have stimulated students about public interest work are the following: civil rights; the draft; riots—most law students are not unlike most members of the bar: they are luminated by student fires rather than by the light of their own intellect; the Vietnam War, not only because of the draft, which affected many students, but also because it is a form of violence that law students, like many other people, understand—that is, raw physical violence, not hunger, brain damage, lead poisoning, pollution—not the silent forms of violence that take so long to prevent.

Why does the Law School graduate go into one field and not another? The questions he might ask are: Is it an intellectual challenge? Does it pay? Is it a normative challenge? Does it provide creative outlet, independence of action? And the answers for the public interest area are all yes with the exception of pay. And what does that boil down to? The materialism syndrome, and that's what it is all about. To what small degree are law graduates willing to sacrifice their material standard of living? The model and year of car, the type of apartment or house, clothes and food, the conspicuous consumption. Ah, the debts, the Law School debts, the strongest argument yet: the way the projections are now, it seems that students will get out of law school with such enormous debts that their risktaking ability will be crippled even further.

One response to that is that you have to begin generating political and other persuasive power so that millions of dollars will start flowing into public interest law work. It is one step to develop student groups, and it *is* a step, but as long as the oil industry gets billions a year out of the government's tax and quota policies and the defense industry many times as much in its inimitable way, as long as subsidies and loopholes flow out into the billions for support of commercial activities, it hardly strains reason to demand a very significant diversion into this area—far, far greater than the OEO budget and neighborhood legal services. If $150 million goes into just one nuclear sub, what is the response to deep-poverty children—that there is only money to defend their misery? Where is their legal right to counsel that will obtain food, health, safety, and a future?

And we have to provide them, and the best way to start on this long road is a small step. The disillusionment, disappointment, and dropping out on the part of some students today is often because of their eagerness to take big fast steps and being told that they can only take small steps. So they don't take any steps. If you can't take big steps you have to take small steps. There is now a necessary modesty to horizons in the public interest area that lays the groundwork for more expensive justice in the future. . . .

There is great merit in breaking down the homogeneity of law students and faculty, not just by encouraging diverse backgrounds, but also by having other people participate who have nothing to do with law. It would be broadening and prodding for law students if the labor unions sent fifty or sixty on-the-line workers to spend a semester at the Law School, and if that kind of residence were established, a host of other occupations could be included. I suspect that if fifteen or twenty farmers had spent a semester at the Law School fifteen years ago, something quite different would be reflected in textbooks and scholarship today. Because very often we can't empathize, we can't project and we can't reduce the agony and the pain to classroom recognition. We can only remotely observe or hear about them, and coming from a law school that used to consider going down to Harvard Square as a trip abroad, coming from a law school that has tunnels linking its buildings underground so that you never have to see the sky, this isolation is a very, very serious and myopic deprivation of the mind.

One doesn't have to want to operate a lathe, serve in a hospital or a restaurant, go down in a coal mine, work deep in the bowels of the federal bureaucracy, or in corporate management, to appreciate that that is where the problems for the law come from. You should never mistake desire with relevance. We can refuse to have anything to do with these kinds of experiences, but that doesn't mean that they are not relevant to us, that they shouldn't provide the wellspring, the insight, the motivation for our chosen profession in redirecting itself in the great catalytic role that it is so important for it to play.

We don't have to be egocentric about the law to believe that it is the primordial profession in the country. There is no other profession where it is acceptable to be a generalist, to deal with a wide range of facts, institutions, and roles, and where it is acceptable to go into other occupations. There is no other profession that deals so intimately with the accumulation, distribution, and defense of power, that draws in the other professions in the formation of public policy, conflict resolution, planning, etcetera. This is a very important profession, not to be demeaned by styles, rigorous trivia, semantic diversions, lack of courage, or lack of sacrifice.

I ask you to look at the official heroes in the Harvard Law School pantheon. How many of them sacrificed? How many of them endured the abrasions and the assaults of an unforgiving or an un-understanding society. How many of them were offensive attorneys for justice? How many of them developed institutions that lasted and that filled brave new roles and needs? How many of them were really pioneers—including the best of them, with their exquisite analytic minds and their great judicial decisions? Those who tried or those who did pioneer are likely to be forgotten.

There is a real world out there starving, starving for this kind of lawyer redeployment. In many ways there is no way to complete these observations; it has to become self-analysis. It really is a personal decision.

But I leave you with this one concluding thought. If there were no marker, determinants—if, no matter what you chose to work on at Law School and afterward, there were only one salary level, what would you do? How would you design a new law school? How would you design your own career? How would you change your thinking and your habits? If you will just go through that exercise and develop this hypothetical model, then you can step back from it and begin asking the questions why, where, and how you should and can redefine your careers. There are too many capable youths who preceded you here who should have been what they might have been if they could have been. Your resolve can avoid that duplication of comparatively wasted human resources.

BELLA ABZUG

—— ★ ——

A New Kind of Southern Strategy

SOUTHERN WOMEN'S CONFERENCE ON EDUCATION FOR
DELEGATE SELECTION, SCARRITT COLLEGE,
NASHVILLE, TENNESSEE; FEBRUARY 12, 1972

The women's movement in the United States was reborn in the 1960s, emerging from the general climate of protests and civil rights agitation. In 1963 Betty Friedan's book The Feminine Mystique *was published, and the National Organization for Women was formed in 1966. Bella Abzug (1920–   ) served as a lawyer for the American Civil Liberties Union, was active in the peace movement, and was an organizer of the National Women's Political Caucus. A U.S. representative from New York in the 1970s, she spoke to a Nashville conference of mostly Democratic party women on "a political strategy for women who have been shut out of power."*

As cochairwoman of the National Women's Political Caucus, I welcome you to the women's political power movement.

I am not an authority on the South, but I suspect that this is the first time a conference such as this has ever been held here. You are making history today.

You are creating a new kind of "Southern strategy" for 1972
. . . a political strategy for women who have been shut out of
power and who are determined that this is the year to win full
citizenship and participation in political decision making for the
women of the South—white and black.

As you come together here to study the techniques of electoral politics, you are part of a nationwide movement. You are
doing what women all across the country are doing, and I
predict that the male politicians are in for some real surprises in
this election year. Reports are coming in of women turning out
in unexpectedly large numbers at political meetings—not just
the big rallies, but the small precinct meetings where the political process starts. And I hear that the women are asking sharp
questions of the candidates and they're not satisfied with plat-
itudes or with having their babies kissed.

I think we can take some credit for that. We've been doing
a lot of political consciousness raising. Since the National
Women's Political Caucus was organized in Washington last
July, women have organized caucuses in more than forty
states. . . .

Our women are as diverse as America itself, as diverse as
you who have come here today. Women who are young and old,
rich and poor, white, black, Chicanas, Puerto Ricans and Indians, women who come from all parties and no parties, women
who are in the United States Congress and women who have
never held office.

Your presence here indicates the conscious unity that binds
you together with thousands of women across the country and
the sense of common wrongs and injustices that exists among
millions of women, whether they work in universities, factories,
offices or in the home.

We are women with many different life-styles. Television
and the other media which thrive on the offbeat and the sensational have tried to depict the women's liberation movement as
an assembly of bra-burning, neurotic, man-hating exhibition-
ists. Don't let them fool you.

I have been to hundreds of women's meetings and I have yet to see a bra burned. But I have met and talked to women who were burning with indignation at the wastefulness and stupidity of a society that makes second-class citizens of half its population.

Women, in fact, are 53 percent of the electorate. Yet throughout our history and now, more than a half-century after we won the vote, women are still almost invisible in government, in elected posts, in high administrative decision-making positions, in the judiciary.

We are determined to change that. And we intend to do it by organizing ourselves and by reaching out to women everywhere. . . .

Wherever I go, and I have traveled a great deal in the past year, I have found a strong community of interest among huge numbers of American women, a strong commitment to changing the direction of our society.

Women are in the forefront of the peace movement, the civil rights and equal rights movements, the environment and consumer movements, the child care movement. This is part of your tradition too. It was Southern ladies who organized the Committee to Stop Lynching here in the South many years ago, and it was a woman who sat in the front of a bus in Montgomery, Alabama, and made history. . . .

I believe that shutting women out of political power and decision-making roles has resulted in a terrible mutilation of our society. It is at least partly responsible for our present crisis of lopsided priorities and distorted values. It is responsible too for the masculine mystique, the obsession with militarism that has made the nuclear missile the symbol of American power and that equates our national honor with continuing the senseless killing in Indochina, continuing a war which American women —in even larger numbers than men—say must be ended.

As you know, some of the most powerful men in the House are from the South. They hold the leadership posts. They head the most important committees—Armed Services, Appropriations, Ways and Means, and others. They are the ones who decide whether we are to build more bombs or more schools. They are there because of the seniority system and because they are reelected year after year without any significant opposition. Women help elect these men, and then men use their power to deny women their most basic needs.

I hope that this is the year when some of you women will begin to challenge these men and put them on notice that they don't have a lifetime hold on those congressional seats. . . .

I would suggest that women are greater authorities on family life than is the president. It is they who bear the children and raise them, many as heads of the family. It is they who work as waitresses, secretaries, hospital aides, factory hands, and in the fields. And it is they who come home and have to clean and cook and care for their children and worry about getting baby-sitters when they go to work the next day or night.

If we had more of these real experts in Congress, they would not let the president get away with pious invocations of a nonreal world. They would insist that instead of raising our military budget to $80 billion, as the president proposes, that we allocate money for child care centers, for training programs and more educational opportunities for women, for basic human needs. . . .

I am not elevating women to sainthood, nor am I suggesting that all women share the same views, or that all women are good and all men are bad. But I do believe that because they have been excluded from political power for so long, they see with more clairvoyant eyes the deficiencies of our society. Their work in the voluntary organizations has made them the compassionate defenders of the victims of our distorted priorities. They know intimately the problems of the aged and the sick, of the neglected, miseducated child, the young soldiers returning home wounded in body or spirit.

There are only eleven of us women in the House. Some of us are Democrats, some Republicans, some liberals and some conservatives. But all of us supported the Mansfield Amendment, which requires all American troops to be withdrawn from

Indochina within six months. I find that very significant and an encouraging omen of things to come.

What is to come? Is this the year when women's political power will come of age? Or are we just going to make noise but no real progress?

I believe that in the seven months of our existence, the National Women's Political Caucus has already achieved a great deal. . . .

As standards for reasonable representation at the conventions, the women's caucus has voted that each state delegation should be comprised of no less than 50 percent women. It has also voted that racial minorities and young people should be present in each delegation in percentages at least as great as their percentage of the total state population.

We have set up task forces within the caucus to meet with representatives of the Republican and Democratic parties to press the issue of representation. Our task force of Republican women is following up on this pledge. . . .

As for the Democratic party, it has a specific commitment to honor the guidelines of the McGovern-Fraser party reform commission, which would ensure reasonable representation at the convention of women, youth, and minorities. . . .

We intend to hold the Democratic party leadership to that commitment. We are now engaged in a national effort to ensure that at least half of the delegates are women, and we are prepared to challenge the credentials of delegations that are not representative. . . .

We want a party and a platform committed to working for a peaceful and humane society that meets the needs of all its people. And to make sure that this comes to pass, we want guarantees that women share equally in committee posts in the party and at the convention.

We want guarantees from the nominee, whoever he or she may be, that women will have an equal share in government —an equal number of Cabinet posts and high administrative offices. And we want an end to the exclusion of women from the

Supreme Court and their almost total exclusion from the lower courts. . . .

We will have more women running this year for local office, for the state legislature, for Congress. Some will run for the experience, and some will run to win. Some are already running. I have been getting phone calls from around the country. A woman is running for governor of Texas. Black women are running for Congress from Texas and California, and there are others who are planning to do so or who have already announced. At some point we're going to get all our women candidates together and introduce them to the nation. . . .

Representatives of young people with a potential strength of twenty-five million new voters met in Chicago recently to organize a Youth Caucus, and they are now setting up caucuses in all the states. The black caucus is well-organized, and other minority groups are also joining together to make their political power count.

I believe that with the organization of these groups we have the components of a New Majority, a majority of women, young people, minority groups, and other Americans—small businessmen, working people, farmers, poor people—who share in our concerns and needs.

Working together, this New Majority has the capacity to change America, to lead us away from war and to work together instead for a society in which human needs are paramount, in which all people—men and women—who can work will have meaningful employment, in which women will have full citizenship and dignity as individuals, in which our children can learn and live free from the atmosphere of hatred and violence that has despoiled our land for so many years.

These are goals to which I believe most women will respond. What you do here this weekend at this historic first political meeting of Southern womanpower will help create that kind of America.

Henry Kissinger

—— ★ ——

Statement to the Senate
Foreign Relations Committee

U.S. Senate, Washington, D.C.;
September 7, 1973

Born in Germany, Henry Kissinger (1923–   ) became a U.S. citizen in 1943 and received a doctorate from Harvard eleven years later. He taught government at Harvard from 1957 to 1969, and during this time he served as a consultant to Presidents Eisenhower, Kennedy, and Johnson. He was President Nixon's national security advisor, presiding over such important events in foreign affairs as the normalization of relations with the People's Republic of China, detente with the Soviet Union, and the ending of the Vietnam War. He received the Nobel Peace Prize in 1973, the year he was appointed and confirmed as secretary of state.

M r. Chairman, and Distinguished Members of the Senate Foreign Relations Committee: After talking to the chairman and most members of the committee, I have the impression that your purposes would best be served if we moved quickly to your questions. Therefore, I shall confine my opening remarks to a statement outlining the attitude I propose to bring to the office of secretary of state if the committee and Senate should confirm my nomination. I take this approach, moreover, because the close and cooperative relationship that we shall seek between the executive and the legislative branches in foreign affairs depends ultimately on the spirit with which it is implemented. . . .

Mr. Chairman, we have come to experience in recent years that peace at home and peace abroad are closely related. How well we perform in foreign policy depends importantly on how purposeful we are at home. America has passed through a decade of domestic turbulence which has deepened divisions and even shaken our national self-confidence in some measure. At the same time, profound changes have occurred in the world around us, a generation after World War II. Our era is marked by both the anxieties of a transitional period and the opportunities of fresh creation.

These challenges, though they appear as practical issues, cannot be solved in technical terms; they closely reflect our view of ourselves. They require a sense of identity and purpose as much as a sense of policy. Throughout our history we have thought of what we did as growing out of deeper moral values. America was not true to itself unless it had a meaning beyond itself. In this spiritual sense, America was never isolationist.

This must remain our attitude.

This is why our international policies must enlist the contributions of our best people regardless of political persuasion. Our task is to define—together—the contours of a new world and to shape America's contribution to it. Our foreign policy cannot be effective if it reflects only the sporadic and esoteric initiatives of a small group of specialists. It must rest on a broad national base and reflect a shared community of values.

With good will on all sides, I deeply believe we can reach this goal. There is no dispute about many of the fundamental objectives of national policy. We are at a crucial point of transition in the international order, with major changes in the global structure promising a more peaceful world.

Successful postwar policies have helped our friends to new strength and responsibilities. We shall work constructively and openly with our partners in Europe and Japan to give new impetus to associations based on shared purposes and ideals. We shall always remember that the vitality of our friendships is the necessary condition for the lowering of tensions with our opponents.

We have developed fresh relationships with adversaries that

can ease us away from confrontation toward cooperation. Tensions have been reduced in many areas. For the first time since the end of World War II, all great nations have become full participants in the international system. There is the hope that the arms race can be arrested and the burden of armaments reduced.

Our most anguishing and divisive problem, the Vietnam War, is behind us. We achieved a negotiated settlement last January. The Congress has since expressed its view on how to terminate our military participation in the last area of conflict—Cambodia. As you gentlemen know, the administration differs with that view. But it will not attempt to circumvent it.

We face unprecedented issues, which transcend borders and ideologies and beckon global cooperation. Many traditional assumptions need adjustment. We have viewed ourselves as blessed with unlimited agricultural surpluses; today we must contemplate scarcity in relation to world needs. We have assumed self-sufficiency in energy; now we face increasing needs for external supply at least for an interim period. Environmental problems used to be considered national issues, if they were considered at all; now many must be met internationally if they are going to be met at all. We need to explore new conceptual frontiers to reflect the new reality produced by both technology and human aspirations: that our planet has become a truly global society.

This administration will continue to adapt America's role to these new conditions. But we cannot take for granted what has been begun. We cannot let irretrievable opportunities slip from our grasp. Just as we have benefited from the efforts of our predecessors, so must we build for our successors. What matters to other countries—and to the world—is not so much the work of one administration as the steadiness of America. So the nation is challenged to render our purposes durable and our performance reliable. This we achieved during most of a generation after the Second World War. We need to continue to do so. . . .

As you know, the president has asked me to retain my position as assistant to the president if I am confirmed as secretary of state. I believe this will benefit the coherence and effectiveness of our foreign policy. The secretary of state will be clearly the principal foreign policy adviser to the president. The locus of authority and the chain of authority will be unambiguous. Bureaucratic friction will be minimized. As the president said in announcing my appointment, the unity of position will underline the traditional principal role of the Department of State in the policy-making process.

There must be, as well, a closer relationship between the executive and legislative branches. It is the president's objective to make policy more accessible to the scrutiny and the views of the Congress. This is the fundamental answer to the question of executive privilege. As you gentlemen know, over an extended period of time when I was fully covered by this principle, I met regularly with the members of this committee, both individually and as a group, and most frequently with the chairman.

In my new capacity, I shall be prepared to testify formally on all my activities. In other words, I shall testify with respect to all matters traditionally covered by secretaries of state and on my duties as assistant to the president concerning interdepartmental issues. I will not claim executive privilege in either capacity except for the one area customarily invoked by Cabinet officers, that is, direct communications with the president or the actual deliberations of the National Security Council. . . .

This process of greater cooperation will not be confined to formal testimony. If confirmed, I will propose to meet immediately with the chairman and the ranking member to work out procedures for enabling the committee to share more fully in the design of our foreign policy. . . .

If our foreign policy is to be truly national, we must deepen our partnership with the American people. This means an open articulation of our philosophy, our purposes, and our actions. We have sought to do this in the president's annual reports to the Congress on foreign policy. Equally, we must listen to the hopes and aspirations of our fellow countrymen. I plan, therefore, on a regular basis, to elicit the views of America's opinion leaders and to share our perspectives freely. . . .

Americans have recently endured the turmoil of assassinations and riots, racial and generational confrontations, and a bitter, costly war. Just as we were emerging from that conflict, we were plunged into still another ordeal.

These traumatic events have cast lengthening shadows on our traditional optimism and self-esteem. A loss of confidence in our own country would inevitably be mirrored in our international relations. Where once we ran the risk of thinking we were too good for the world, we might now swing to believing we are not good enough. Where once a soaring optimism tempted us to dare too much, a shrinking spirit could lead us to attempt too little. Such an attitude—and the foreign policy it would produce—would deal a savage blow to global stability.

But I am hopeful about our prospects. America is resilient. The dynamism of this country is irrepressible. Whatever our divisions, we can rally to the prospects of building a world at peace and responsive to humane aspirations. In so doing, we can replenish our reservoir of faith.

This is our common challenge:

To distinguish the fundamental from the ephemeral.

To seek out what unites us, without stifling the healthy debate that is the lifeblood of democracy.

To promote the positive trends that are the achievements not just of this administration but also of those who came before.

To shape new initiatives that will serve not just the next forty months but also the decades to follow.

A few years before he died, one of our most distinguished secretaries of state, Dean Acheson, entitled his memoirs *Present at the Creation.* He chose that title because he was one of the leading participants in the creation of the postwar international system. The challenge before our country now is whether our generation has the vision—as Dean Acheson's did more than two decades ago—to turn into dynamic reality the hopeful beginnings we have made toward a more durable peace and a more benevolent planet.

Mr. Chairman and gentlemen of the committee, I am confident that working together we can speed the day when all of us will be able to say that we were "present at the creation" of a new era of peace, justice, and humanity.

Thank you.

MARGARET MEAD

——— ★ ———

The Planetary Crisis and the Challenge to Scientists

ANNUAL MEETING OF THE NEW YORK ACADEMY OF
SCIENCES, AMERICAN MUSEUM OF NATURAL HISTORY,
NEW YORK, NEW YORK; DECEMBER 6, 1973

Perhaps the best-known anthropologist of her day, Margaret Mead (1901–1978) began her long association with the American Museum of Natural History in New York in 1926 and with Columbia University in 1954. She served in an executive capacity with numerous scientific organizations, including the American Anthropological Association, the New York Academy of Sciences, and the American Association for the Advancement of Science. Her writings reflect her series of expeditions, from the 1930s onward, to New Guinea and Bali. In her 1973 speech to the New York Academy of Sciences, Mead addressed the growing energy crisis and called for "a transformed life-style which will be as different from our present wasteful, shortsighted, reckless use of the earth's treasures as the present twentieth-century world is from the agrarian world of the past."

The energy crunch, which is being felt around the world —in Japan, in Europe, in the United States—has dramatized for us a worldwide situation and a worldwide opportunity to take stock of how the reckless despoiling of the earth's resources—here in America and all over the world—has brought the whole world to the brink of disaster. It also provides the United States, its citizens, its government, its scientists, and its leaders of business and labor with a magnificent opportunity to initiate a transformation in our present way of life.

Our present way of life was conceived in a spirit of progress, in an attempt to improve the standard of living of all Americans through the increasing capability of technological development to bring previously undreamed-of amenities within reach of the common man. But this search for a better life has—especially since World War II—taken a form which is untenable and which this planet cannot support. The overdevelopment of motor transport, with its spiral of more cars, more cement highways, more pollution, more suburbs, more commuting, has contributed to the near destruction of our great cities, the disintegration of the family, the isolation of the old, the young, and the poor, and the pollution not only of local air, but also of the earth's atmosphere. Our terribly wasteful use of electricity and of nonrenewable resources are likewise endangering our rivers, our oceans, and the atmosphere which protects the planet.

The realization that a drastic transformation is needed has steadily increased. But the problem has been how to turn around? How to alter our dependence on motor transport? How to persuade the individual citizen enmeshed in a system in which he and his wife and children are imprisoned without one car, two cars, three cars, that change is possible? How to stop building enormous, uneconomical buildings which waste electricity night and day, all year long?

Even though the present rate of development of energy use and resource use is only some twenty-five years old, it has been so much taken for granted in the industrialized countries that it has seemed almost impossible to turn around short of some major catastrophe, some catastrophe which would destroy millions of lives.

The catastrophe has now arrived, not in the form of the death of millions in an inversion over a large city, but in the energy crunch. . . . The crisis is here and some kind of crisis activities will be undertaken. Some measures have been taken. More are underway. But we have the opportunity to use the crisis to transform our own economy, to take the lead in a transformation which is needed right around the world, to aim not for a shallow independence but for a genuine responsibility. We must not be content with half-measures, with small, mean palliatives, following the administration's assurance that all that is needed is fewer Sunday drives to visit mother-in-law and lowered lights on Christmas trees—to be followed very soon by a return to normal waste and pollution. We must not return to complacency over a situation in which our major nutritional disease is *over*nutrition, while millions of Americans are on the verge of starvation and while we are only 6 percent of the world's population, we are using 30 percent of available energy resources. The crisis can and must be used constructively.

During the inevitable disorganization of everyday life, business, industry, and education, we will be taking stands, making decisions, learning new habits and new ways of looking at things, and initiating new research into alternative technologies in transportation, agriculture, architecture, and town planning. It is vital that these activities move us forward into a new era, in which the entire nation is involved in a search for a new standard of living, a new quality of life, based on conservation not waste, on protection not destruction, on human values rather than built-in obsolescence and waste.

As scientists who know the importance of accurate information, we can press immediately for the establishment of an enquiry with subpoena power to ascertain from the energy industries the exact state of supplies and reserves in this country. As scientists, concerned with direction of research and the application of scientific knowledge to a technology devoted to human ends, we can press for a massive project on alternative and environmentally safe forms of energy—solar energy, fusion, other forms. Such a project should be as ambitious as the Manhattan Project or NASA, but there would be no need for secrecy. It would be aimed not at destroying or outdistancing other countries, but at ways of conserving our resources in new technologies which would themselves provide new activities for those industries whose present prosperity is based on oil and motor transport and energy-wasting, expensive synthetic materials.

Those of us who are social scientists have a special responsibility for the relationship between measures that are to be taken and the way in which the American people and American institutions will respond. For example, we have abundant information on the responses of Americans to rationing during World War II. If there is to be gasoline rationing, we have to consider the importance of built-in flexibility and choice. In the United States, a rationing system will only be experienced as fair and just if it discriminates among the needs of different users; recognizes that workers have to get to work, that many people work on Sundays, that different regions of the country will need different measures. Without rationing, we will set one set of users against another, one part of the country against another, encouraging such narrowly partisan measures as severance taxes through which oil-rich states will benefit at the expense of the residents of oil-less states. Rationing is a way of making the situation genuinely national, involving each American in the fate of all Americans.

But while some form of rationing or allotment—or the same procedure by some other name—will be necessary, it will be important to consider that the American people have experienced rationing only as a temporary measure in wartime or as an abhorrent practice of totalitarian countries. There will be danger that rationing may simply accentuate the desire to get back to normal again, with "normal" defined as where we were when the shortage hit us. What we need to do is to define all measures taken not as temporary but as *transitional* to a saner, safer, more human life-style. How can we make the present period into a period of tooling up for smaller cars, rapid research, and preparation for entirely new forms of transportation, of utilities, of energy generators? Such mechanisms can be found. In the past, war, revolution, and depressions have provided the dire circumstances within which society's technologies and social institutions have been transformed.

Our present situation is unlike war, revolution, or depression. It is also unlike the great natural catastrophes of the past—famine, earthquake, and plague. Wars are won or lost, revolutions succeed or fail, depressions grind to an end, famine and plagues are over after millions have died. A country rebuilds, too often in the same spot, after an earthquake. The situation we are in is profoundly different. An interdependent, planetary, man-made system of resource exploitation and energy use has brought us to a state where long-range planning is crucial. What we need is not a return to our present parlous state, which endangers the future of our country, our children, and our earth, but a movement forward to a new norm—so that the developed and the developing countries will be able to help each other. The developing countries have less obsolescence, fewer entrenched nineteenth-century industrial forms to overcome; the developed countries have the scientists and the technologists to work rapidly and effectively on planetary problems.

This country has been reeling under the continuing exposures of loss of moral integrity and the revelation that ubiquitous lawbreaking, in which unenforceable laws involve every citizen, has now reached into the highest places in the land. There is a strong demand for moral reinvigoration and for some commitment that is vast enough and yet personal enough to enlist the loyalty of all. In the past it has been only in a war in defense of their own country and their own ideals that any people have been able to invoke total commitment—and then it has always been on behalf of one group against another.

This is the first time in history that the American people have been asked to defend themselves and everything that we hold dear in cooperation with all the other inhabitants of this planet, who share with us the same endangered air and the same endangered oceans. This time there is no enemy. There is only a common need to reassess our present course, to change that course and to devise new methods through which the whole world can survive. This is a priceless opportunity.

To grasp it, we need a widespread understanding of the nature of the crisis confronting us—and the world—a crisis that is no passing inconvenience, no byproduct of the ambitions of the oil-producing countries, no figment of environmentalists' fears, no byproduct of any present system of government— whether free enterprise, socialist, or communist, or any mixture thereof. What we face is the outcome of the inventions of the last four hundred years. What we need is a transformed life-style which will be as different from our present wasteful, short-sighted, reckless use of the earth's treasures as the present twentieth-century world is from the agrarian world of the past. This new life-style can flow directly from the efforts of science and the capabilities of technology, but its acceptance depends on an overriding citizen commitment to a higher quality of life for the world's children and future generations on our planet.

BARBARA JORDAN

———— ★ ————

On the Impeachment of
the President

HEARINGS ON ARTICLES OF IMPEACHMENT BY
THE COMMITTEE ON THE JUDICIARY OF
THE HOUSE OF REPRESENTATIVES,
WASHINGTON, D.C.; JULY 26, 1974

*As a lawyer and Texas legislator, Barbara Jordan (1936–   )
rose to prominence within the Democratic party with her election as U.S. representative from Texas in 1974 and by virtue of
her eloquence as a public speaker. On July 26, 1974, she spoke
in favor of the impeachment of President Richard Nixon, whose
administration had labored under the cloud of the Watergate
scandal since June 1972. She reasoned that "the president has
engaged in a series of public statements and actions designed to
thwart the lawful investigation by government prosecutors . . .
[and] has made public announcements and assertions . . . which
the evidence will show he knew to be false."*

E arlier today we heard the beginning of the Preamble to the
Constitution of the United States, "We, the people." It is a
very eloquent beginning. But when that document was completed on the seventeenth of September in 1787 I was not included in that "We, the people." I felt somehow for many years
that George Washington and Alexander Hamilton just left me
out by mistake. But through the process of amendment, interpretation, and court decision I have finally been included in
"We, the people."

Today, I am an inquisitor; I believe hyperbole would not be
fictional and would not overstate the solemnness that I feel right
now. My faith in the Constitution is whole, it is complete, it is

total. I am not going to sit here and be an idle spectator to the diminution, the subversion, the destruction of the Constitution.

"Who can so properly be the inquisitors for the nation as the representatives of the nation themselves?"—*The Federalist,* number 65. The subject of its jurisdiction are those offenses which proceed from the misconduct of public men. That is what we are talking about. In other words, the jurisdiction comes from the abuse or violation of some public trust. It is wrong, I suggest, it is a misreading of the Constitution for any member here to assert that for a member to vote for an article of impeachment means that that member must be convinced that the president should be removed from office. The Constitution doesn't say that. The powers relating to impeachment are an essential check in the hands of this body, the legislature, against and upon the encroachment of the executive. In establishing the division between the two branches of the legislature, the House and the Senate, assigning to the one the right to accuse and to the other the right to judge, the framers of this Constitution were very astute. They did not make the accusers and the judges the same person.

We know the nature of impeachment. We have been talking about it awhile now. "It is chiefly designed for the president and his high ministers" to somehow be called into account. It is designed to "bridle" the executive if he engages in excesses. "It is designed as a method of national inquest into the conduct of public men"—Hamilton, *The Federalist,* number 65. The framers confined in the Congress the power, if need be, to remove the president in order to strike a delicate balance between a president swollen with power and grown tyrannical and preservation of the independence of the executive. The nature of impeachment is a narrowly channeled exception to the separation of powers maxim—the federal convention of 1787 said that. It limited impeachment to high crimes and misdemeanors and discounted and opposed the term "maladministration." "It is to be used only for great misdemeanors," so it was said in the North Carolina ratification convention. And in the Virginia ratification convention: "We do not trust our liberty to a particular branch. We need one branch to check the others."

The North Carolina ratification convention: "No one need be afraid that officers who commit oppression will pass with immunity."

"Prosecutions of impeachments will seldom fail to agitate the passions of the whole community," said Hamilton in *The Federalist,* number 65. "And to divide it into parties more or less friendly or inimical to the accused." I do not mean political parties in that sense.

The drawing of political lines goes to the motivation behind impeachment; but impeachment must proceed within the confines of the constitutional term "high crime and misdemeanors."

Of the impeachment process, it was Woodrow Wilson who said that "nothing short of the grossest offenses against the plain law of the land will suffice to give them speed and effectiveness. Indignation so great as to overgrow party interest may secure a conviction; but nothing else can."

Common sense would be revolted if we engaged upon this process for petty reasons. Congress has a lot to do. Appropriations, tax reform, health insurance, campaign finance reform, housing, environmental protection, energy sufficiency, mass transportation. Pettiness cannot be allowed to stand in the face of such overwhelming problems. So today we are not being petty. We are trying to be big because the task we have before us is a big one.

This morning in a discussion of the evidence we were told that the evidence which purports to support the allegations of misuse of the CIA by the president is thin. We are told that that evidence is insufficient. What that recital of the evidence this morning did not include is what the president did know on June 23, 1972. The president did know that it was Republican money, that it was money from the Committee for the Reelection of the President, which was found in the possession of one of the burglars arrested on June 17.

What the president did know on June 23 was the prior activities of E. Howard Hunt, which included his participation in the break-in of Daniel Ellsberg's psychiatrist, which included Howard Hunt's participation in the Dita Beard ITT affair, which included Howard Hunt's fabrication of cables designed to discredit the Kennedy administration.

We were further cautioned today that perhaps these proceedings ought to be delayed because certainly there would be new evidence forthcoming from the president of the United States. There has not even been an obfuscated indication that this committee would receive any additional materials from the president. The committee subpoena is outstanding and if the president wants to supply that material, the committee sits here.

The fact is that on yesterday, the American people waited with great anxiety for eight hours, not knowing whether their president would obey an order of the Supreme Court of the United States.

At this point I would like to juxtapose a few of the impeachment criteria with some of the president's actions.

Impeachment criteria, James Madison, from the Virginia ratification convention: "If the president be connected in any suspicious manner with any person and there be grounds to believe that he will shelter him, he may be impeached."

We have heard time and time again that the evidence reflects payment to the defendants of money. The president had knowledge that these funds were being paid and that these were funds collected for the 1972 presidential campaign.

We know that the president met with Mr. Henry Petersen twenty-seven times to discuss matters related to Watergate and immediately thereafter met with the very persons who were implicated in the information. Mr. Petersen was receiving and transmitting to the president. The words are: "If the president be connected in any suspicious manner with any person and there be grounds to believe that he will shelter that person, he may be impeached."

Justice Story: "Impeachment is intended for occasional and

extraordinary cases where a superior power acting for the whole people is put into operation to protect their rights and rescue their liberties from violations."

We know about the Huston plan. We know about the break-in of the psychiatrist's office. We know that there was absolute complete direction in August 1971 when the president instructed Ehrlichman to "do whatever is necessary." This instruction led to a surreptitious entry into Dr. Fielding's office.

"Protect their rights." "Rescue their liberties from violation."

The South Carolina ratification convention impeachment criteria: Those are impeachable "who behave amiss or betray their public trust."

Beginning shortly after the Watergate break-in and continuing to the present time the president has engaged in a series of public statements and actions designed to thwart the lawful investigation by government prosecutors. Moreover, the president has made public announcements and assertions bearing on the Watergate case which the evidence will show he knew to be false.

These assertions, false assertions, impeachable, those who misbehave—those who "behave amiss or betray their public trust."

James Madison again at the constitutional convention: "A president is impeachable if he attempts to subvert the Constitution."

The Constitution charges the president with the task of taking care that the laws be faithfully executed, and yet the president has counseled his aides to commit perjury, willfully disregarded the secrecy of grand jury proceedings, concealed surreptitious entry, attempted to compromise a federal judge while publicly displaying his cooperation with the processes of criminal justice.

"A president is impeachable if he attempts to subvert the Constitution."

If the impeachment provision in the Constitution of the

United States will not reach the offenses charged here, then perhaps that eighteenth-century Constitution should be abandoned to a twentieth-century paper shredder. Has the president committed offenses and planned and directed and acquiesced in a course of conduct which the Constitution will not tolerate? That is the question. We know that. We know the question. We should now forthwith proceed to answer the question. It is reason, and not passion, which must guide our deliberations, guide our debate, and guide our decision.

Richard M. Nixon

— ★ —

Resignation Speech

BROADCAST ADDRESS TO THE NATION;
AUGUST 8, 1974

---

*Richard Nixon's political career, from his election to the U.S.
House of Representatives in 1946 to his resignation from the
presidency in 1974, was filled with triumphs, defeats, and come-
backs. He was Eisenhower's vice president for two terms but was
almost forced to resign for accepting questionable contributions.
In the presidential election of 1960, Kennedy narrowly defeated
him, and he lost again when he ran for California governor in 1962.
Nixon (1913–   ), returning as the Republican candidate for
president in 1968, promised "peace with honor" in the Vietnam
conflict and defeated Democrat Hubert Humphrey. In the midst of
his campaign for reelection—which he won by a landslide in
1972—five burglars were caught bugging Democratic party headquarters in the Watergate building. The 1973 trial of the burglars
revealed a conspiracy to conceal the administration's involvement,
and during the coming months resignations, charges of coverup,
and revelations of tapes tampered with or withheld were continuing occurrences. In late July 1974, the House Judiciary Committee voted three articles of impeachment. On August 8, Nixon
addressed the nation for the last time as president.*

Good evening. This is the thirty-seventh time I have spoken
to you from this office in which so many decisions have
been made that shape the history of this nation.

Each time I have done so to discuss with you some matters
that I believe affected the national interest. And all the decisions
I have made in my public life I have always tried to do what was
best for the nation.

Throughout the long and difficult period of Watergate, I
have felt it was my duty to persevere, to make every possible

effort to complete the term of office to which you elected me. In the past few days, however, it has become evident to me that I no longer have a strong enough political base in the Congress to justify continuing that effort.

As long as there was such a base, I felt strongly that it was necessary to see the constitutional process through to its conclusion; that to do otherwise would be unfaithful to the spirit of that deliberately difficult process, and a dangerously destabilizing precedent for the future. But with the disappearance of that base, I now believe that the constitutional purpose has been served. And there is no longer a need for the process to be prolonged.

I would have preferred to carry through to the finish whatever the personal agony it would have involved, and my family unanimously urged me to do so. But the interests of the nation must always come before any personal considerations. From the discussions I have had with congressional and other leaders I have concluded that because of the Watergate matter I might not have the support of the Congress that I would consider necessary to back the very difficult decisions and carry out the duties of this office in the way the interests of the nation will require.

I have never been a quitter. To leave office before my term is completed is opposed to every instinct in my body. But as president I must put the interests of America first.

America needs a full-time president and a full-time Congress, particularly at this time with problems we face at home and abroad. To continue to fight through the months ahead for my personal vindication would almost totally absorb the time and attention of both the president and the Congress in a period when our entire focus should be on the great issues of peace abroad and prosperity without inflation at home.

Therefore, I shall resign the presidency effective at noon tomorrow.

Vice President Ford will be sworn in as president at that hour in this office.

As I recall the high hopes for America with which we began this second term, I feel a great sadness that I will not be here in this office working on your behalf to achieve those hopes in the next two and a half years.

But in turning over direction of the government to Vice President Ford I know, as I told the nation when I nominated him for that office ten months ago, that the leadership of America will be in good hands.

In passing this office to the vice president I also do so with the profound sense of the weight of responsibility that will fall on his shoulders tomorrow, and therefore of the understanding, the patience, the cooperation he will need from all Americans. As he assumes that responsibility he will deserve the help and the support of all of us. As we look to the future, the first essential is to begin healing the wounds of this nation—to put the bitterness and divisions of the recent past behind us and to rediscover those shared ideals that lie at the heart of our strength and unity as a great and as a free people.

By taking this action, I hope that I will have hastened the start of that process of healing which is so desperately needed in America.

I regret deeply any injuries that may have been done in the course of the events that led to this decision. I would say only that if some of my judgments were wrong—and some were wrong—they were made in what I believed at the time to be the best interests of the nation.

To those who have stood with me during these past difficult months, to my family, my friends, the many others who've joined in supporting my cause because they believed it was right, I will be eternally grateful for your support.

And to those who have not felt able to give me your support, let me say I leave with no bitterness toward those who have opposed me, because all of us in the final analysis have been concerned with the good of the country however our judgments might differ.

So let us all now join together in affirming that common

commitment and in helping our new president succeed for the benefit of all Americans.

I shall leave this office with regret at not completing my term but with gratitude for the privilege of serving as your president for the past five and a half years.

These years have been a momentous time in the history of our nation and the world. They have been a time of achievement in which we can all be proud—achievements that represent the shared efforts of the administration, the Congress and the people. But the challenges ahead are equally great.

And they, too, will require the support and the efforts of a Congress and the people, working in cooperation with the new administration.

We have ended America's longest war. But in the work of securing a lasting peace in the world, the goals ahead are even more far-reaching and more difficult. We must complete a structure of peace, so that it will be said of this generation—our generation of Americans—by the people of all nations, not only that we ended one war but that we prevented future wars.

We have unlocked the doors that for a quarter of a century stood between the United States and the People's Republic of China. We must now insure that the one quarter of the world's people who live in the People's Republic of China will be and remain, not our enemies, but our friends.

In the Middle East, one hundred million people in the Arab countries, many of whom have considered us their enemies for nearly twenty years, now look on us as their friends. We must continue to build on that friendship so that peace can settle at last over the Middle East and so that the cradle of civilization will not become its grave.

Together with the Soviet Union we have made the crucial breakthroughs that have begun the process of limiting nuclear arms. But, we must set as our goal, not just limiting but reducing and finally destroying these terrible weapons so that they cannot destroy civilization.

And so that the threat of nuclear war will no longer hang

over the world and the people, we have opened a new relation with the Soviet Union. We must continue to develop and
expand that new relationship so that the two strongest nations
of the world will live together in cooperation rather than
confrontation.

Around the world—in Asia, in Africa, in Latin America, in
the Middle East—there are millions of people who live in terrible poverty, even starvation. We must keep as our goal turning
away from production for war and expanding production for
peace so that people everywhere on this earth can at last look
forward, in their children's time if not in our time, to having the
necessities for a decent life.

Here in America we are fortunate that most of our people
have not only the blessings of liberty but also the means to live
full and good, and by the world's standards even abundant,
lives.

We must press on, however, toward a goal not only of more
and better jobs but of full opportunity for every man, and of
what we are striving so hard right now to achieve—prosperity
without inflation.

For more than a quarter of a century in public life, I have
shared in the turbulent history of this evening.

I have fought for what I believe in. I have tried, to the best
of my ability, to discharge those duties and meet those responsibilities that were entrusted to me.

Sometimes I have succeeded. And sometimes I have failed.
But always I have taken heart from what Theodore Roosevelt
said about the man in the arena whose face is marred by dust
and sweat and blood, who strives valiantly, who errs and comes
short again and again because there is not effort without error
and shortcoming, but who does actually strive to do the deed,
who knows the great devotion, who spends himself in a worthy
cause, who at the best knows in the end the triumphs of high
achievements and with the worst if he fails, at least fails while
daring greatly.

I pledge to you tonight that as long as I have a breath of life in my body I shall continue in that spirit. I shall continue to work for the great causes to which I have been dedicated throughout my years as a congressman, a senator, vice president, and president, the cause of peace—not just for America but among all nations—prosperity, justice, and opportunity for all of our people.

There is one cause above all to which I have been devoted and to which I shall always be devoted for as long as I live.

When I first took the oath of office as president five and a half years ago, I made this sacred commitment: to consecrate my office, my energies, and all the wisdom I can summon to the cause of peace among nations.

As a result of these efforts, I am confident that the world is a safer place today, not only for the people of America but for the people of all nations, and that all of our children have a better chance than before of living in peace rather than dying in war.

This, more than anything, is what I hoped to achieve when I sought the presidency. This, more than anything, is what I hope will be my legacy to you, to our country, as I leave the presidency.

To have served in this office is to have felt a very personal sense of kinship with each and every American. In leaving it, I do so with this prayer: May God's grace be with you in all the days ahead.

RONALD REAGAN

——— ★ ———

First Inaugural Address

CAPITOL, WASHINGTON, D.C.; JANUARY 20, 1981

Ronald Reagan (1911–   ), who had sought his party's nomination for president in 1976, ran as the Republican candidate in 1980, thwarting the reelection bid of Jimmy Carter. Reagan's deficits—his age and reputation as an extreme conservative—were not considered significant by an electorate weary of double-digit inflation and the nightmare of Americans held hostage in Iran for the past year. On the day Reagan was sworn in as president, the Iranian government released the hostages. With this dramatic and symbolic event as a backdrop, Reagan unveiled a path of revolutionary economic policies guided by the principle that "government is not the solution to our problem; government is the problem." President Reagan's success as "the great communicator" derived from his projection of genial optimism and strength of conviction, as well as from speeches filled with anecdotes, simple concepts, and patriotic effusion.

To a few of us here today this is a solemn and most momentous occasion, and yet in the history of our nation it is a commonplace occurrence. The orderly transfer of authority as called for in the Constitution routinely takes place, as it has for almost two centuries, and few of us stop to think how unique we really are. In the eyes of many in the world, this every-four-year-ceremony we accept as normal is nothing less than a miracle. . . .

The business of our nation goes forward. These United States are confronted with an economic affliction of great proportions. We suffer from the longest and one of the worst sustained inflations in our national history. It distorts our economic decisions, penalizes thrift, and crushes the struggling young and the fixed-income elderly alike. It threatens to shatter the lives of millions of our people.

Idle industries have cast workers into unemployment, human misery, and personal indignity. Those who do work are denied a fair return for their labor by a tax system which penalizes successful achievement and keeps us from maintaining full productivity.

But great as our tax burden is, it has not kept pace with public spending. For decades we have piled deficit upon deficit, mortgaging our future and our children's future for the temporary convenience of the present. To continue this long trend is to guarantee tremendous social, cultural, political, and economic upheavals.

You and I, as individuals, can, by borrowing, live beyond our means, but for only a limited period of time. Why, then, should we think that collectively, as a nation, we're not bound by that same limitation? We must act today in order to preserve tomorrow. And let there be no misunderstanding: we are going to begin to act, beginning today.

The economic ills we suffer have come upon us over several decades. They will not go away in days, weeks, or months, but they will go away. They will go away because we as Americans have the capacity now, as we've had in the past, to do whatever needs to be done to preserve this last and greatest bastion of freedom.

In this present crisis, government is not the solution to our problem; government is the problem. From time to time we've been tempted to believe that society has become too complex to be managed by self-rule, that government by an elite group is superior to government for, by, and of the people. Well, if no one among us is capable of governing himself, then who among us has the capacity to govern someone else? All of us together, in and out of government, must bear the burden. The solutions we seek must be equitable, with no one group singled out to pay a higher price.

We hear much of special interest groups. Well, our concern

must be for a special interest group that has been too long neglected. It knows no sectional boundaries or ethnic and racial divisions, and it crosses political party lines. It is made up of men and women who raise our food, patrol our streets, man our mines and factories, teach our children, keep our homes, and heal us when we're sick—professionals, industrialists, shop-keepers, clerks, cabbies, and truck-drivers. They are, in short, "We the people," this breed called Americans.

Well, this administration's objective will be a healthy, vigor-ous, growing economy that provides equal opportunities for all Americans, with no barriers born of bigotry or discrimination. Putting America back to work means putting all Americans back to work. Ending inflation means freeing all Americans from the terror of runaway living costs. All must share in the productive work of this "new beginning," and all must share in the bounty of a revived economy. With the idealism and fair play which are the core of our system and our strength, we can have a strong and prosperous America, at peace with itself and the world.

So, as we begin, let us take inventory. We are a nation that has a government—not the other way around. And this makes us special among the nations of the earth. Our government has no power except that granted it by the people. It is time to check and reverse the growth of government, which shows signs of having grown beyond the consent of the governed.

It is my intention to curb the size and influence of the federal establishment and to demand recognition of the distinction be-tween the powers granted to the federal government and those reserved to the states or to the people. All of us need to be reminded that the federal government did not create the states; the states created the federal government. . . .

We have every right to dream heroic dreams. Those who say that we're in a time when there are not heroes, they just don't know where to look. You can see heroes every day going in and out of factory gates. Others, a handful in number, produce enough food to feed all of us and then the world beyond. You meet heroes across a counter, and they're on both sides of that counter. There are entrepreneurs with faith in themselves and faith in an idea who create new jobs, new wealth, and opportunity. They're individuals and families whose taxes support the government and whose voluntary gifts support church, charity, culture, art, and education. Their patriotism is quiet, but deep. Their values sustain our national life. . . .

I'm told that tens of thousands of prayer meetings are being held on this day, and for that I'm deeply grateful. We are a nation under God, and I believe God intended for us to be free. It would be fitting and good, I think, if on each inaugural day in future years it should be declared a day of prayer.

This is the first time in our history that this ceremony has been held, as you've been told, on this west front of the Capitol. Standing here, one faces a magnificent vista, opening up on this city's special beauty and history. At the end of this open mall are those shrines to the giants on whose shoulders we stand.

Directly in front of me, the monument to a monumental man, George Washington, father of our country—a man of humility who came to greatness reluctantly. He led America out of revolutionary victory into infant nationhood. Off to one side, the stately memorial to Thomas Jefferson. The Declaration of Independence flames with his eloquence. And then, beyond the Reflecting Pool, the dignified columns of the Lincoln Memorial. Whoever would understand in his heart the meaning of America will find it in the life of Abraham Lincoln.

Beyond those monuments to heroism is the Potomac River, and on the far shore the sloping hills of Arlington National Cemetery, with its row upon row of simple white markers bearing crosses or stars of David. They add up to only a tiny fraction of the price that has been paid for our freedom.

Each one of those markers is a monument to the kind of hero I spoke of earlier. Their lives ended in places called Belleau Wood, the Argonne, Omaha Beach, Salerno, and halfway around the world on Guadalcanal, Tarawa, Pork Chop Hill, the

Chosin Reservoir, and in a hundred rice paddies and jungles of a place called Vietnam.

Under one such marker lies a young man, Martin Treptow, who left his job in a small town barbershop in 1917 to go to France with the famed Rainbow Division. There, on the western front, he was killed trying to carry a message between battalions under heavy artillery fire.

We're told that on his body was found a diary. On the flyleaf under the heading "My Pledge" he had written these words: "America must win this war. Therefore I will work, I will save, I will sacrifice, I will endure, I will fight cheerfully and do my utmost, as if the issue of the whole struggle depended on me alone."

The crisis we are facing today does not require of us the kind of sacrifice that Martin Treptow and so many thousands of others were called upon to make. It does require, however, our best effort and our willingness to believe in ourselves and to believe in our capacity to perform great deeds, to believe that together with God's help we can and will resolve the problems which now confront us.

And after all, why shouldn't we believe that? We are Americans.

God bless you, and thank you.

MARIO CUOMO

—— ★ ——

A Case for the Democrats:
A Tale of Two Cities

DEMOCRATIC NATIONAL CONVENTION,
SAN FRANCISCO, CALIFORNIA; JULY 16, 1984

Jimmy Carter's vice president, Walter Mondale, was the Democratic party's presidential nominee in 1984. Amid characteristic factional strife, the Democratic National Convention heard a keynote speech delivered by New York Governor Mario Cuomo (1932–   ). Cuomo's stirring, literate oratory electrified the convention and impressed the media and the public. In language both direct and poetic, Cuomo extolled the diversity found under the Democratic umbrella and called for his party to unify despite the divisions. Mario Cuomo became a national figure, but Walter Mondale was defeated by Ronald Reagan in a landslide.

Ten days ago, President Reagan admitted that although some people in this country seemed to be doing well nowadays, others were unhappy, and even worried, about themselves, their families, and their futures. The president said he didn't understand that fear. He said, "Why, this country is a shining city on a hill." The president is right. In many ways we are "a shining city on a hill." But the hard truth is that not everyone is sharing in this city's splendor and glory.

A shining city is perhaps all the president sees from the portico of the White House and the veranda of his ranch, where everyone seems to be doing well. But there's another part of the city, the part where some people can't pay their mortgages and most young people can't afford one, where students can't afford the education they need and middle-class parents watch dreams they hold for their children evaporate.

298

In this part of the city there are more poor than ever, more families in trouble. More and more people who need help but can't find it. Even worse: there are elderly people who tremble in the basements of the houses there. There are people who sleep in the city's streets, in the gutter, where the glitter doesn't show. There are ghettos where thousands of young people, without an education or a job, give their lives away to drug dealers every day. There is despair, Mr. President, in faces you never see, in places you never visit in your shining city.

In fact, Mr. President, this nation is more a "Tale of Two Cities" than it is a "Shining City on a Hill." Maybe if you visited more places, Mr. President, you'd understand.

Maybe if you went to Appalachia where some people still live in sheds and to Lackawanna where thousands of unemployed steel workers wonder why we subsidized foreign steel while we surrender their dignity to unemployment and to welfare checks; maybe if you stepped into a shelter in Chicago and talked with some of the homeless there; maybe, Mr. President, if you asked a woman who'd been denied the help she needs to feed her children because you say we need the money to give a tax break to a millionaire or to build a missile we can't even afford to use—maybe then you'd understand. Maybe, Mr. President. But I'm afraid not. Because the truth is, this is how we were warned it would be.

President Reagan told us from the beginning that he believed in a kind of social Darwinism. Survival of the fittest. Government can't do everything, we were told. So it should settle for taking care of the strong and hope that economic ambition and charity will do the rest. Make the rich richer and what falls from their table will be enough for the middle class and those trying to make it into the middle class.

The Republicans called it trickle-down when Hoover tried it. Now they call it supply side. It is the same shining city for those relative few who are lucky enough to live in its good neighborhoods. But for the people who are excluded—locked out—all they can do is to stare from a distance at that city's glimmering towers.

It's an old story. As old as our history.

The difference between Democrats and Republicans has always been measured in courage and confidence. The Republicans believe the wagon train will not make it to the frontier unless some of our old, some of our young, and some of our weak are left behind by the side of the trail. The strong will inherit the land!

We Democrats believe that we can make it all the way with the whole family intact. We have. More than once. Ever since Franklin Roosevelt lifted himself from his wheelchair to lift this nation from its knees. Wagon train after wagon train. To new frontiers of education, housing, peace. The whole family aboard. Constantly reaching out to extend and enlarge that family. Lifting them up into the wagon on the way. Blacks and Hispanics, people of every ethnic group, and Native Americans—all those struggling to build their families claim some share of America. . . .

We speak for the minorities who have not yet entered the mainstream: for ethnics who want to add their culture to the mosaic that is America; for women indignant that we refuse to etch into our governmental commandments the simple rule "thou shalt not sin against equality," a commandment so obvious it can be spelled in three letters: E.R.A.; for young people demanding an education and a future, for senior citizens terrorized by the idea that their only security, their Social Security, is being threatened; for millions of reasoning people fighting to preserve our environment from greed and stupidity. And fighting to preserve our very existence from a macho intransigence that refuses to make intelligent attempts to discuss the possibility of nuclear holocaust with our enemy. Refusing because they believe we can pile missiles so high that they will pierce the clouds and the sight of them will frighten our enemies into submission.

We're proud of this diversity. Grateful we don't have to

manufacture its appearance the way the Republicans will next month in Dallas, by propping up mannequin delegates on the convention floor.

But we pay a price for it. The different people we represent have many points of view. Sometimes they compete and then we have debates, even arguments. That's what our primaries were. . . .

Inflation is down since 1980. But not because of the supply-side miracle promised by the president. Inflation was reduced the old-fashioned way, with a recession, the worst since 1932. More than 55,000 bankruptcies. Two years of massive unemployment. Two hundred thousand farmers and ranchers forced off the land. More homeless than at any time since the Great Depression. More hungry, more poor—mostly women—and a nearly $200 billion deficit threatening our future. . . .

And what about foreign policy? They said they would make us and the whole world safer. They say they have. By creating the largest defense budget in history, one even they now admit is excessive, failed to discuss peace with our enemies. By the loss of 279 young Americans in Lebanon in pursuit of a plan and a policy no one can find or describe. We give monies to Latin American governments that murder nuns, and then lie about it. We have been less than zealous in our support of the only real friend we have in the Middle East, the one democracy there, our flesh-and-blood ally, the state of Israel.

Our policy drifts with no real direction, other than a hysterical commitment to an arms race that leads nowhere, if we're lucky. If we're not—could lead us to bankruptcy or war. . . .

How high will we pile the missiles? How much deeper will be the gulf between us and our enemies? Will we make meaner the spirit of our people?

This election will measure the record of the past four years. But more than that, it will answer the question of what kind of people we want to be.

We Democrats still have a dream. We still believe in this nation's future. And this is our answer, our credo: We believe in only the government we need, but we insist on all the government we need.

We believe in a government characterized by fairness and reasonableness, a reasonableness that goes beyond labels, that doesn't distort or promise to do what it knows it can't do. A government strong enough to use the words "love" and "compassion" and smart enough to convert our noblest aspirations. . . .

We believe, as Democrats, that a society as blessed as ours, the most affluent democracy in the world's history, that can spend trillions on instruments of destruction, ought to be able to help the middle class in its struggle, ought to be able to find work for all who can do it, room at the table, shelter for the homeless, care for the elderly and infirm, hope for the destitute.

We proclaim as loudly as we can the utter insanity of nuclear proliferation and the need for a nuclear freeze, if only to affirm the simple truth that peace is better than war because life is better than death.

We believe in firm but fair law and order, in the union movement, in privacy for people, openness by government, civil rights, and human rights. . . .

That struggle to live with dignity is the real story of the shining city. It's a story I didn't read in a book or learn in a classroom. I saw it and lived it. Like many of you.

I watched a small man with thick calluses on both hands work fifteen and sixteen hours a day. I saw him once literally bleed from the bottoms of his feet, a man who came here uneducated, alone, unable to speak the language, who taught me all I needed to know about faith and hard work by the simple eloquence of his example. I learned about our kind of democracy from my father. I learned about our obligation to each other from him and from my mother. They asked only for a chance to work and to make the world better for their children and to be protected in those moments when they would not be able to protect themselves. This nation and its government did that for them.

And on January 20, 1985, it will happen again. Only on a much grander scale. We will have a new president of the United States, a Democrat born not to the blood of kings but to the blood of immigrants and pioneers.

We will have America's first woman vice president, the child of immigrants, a New Yorker, opening with one magnificent stroke a whole new frontier for the United States.

It will happen, if we make it happen.

I ask you, ladies and gentlemen, brothers and sisters—for the good of us all, for the love of this great nation, for the family of America, for the love of God. Please make this nation remember how futures are built.

Jesse Jackson

— ★ —

Democratic Convention Speech

Democratic National Convention, New York, New York; July 14, 1992

Jesse Jackson (1941–   ), a Baptist minister since 1968, was the national director of the Southern Christian Leadership Conference's Operation Breadbasket Project from 1967 to 1971. He founded Operation PUSH (People United to Serve Humanity) in Chicago in 1971. In the 1980s Jackson established an international profile as a leader in minority, poor, third-world, and liberal causes, and particularly in increased voter registration. A worldwide lecturer with imposing oratorical powers, Jackson created the National Rainbow Coalition in Chicago and was a Democratic party candidate for the presidency in 1984 and 1988. Jackson's address at the Democrats' 1992 convention emphasized his traditional themes of the party's commitment to economic justice for working people and the poor and offered a vision of hope and empowerment.

W e stand as witnesses to a pregnant moment in history. Across the globe, we feel the pain that comes with new birth. Here in our country, pain abounds. We must be certain that it too leads to new birth and not a tragic miscarriage of opportunity.

We must turn pain to power, pain into partnership—not pain into polarization.

The great temptation in these difficult days of racial polarization and economic injustice is to make political arguments black and white and miss the moral imperative of wrong and right. Vanity asks—is it popular? Politics asks—will it win? Morality and conscience ask—is it right?

We are part of a continuing struggle for justice and decency, links in a chain that began long before we were born and will extend long after we are gone. History will remember us not for our positioning but for our principles. Not by our move to the political center, left or right, but rather by our grasp on the moral and ethical center of wrong and right.

We who stand with working people and poor have a special burden. We must stand for what is right, stand up to those who have the might. We do so grounded in the faith that that which is morally wrong will never be politically right. But if it is morally sound, it will eventually be politically right.

When I look at you gathered here today, I hear the pain and see the struggles that prepared the ground that you stand on. We have come a long way from where we started.

A generation ago, in 1964, Fanny Lou Hamer had to fight even to sit in this convention. Tonight, twenty-eight years later, the chair of the party is Ron Brown from Harlem; the manager is Alexis Herman, an African-American woman from Mobile, Alabama. We have come a long way from where we started.

We are more interdependent than we realize. Not only African Americans benefited from the movement for justice. It was only when African Americans were free to win and sit in these seats that Bill Clinton and Al Gore from the new South could be able to stand on this rostrum. We are inextricably bound together in a single garment of destiny.

Tonight we face another challenge. Ten million Americans are unemployed, 25 million on food stamps, 35 million in poverty, 40 million have no health care. From the coal miners in Bigstone Gap, Virginia, to the loggers and environmentalists in Roseburg, Oregon, from displaced textile workers in my home town of Greenville, South Carolina, to plants closing in Van Nuys, California, pain abounds. Plants are closing, jobs leaving on a fast track, more are working for less, trapped by repressive antilabor laws. The homeless are a source of national shame and disgrace.

There is a harshness to America that comes from not seeing

and a growing mindless materialism. Our television sets bring the world into our living rooms, but too often we overlook our neighbors. . . .

Now is the time to rebuild America. We must be the party with the plan and the purpose. Four years ago, we fought for a program to reinvest in America, paid for by fair taxes on the rich and savings from the military. This year, Governor Bill Clinton has taken a substantial step in that direction. He has expressed Democratic support for D.C. statehood, same-day on-site universal voter registration. D.C. has more people than five states, we pay more taxes than ten states, and we sent more youth to the Persian Gulf than twenty states; we deserve the right to vote. Governor Clinton has vowed to challenge corporations to invest at home, retrain their workers, and pay their share of taxes. He has made a commitment to raising and indexing the minimum wage. We must build upon that direction and go further still. . . .

We must have a plan on a scale that corresponds with the size of the problems we face. Taiwan has a $1 trillion plan—it is the size of Pennsylvania. Japan has a $3 trillion plan over ten years. We found the money to help rebuild Europe and Japan after World War II; we found the money to help Russia and Poland. We found $600 billion to bail out the mess left by the buccaneer bankers. Surely we can find the money to rebuild America and put people back to work.

We must have a vision sufficient to correspond with the size of our opportunity. Across the world, walls are coming down. The cold war is over; the Soviet Union is no more. Russia wants to join NATO. We can change our priorities, reinvest in educating our children, train our workers, rebuild our cities. Today Japan makes fast trains; we make fast missiles. If we change our priorities and build a high-speed national railroad, we could go from New York to L.A. in eight hours. We could make the steel, lay the rail, build the cars and drive them. Scientists can stop devising weapons we don't need and start working on environmental advances we can't live without.

We must have an imagination strong enough to see beyond

war. In Israel, Prime Minister Rabin's election is a step toward greater security and peace for the entire region. Rabin's wisdom in affirming negotiation over confrontation, land for peace, bargaining table over battlefield has inspired hope, not only in the hearts of democratic Israel, but on the West Bank. Israeli security and Palestinian self-determination are inextricably bound, two sides of the same coin. With the effort at talk between Syria and Jordan, with a stable partner in King Fahd of Saudi Arabia and President Hosni Muburak of Egypt, there is hope. . . .

In Africa today, democracy is on the march. In Nigeria, under President Babanguida we witnessed successful elections last week. But democracy cannot flourish amid economic ruins. Democracy protects the right to vote; it does not insure that you can eat. . . .

We must understand that development in the Third World and economic prosperity at home are inextricably bound. We can be a force for peace in the Middle East, development in Africa and Latin America, hope in Eastern Europe and the former Soviet Union. . . .

We hear a lot of talk about family values, even as we spurn the homeless on the street. Remember, Jesus was born to a homeless couple, outdoors in a stable, in the winter. He was the child of a single mother. When Mary said Joseph was not the father, she was abused. . . . But Mary had family values. It was Herod—the Quayle of his day—who put no value on the family.

We who would be leaders must feel and be touched by people's pain. How can you be a doctor and not touch the sick? How can you be a leader and not touch the hurt? Gandhi adopted the untouchables. Dr. King marched with violent gang members, hoping to turn them to the discipline of nonviolence.

Above all, we must reach out and touch our children. Our children are embittered and hurt, but it is not a congenital disease. They were not born that way. They live amid violence and rejection, in broken streets, broken glass, broken sidewalks, broken families, broken hearts. Their music, their rap, their video, their art reflects their broken world. We must reach out and touch them. . . .

Too many of our children see jail as a relief station and death as a land beyond pain. We must reach out and touch them. Surely, it is better to have dirty hands and clean hearts than clean hands and a dirty heart.

If we reach out, we can win—and deserve to win. We will win only if we put forth a vision that corresponds with the size of our problems and the scope of our opportunity, if we reach out to those in despair and those who care, reach across the lines that divide by race, region, or religion. . . .

In L.A., they focused on Rodney King beaten by white officers, who were acquitted by an all-white jury. But it was a white man who had the instinct and the outrage to film it and take it public. The media focus was on the white truck driver beaten by black youth. But it was four young black youth who stepped in and saved his life, good samaritans.

In the final analysis it comes down to a question of caring. On a small Southern college campus, I once observed a lesson never to be forgotten. I saw a dwarf and a giant walking together—they were an odd couple. He was six feet three; she was three feet tall. When they reached the parting paths, they embraced. He handed her books and she skipped down the path. It looked to be romantic. I asked the president, What is this I am seeing? He said, I thought you would ask; you see, that is his sister, in fact his twin sister. By a twist of fate he came out a giant, she a dwarf. All the big schools offered him athletic scholarships. The pros offered him money. But he said I can only go where my sister can go. And so he ended up here with us.

Somewhere that young man learned ethics, caring for others. Few of us are driven by a tailwind. Most of us struggle with headwinds. Not all of us can be born tall, some are born short, motherless, abandoned, hungry, orphaned. Somebody has to care. It must be us. And if we do, we will win, and deserve to win.

Keep hope alive.